In this far-ranging and innovative study Christopher Berry explores the meanings and ramifications of the idea of luxury. Insights from political theory, philosophy and intellectual history are utilised in a sophisticated conceptual analysis that is complemented by a series of specific historical investigations. Dr Berry suggests that the value attached to luxury is a crucial component in any society's self-understanding, and shows how luxury has changed from being essentially a negative term, threatening social virtue, to a guileless ploy supporting consumption. His analytic focus upon the interplay between the notions of need and desire suggests that luxuries fall into four categories – sustenance, shelter, clothing and leisure – and these are exemplified in sources as diverse as classical philosophy and contemporary advertising.

IDEAS IN CONTEXT

Edited by Quentin Skinner (General Editor), Lorraine Daston, Wolf Lepenies, Richard Rorty and J. B. Schneewind

The books in this series will discuss the emergence of intellectual traditions and of related new disciplines. The procedures, aims and vocabularies that were generated will be set in the context of the alternatives available within the contemporary frameworks of ideas and institutions. Through detailed studies of the evolution of such traditions, and their modification by different audiences, it is hoped that a new picture will form of the development of ideas in their concrete contexts. By this means, artificial distinctions between the history of philosophy, of the various sciences, of society and politics, and of literature may be seen to dissolve.

The series is published with the support of the Exxon Foundation.

A list of books in the series will be found at the end of the volume.

IDEAS IN CONTEXT

THE IDEA OF LUXURY

THE IDEA OF LUXURY

A conceptual and historical investigation

CHRISTOPHER J. BERRY

Department of Politics, University of Glasgow

CAMBRIDGE
UNIVERSITY PRESS

Published by the Press Syndicate of the University of Cambridge
The Pitt Building, Trumpington Street, Cambridge CB2 1RP
40 West 20th Street, New York, NY 10011-4211, USA
10 Stamford Road, Oakleigh, Melbourne 3166, Australia

First published 1994

A catalogue record for this book is available from the British Library

Library of Congress cataloguing in publication data
Berry, Christopher J.
The idea of luxury: a conceptual and historical investigation /
Christopher J. Berry.
p.   cm. – (Ideas in context: 30)
Includes bibliographical references and index.
ISBN 0 521 45448 4 (hbk).   ISBN 0 521 46621 1 (pbk)
1. Luxury–History.   I. Title.   II. Series.
HB841.B47   1994
330.1'6 – dc20   93-32166   CIP

ISBN 0 521 454484 hardback
ISBN 0 521 466911 paperback

Transferred to digital printing 1999

To
Craig Adrian and Paul Duncan
and
Christine

Contents

Preface

As its title indicates this study is a mixture of historical investigation and conceptual analysis. The focus of the latter is upon the interplay between the notions of 'need' and 'desire'. The former limns out certain crucial episodes in the intellectual career of the idea of luxury. To say that the investigation is 'episodic' is to admit, implicitly, that no attempt at an exhaustive survey is being attempted. Baudrillart tried that in the late nineteenth century and produced four enormous volumes of which, even if it is a truculent exaggeration, Sombart's judgment that one learns from it almost nothing, does suggest that both a more selective and more focused approach is warranted. My conceptual analysis is intended, in part, to assist to that end. Of course, any 'episodic' treatment leaves itself open to cavils about inclusions and exclusions; certainly a strong case can be made for giving Aristotle and, especially, Rousseau more prominence than they will actually receive in what follows.

One other book deserves a mention at this point. John Sekora has written a good book on the idea of luxury to which I am indebted more than my relatively few references might indicate. My task, however, is different from his. Sekora's own agenda was to fill in the intellectual/historical background to a study of Smollett; my concerns are less chronologically specific as well as being in a general sense more 'political'. At its broadest, my investigation and analysis of luxury is undertaken because the topic provides an illuminating entrée into a basic political issue, namely, the nature of social order. That issue is itself clearly very general and what makes luxury so potentially illuminating is that it, as a topic, straddles various academic disciplines, bringing together issues of philosophy, history, anthropology, theology and economics as well as politics. This should not be taken to mean that the study of luxury is of only instrumental value. It is also an intrinsically worthwhile subject. This worth lies partly in an account of why it is indeed apparently so ubiquitous, cropping up in these various disciplines. It lies also in the change in contextual meaning that the term has undergone. In its own way it acts as a barometer of the movement from the classical and medieval world-view to that of modernity. Of course it shares that role with many other notions – reason and nature to name but the two most dramatic.

As a response to the topic's wide-ranging quality, this study quite deliberately adopts an eclectic mode of investigation and analysis. Hence I provide some detailed textual analyses, of Plato and Barbon for example, as well as undertaking some synoptic overviews, of post-Augustinian Christianity and the Enlightenment for example. For the same reason, I draw upon disparate sources of evidence, ranging from contemporary commercial advertising to analytical philosophy to histories of Gothic architecture to regulations governing the taxation of children's clothing. My hope is that this constitutes not a confusing mish-mash but rather a mosaic, which when assembled or taken together reveals some design.

This eclecticism in its own way supposes certain methodological claims. Since it appears to have become a virtual requirement to make some comments about such claims, I here wish to enter two general disclaimers. The requirement itself seems to be a product of a commendable self-consciousness, so much so that 'the methodology of the history of ideas' has become an area of study in its own right, generating its own debates and canon – Lovejoy, Gadamer, Koselleck, Pocock, Skinner *et alii*. My initial disclaimer is that I am not participating directly in these discussions. The reason for this diffidence is that I do not wish the methodological tail to wag the substantive dog. I am not here engaged in treating luxury as a test-case for evaluating, say, the tenability of *Begriffsgeschichte*. Of course, as I have allowed, I cannot but make certain methodological commitments. Since I am interested in the changing 'place' of luxury within societal self-understandings of the nature of social order, then it is because these are *understandings* that the investigation focuses on broadly conceptual issues. And it is because of this focus that the historical dimension concentrates (episodically) upon what I called above its 'intellectual career'. In line with my eclecticism, how this 'career' is mapped in the different episodes varies but there is a general acceptance of the view that it is contemporary understandings, implicit and explicit, that constitute the most appropriate context.

I earlier characterised my eclecticism as constituting a mosaic. A mosaic is not a seamless web – there are observable joins, which, indeed, become more obvious the closer one looks. What this means in practice, and here is my second disclaimer, is that the juxtaposition of, say, analytical philosophy, contemporary unreflective usage and historical investigation is not so integrated that one blends indiscernibly into another. What I do attempt to do is bring the various aspects to bear on each other when I believe mutual enlightenment will ensue. The appropriate judgment is the extent to which, more or less, this works, not the fact that the join is discernible.

The book is divided into four Parts. The first utilises contemporary popular usage to provide a general framework. Building upon an analysis of the differences between needs and desires, I claim that luxuries fall into four categories. I also introduce or 'signpost' various issues and themes which are taken up in later chapters. Part II consists of three chapters – on Plato, the Romans and early Christianity – which together establish the 'classical paradigm'. Within this paradigm luxury is a pejorative term because it stands for the corruption of a virtuous manly life. Part III also consists of three chapters. These chart the ways in which luxury becomes 'de-moralised' (Chapter 5), its links with the vindication of a commercial society in the work of Smith and others (Chapter 6) and the impact upon the paradigm of a general shift toward the historicisation of values (Chapter 7). The final Part returns more openly to conceptual analysis and contemporary issues.

In Part IV, Chapter 8 deals with the intersections between luxury and necessity as manifest in taxation policy and debates over the meaning of poverty. This chapter also re-addresses the issue of luxury's pejorativeness. The final chapter deals abstractly with the way the distinction between luxury and necessity informs the ideas of social order and social identity. Although the various chapters are grouped in this way, they do to some extent stand on their own. However, this book is not intended to be a set of nine discrete essays – certain inter-linking themes are overtly present and others are to be discerned (I hope) as the mosaic and overall design takes shape.

Serious work on this study was begun when I was awarded an ESRC Personal Research Grant (E 00242057). This provided me with an academic year free of teaching and administration and enabled me to break the ground so that this book might in due course come forth. I am grateful to the ESRC for providing me with this opportunity and to all those who were instrumental in my gaining the grant. The basic outline and substance of the book were completed by the end of 1991. The following year was spent upon elaborating and some re-thinking, aided by the helpful comments of two anonymous readers. At other times, and in some very different guises, some of the themes and arguments herein have benefited from comments received in Edinburgh, York, Oxford as well as Glasgow. Earlier workings of Chapter 2, Chapter 3 and part of Chapter 6 appeared, respectively, in *Polis* 8 (1989), *History of Political Thought*, vol. 10, pp. 597–613, © 1989 Imprint Academic, Exeter, UK, and *Virtue (Nomos 34)*, J. Chapman and W. Galston (eds.), © New York University Press, 1992. I am grateful for permission to re-utilise this material. Between its inception and completion both my parents died and I dedicate this book to their two grandsons, and to Christine, again.

PART I
Preliminary essay

CHAPTER I

Luxury goods

On 31 December 1987 *The Times* carried the following report,

A Lake District Hotel is offering weekend breaks costing nearly £1,000 a day. Guests paying £1,995 each will be served grouse, venison, fillet steak, lobster, caviar, truffles and pâté de foie gras. Miss Carolyn Graves, a director of the hotel, said,
   'The big-spending break is for people who work so hard that holidays are a rarity and have to be crammed full of a year's worth of pleasure.' . . .
   Those include return helicopter travel from up to 200 miles, a self-drive or chauffeur driven Rolls-Royce, the hotel's luxury suite with its spa bath and sunbathing tower, a case of champagne per person, the pick of the cellar, a personal chef to cook whatever takes the guests' fancy, and two sheepskin coats and personalized crystal decanter and glasses as souvenirs.

The Times called this a 'luxury weekend' and it does indeed represent, even to the possible extent of self-parody, what would appear to be commonly conjured up by the use of the word 'luxury'.

Open any newspaper or magazine, turn to the advertisements placed by commercial retailers, and the word 'luxury' will recur and recur. Since this is a commercial context, we can be reasonably confident that this rhetoric must be thought to be a selling-point. Obviously in the competitive market-place advertisers are not going to proclaim their products deficient, inadequate or even average. It is, therefore, fair to infer that labelling a consumption good ('capital' goods such as steel mills or power stations are not at issue) or a service as a 'luxury' is also to make a claim about its 'desirability'.

At this superficial level there seems to be a definite connexion between a good being a luxury and it being an object of desire. Since it is being publicly proclaimed, the implication is that this connexion is thought to be innocent or innocuous. From a historical perspective the fact that the desire for luxury goods can be assumed to be innocuous is a point of considerable significance. From the Greeks

3

onwards, luxury had always been associated with desire but, up until the eighteenth century, this association had been deemed pernicious and harmful. While an important evaluative change occurred at that time, a morally censorious attitude toward luxury persisted throughout the nineteenth century, attaining a prominent place in France in the last decade of the century (see, for example, Laveleye, *Luxury*) and echoes can be heard in some aspects of contemporary cultural criticism. I will examine these issues in Parts II and IV. In this chapter I explore contemporary usage to the end of establishing both a general conceptual framework and a *terminus ad quem*. I also introduce or 'signal' many of the themes that will be adopted in fuller detail in later chapters. In that sense this chapter is a preliminary to what follows.

While my exploration will, in the course of establishing the framework, aim to explicate the presence of certain standard assumptions, the bulk of contemporary usage is, of course, generally unreflective. Although this does not absolve me from heeding possible contrary cases, the exploration does not pretend to fit all usages into some conceptual straitjacket. That would be a pointless task because it is inherent in the very use of language that it is fluid; the expression 'play on words' is very apt. Nevertheless it is reasonable to maintain that much of such 'playfulness' relies on existing received meanings: it is those meanings that are being inventively exploited through irony, pun, hyperbole, litotes and so on. Similarly while 'luxury' may well be an ingredient in what is dismissively labelled 'adspeak', along with terms like 'executive' or 'premium', the choice of the term is not purely arbitrary; it rests upon or exploits certain assumed connotations. The following analysis of 'luxury' thus fixes upon the standard (whether direct or oblique) usage and its assumptions.

THE CATEGORIES OF LUXURY GOODS

I open by pursuing an implication of the salience of the label 'luxury' in contemporary advertising. The initial response would seem to be that we are dealing with a paradox. On the one hand retailers want to sell as much of their product as they can while, on the other hand, their very object in proclaiming their product a 'luxury' might seem to imply exclusiveness. It is in line with this exclusivity that luxury goods are seemingly to be associated with expensiveness and rarity. I want to argue, however, firstly and unremarkably, that the image of the 'exclusive' luxury good is a gambit to increase consumption and, secondly and perhaps less obviously, that neither expense nor rarity are of themselves sufficient conditions for a good to be accounted a 'luxury'.

If we reflect upon the argument that the label 'luxury' is an inducement to consumption, then clearly for that to be effective it must be assumed that the good in question is not only desired but widely desired. The image is that although only a (select) 'few' now enjoy (I will return to the aptness of that verb) the good, many others would also like to enjoy it. Here we can discern one reason why rarity is not a sufficient condition. For example, (though I shall have to come back to this) it is possible to purchase a first edition of Hobbes's *De Cive* for a couple of thousand pounds, but the bookseller, while declaring that the copy was 'scarce' (*Blackwell's Rare Book Catalogue*, January 1989) did not proclaim it a 'luxury'.

This example reveals an important distinction. A desire can be characterised either by its general incidence, the extent of its diffusion, or by the intensity with which it is held. Accordingly while few desire a copy of *De Cive*, a book-collector might crave a first edition. As we will now see it is this factor of extensiveness or general desirability that enables us to identify the range of goods to which, in contemporary society, the term 'luxury' is standardly applied. We can make a start by returning to the package offered by that Lake District hotel. In this package four categories of luxury goods can be discerned.

The first category is *sustenance* or food and drink. The hotel makes much of its menu – caviar, champagne – as well as the provision of a personal chef to cook whatever is the guest's fancy. The second category is *shelter*. The hotel itself is offering accommodation with its spa bath, sunbathing tower and presumably also the other standard features provided by luxury hotels ('luxury' applied to and by hotels about themselves is one of the commonest of current usages). The third category is only vestigially present in this package in the form of the 'gift' of sheepskin coats, that is, the third category is *clothing* or apparel, with their various accessories like jewellery and also – though the link is admittedly more tenuous – perfume. The final category is *leisure*. This package is most ostensibly provided by the hotel as a holiday. Under this category is also to be included various entertainment and sporting goods like videos and polo ponies.

The list of categories of luxury goods is thus sustenance, shelter, clothing and leisure. We shall have more to say later about other possible categories and the extent to which these four *as categories* are able to subsume other putative candidates. In the meantime I take it as some corroboration of this list that W. Hamish Fraser in his *The Coming of the Mass Market* states that from the mid-nineteenth century, when the British had some surplus to spend it was expended on 'more and better food, on a wider range of clothing, on more elaborate furnishing for their homes and on a greater variety of leisure pursuits' (1981: p. ix). My claim therefore is that the goods that advertisers prefix with the label 'luxury' fall into one or other of these categories. Why should that be?

As a preliminary to the answer to that question it will be fruitful to address another, namely, what other sorts of consumption goods are there? Is anything here being ruled out? It is important that very little is excluded and apparent examples like 'health goods', as we shall see, are inappropriately labelled 'luxuries'. The importance of the inclusivity of the four categories stems from its negative implications. The fact that almost any consumption good can be a 'luxury good' means that luxury goods do not constitute a discrete, separate category superadded to some other category, such as 'necessities'. This latter notion would imply that luxury expenditure is residual, but this implication is to be resisted on two grounds. First, it gives to 'necessity' some fixed or determinate sense as, for example, in the Stoic notion of a 'natural life' or the idea of 'subsistence' in classical economics (cf. Levine, 1988: pp. 5–6), but such determinacy is unsustainable. Second, it axiomatically yet unwarrantedly prioritises needs over desires. Both of these arguments will be taken up in later chapters.

The relationship between needs and desires is fundamental to this enquiry. This relationship is at the heart of the answer to the initial question: why do advertised 'luxuries' fall into the four identified categories? The vital element in the answer to this question is the extensiveness or generality of the desires for luxury goods. The source of this extensiveness is the fact that the above four categories all relate to satisfactions that are universally experienced. It is the nature of this relationship that is crucial.

We can elicit just why this is so crucial if instead of 'universally experienced satisfactions' we refer to needs. Sustenance, shelter, clothing and leisure are all needs and, for reasons that we shall shortly bring out, because of their 'universality' they can be identified as 'basic needs'. There has been a remarkably consistent agreement that the first three of my quartet are needs of that sort. From Plato and

Seneca in the Classical period to Steuart in the eighteenth century to Kropotkin in the early twentieth century, food, clothing and shelter are time and again cited as basic needs.

The fourth category – leisure – is arguably more problematic. In particular there is the fact that a common understanding of leisure is as a residual rather than a basic category. On this understanding, leisure is that sphere of life remaining after 'the practical necessities of life have been attended to' (*Dictionary of Sociology*, quoted in Parker, 1972: p. 21). But this definition imposes too sharp a division. In many societies work (practical necessity) is not distinguished from leisure. Keith Thomas (1964: p. 51) cites the case of the Dogans of Sudan who use the same word to indicate both cultivation of the ground and ceremonial dancing.

Leisure activities are not, I am claiming, to be understood as residual but as activities that are rooted in the universal requirements of human life – just as eating, being clothed and sheltered are. Of course, these requirements differ from age to age and culture to culture but no more so for leisure than for diet, forms of dress or modes of abode (cf. Herskovits, 1952: pp. 271–5). Accordingly, just as humans have always had to eat, be clothed in some measure and be sheltered so too have they always given expression to 'leisure'. One indication (no more) of this is that holidays and feast days are known throughout all human cultures. More generally the element of 'play' is similarly ubiquitous. There is no need to endorse fully Huizinga's thesis that civilisation itself arose in and as play to recognise its universal dimension (1949: p. 172). Moreover, if it is thought a defect in this fourth category that it lacks a historical pedigree, Huizinga supplies a citation from Plato's *Laws* (7.830) in support of his notion of *homo ludens*.

Regardless of its historical antecedents, leisure, in my categorical sense, is now generally included in lists of human needs. (I shall take up later the importance of these being 'human needs'.) David Braybrooke, for example, not only has a need for recreation amongst his list of course-of-life needs but also includes needs for periodic rest and exercise (1987: p. 36). Nor is this recognition confined to academic theory. In a 1980s survey many respondents regarded a hobby or leisure activity as a necessity (Mack & Lansley, 1985: p. 126). In our terms these activities are universally experienced satisfactions which can thus establish categorically the basis for a widespread desire for goods to meet those satisfactions.

Before proceeding to analyse the relationship between needs and desires we have to ask the question, given that these four are basic needs, why this four? The assumption behind the question is that there are other basic needs. There is no simple straightforward answer to the question but, as a 'working hypothesis', we can hold that this quartet has in common a reference to physical or bodily satisfactions. The consequence of this is to exclude what can be loosely called 'mental needs' such as 'autonomy' (Plant, 1991), 'creative consciousness' (Doyal & Gough, 1984), 'plans of life' (Miller, 1976) or 'freedom and justice' (Simpson, 1982). This is not an arbitrary exclusion as I shall hope to vindicate as the argument proceeds. However, two observations can be made at this juncture.

First, this restriction to physical needs is warranted by the fact that throughout its history 'luxury' has been closely associated with physical or sensory enjoyment. Originally this association was a ground for complaint but later it became, as contemporary advertising exemplifies, a connexion to be celebrated. Second, the identification of needs is not unproblematic, which is one of the reasons why there is no simple answer to the question. Thinking about needs has a history itself, and one feature of that history is particularly pertinent. Traditionally, 'attributes' such as autonomy were not thought of as *needs*. One implication of this tradition is a rejection of the initial assumption that there are other basic needs of a 'mental' sort. Indeed the notion of 'mental' needs was invoked deliberately to counter the traditional accounts, which were thought to over-emphasise the physicality of needs. We shall have more to say about needs-theorising in Chapters 7 and 8.

NEEDS AND DESIRES

I now explore the precise nature of this crucial relationship between needs and luxury goods. I shall aim to bring out certain features common to all four categories. But, of course, it follows from this that there is more to say about each category than I will cover here.

Let us start our guided tour in the kitchen. Food is both a need and, as a category of luxury good, an object of desire. Prima facie this dual character appears uncontentious for it seems self-evident that we both need and want food. This appearance is, however, deceptive. It was because of this deceptiveness that I earlier deliberately referred to the *relationship* between needs and luxury goods. To uncover the source of the deception it is necessary to heed the more general, and for us fundamental, relationship between needs and desires or wants (for my purposes I shall take these latter two terms as synonyms). This is an involved and complex question. All I wish to do at this preliminary stage is outline in a non-definitive way certain central arguments and draw attention to some distinctions (later chapters will elaborate the arguments and explore further the distinctions).

One central aspect of the analysis of need is to differentiate it from 'wanting'. This is a conceptual and not merely a semantic differentiation. That is to say there is a conceptual difference even if the common usage does not invariably reflect it. To similar effect, *besoin* and *Bedürfnis* can in context be translated as either 'need' or 'want' but that does not make these terms conceptually conterminous. Among the various (inter-related) criteria put forward to differentiate them, two are particularly apposite.

First, wants, unlike needs, are intentional. Wiggins's observations are here typical. He writes,

What I need depends not on thought or the workings of my mind (or not only on these) but on the way the world is. Again, if one wants something because it is F, one believes or suspects that it is F. But if one needs something because it is F, it must really be F, whether or not one believes that it is. (1985: pp. 152–3)

In less technical language, wants are privileged. If I say that I want cherry pie you cannot contradict that by declaring that I want apple pie. Needs, by contrast, are not privileged. Thus, unlike wants, others can know better than you what your needs are. For example, you *need* vitamin C (that is the way the world is) to avoid scurvy whether or not you believe this and, hence, whether or not you *want* to consume fruit. This now broaches the second criterion. Needs, unlike wants, are objective or universal; they are attributes of us not *qua* individuals but *qua* 'generic men' (Minogue, 1963: p. 112).

These two criteria of non-intentionality and universality are what characterise basic (or, as they are sometimes called, absolute or fundamental) needs. As we have seen, sustenance, shelter, clothing and leisure can be so characterised. What makes these needs 'basic' is that they embody a stringency such that they are necessary rather than contingent features of human life. They are, by virtue of this stringency, not in their entirety reducible to any possible voluntary set of circumstances or purposive goals.

This analysis, however, does not exhaust the contexts within which the language of needs is employed. This language possesses other idioms. A good can, for example, be needed as an instrumental means to an end. This instrumentalist sense is, perhaps, the predominant use of the word 'need'. These usages concern volitional or purely instrumental needs; in contrast to 'basic needs' they are entirely reducible to purposive or intentional goals. For example, I need a pen so that I might fill in my pools coupon; but I want to fill in my pools coupon so that I might win a large sum of money which will enable me to enjoy a life of luxury. It is clear from this example that the need in question (for a pen) is subordinate to the desire. Although subordinate, the pen is still 'needed' in the strict sense that without it my coupon will remain empty. Moreover, regardless of any belief I might entertain, I need a pen for this task and not a stick of celery since, given 'the way the world is', only the former, and not the latter, will enable me to complete the coupon. However, unlike the putatively basic needs, this need is only called forth by virtue of the prior desire or want. Hence, while the possession of basic needs is involuntary or necessary, instrumental needs arise as a consequence of some volition and are thus possessed contingently. I shall, as promised, return to these questions. There is another issue which, again, at this point can merely be noted. Needs are an important element in moralistic discourse and the extent to which a particular need can be judged to be morally compelling will be affected by whether it is judged to be a fundamental or 'merely' an instrumental need.

For the moment I wish to use this analysis to demonstrate why it can be misleading to say we both need and want food. Such a statement conflates two different levels of generality. To identify basic needs is to identify certain abstract universals. The task that these identifications perform is to categorise certain postulated constants in human life and, generally, to impart to them moral significance. What they do not do is differentiate concretely between particular foodstuffs or particular fabrics or particular shelters or particular pursuits. We all possess needs for (to repeat) food, clothing, shelter and leisure; these possessions are states of the world, they are not principles of action (cf. Thomson, 1987: p. 16). By contrast, wants are principles of action as they specify or particularise the need; we have, accordingly, desires for lamb or pork, for a suit or a sports-jacket, for a flat or a detached villa, for soccer or opera.

Although all desires specify in this manner, they are not all of a piece. We have, therefore, to locate the desires for luxury goods more precisely. This will be a lengthy process. We can commence by elaborating further the idea of 'desire'. By means of this elaboration we can identify two characterising formal features: luxury goods are refined and positively pleasing. These characterise luxury, they are not sufficient of themselves to *define* it.

REFINEMENT

The first feature is that the desires for luxury goods are desires for (what I shall term) increasingly 'refined' goods.[1] The specificity definitive of desiring expresses itself in the greater refinement of the goods that serve generically to meet universally experienced satisfactions or needs. This increasing refinement imparts a dynamism to luxuries. One consequence of this dynamism is that it also imparts a basic transience to the status of a luxury good.

The refinements that characterise luxuries are the qualitative or adjectival aspects of goods. The clearest example of this principle is provided by food. The stomach can only hold so much – there is a natural limit to its capacity (an important idea as we shall see in later chapters). Although the Romans did their best to increase these limits quantitatively in as much as it was common for guests to be sick in the middle of a banquet, so that they might continue to gorge themselves, the scope for such increase is severely circumscribed. Accordingly the increase is to be understood qualitatively.

But once the qualitative dimension is broached then limits are evanescent. It is not now a question of need – bread to assuage hunger – but of desire – for fresh bread (the example is Seneca's). The same applies to clothing or housing or leisure: not a goatskin for warmth but a cashmere coat, not a wattle-and-daub dwelling for protection but a Georgian town-house, not a sing-song round the fire for entertainment but a compact-disc player. Since it is in principle never possible to give a complete description – it is always possible to add another adjective or qualify an existing qualification – then the process of refinement is itself in principle infinite (cf. Hampshire,

[1] I have chosen this terminology in order in part to echo two 'classical' discussions – that of Hume, who changed the title of his essay 'Of Luxury' to 'Of Refinement in the Arts' (see Chapter 6), and that of Sombart (1913: p. 72), who makes a historical link between luxury goods and refined goods.

1965: p. 21). Hence bread that is not simply fresh, but wholemeal, or rye, or stone-ground, or made from organically grown grain, or oval-shaped or baked by Dusty Miller and so on and on. And when we recall that 'the need' is but an abstract category then the initial example of bread is exactly that, 'an example'; it is itself a choice (the refinement of desire) from amongst all that which, inexhaustibly, constitutes the edible. The upshot is that, unlike the supposed fixity of needs (the importance of this 'supposition' will be brought out in Part II), the desires for luxury goods are inherently fluid and dynamic.

POSITIVE PLEASURE AND DESIRE

The second formal feature that characterises the specificity of the desires for luxury goods refers to the presence of a belief. For any good to be desired as a luxury, it must be believed that possession of that good is 'pleasing'. (Recall here Miss Graves's statement that her weekend was designed to be crammed full of 'pleasures'.) This necessary connexion between luxury and what is believed to please explains why it is apt to speak of 'enjoying' luxury goods. The pleasures in question will be those that relate to our four categories which, as we have noted, are associated with bodily or sensory satisfactions. When a prisoner was convicted of bribing a prison-officer to serve him smoked salmon and champagne, the judge commented 'If prisoners live in luxury the whole concept of punishment is undermined' (*Sunday Telegraph*, 25/9/88). In our terminology, in this example, food *qua* abstract universal has in the form of the salmon become a specific object of desire – a luxury good. Luxury food is desired because it is thought to be pleasing to the palate (that is not to say that there may not also be extrinsic reasons why such a dish is desired). It would be pathological or deliberately perverse (as in a notorious film starring Divine) to consider eating dog turd as an object of desire. It is because there is a warranted naturalistic assumption that certain goods are not merely necessarily desired as pleasing but are, in fact, widely desired that these goods are liable to be labelled 'luxuries'. I will return to the relationship between that assumption and such labelling.

It is not vital to this enquiry to enter into the various disputes about the appropriate characterisation of 'desire'. But it is worth making one observation. We can distinguish between negative and positive desires. An appropriate illustration is provided by Francis Hutcheson in the eighteenth century. Hutcheson, in his *Observations on the Fable of the Bees* (p. 60) in the context of a discussion of Mandeville's account of luxury, distinguishes between what is desired 'chiefly in order to remove the pain' and what is desired because of 'a previous opinion of good in the object'. Hutcheson links the former (negative desire) with meeting the bare necessaries of life and the latter (positive desire) with pleasures above necessity, as when humans 'desire something more in dress, houses, furniture than mere warmth or necessary use' (ibid.: p. 62). Following this analysis, we can say that desires for luxuries are positive desires for what pleases – or desires for positive pleasures.

A distinction along these lines has prompted some writers to distinguish 'pleasure' and 'comfort'. Scitovsky, for example, links the latter with cessation of pain (Hutcheson's first sense of desire) and contrasts this, as a passive state, with the former as an active state of change (1976: ch. 4). A somewhat similar active/passive distinction is made by Campbell (1987). He links the former with desire and pleasure, the latter with need and satisfaction (ibid.: p. 60). In line with our earlier use of Wiggins, Campbell notes (drawing on Ryle) that while 'satisfactoriness' is a state that is open to others to assess, the experiencing of something as pleasant is inseparable from our paying attention to it (ibid: p. 62). Like Scitovsky, Campbell links comfort with satisfaction while he looks upon luxuries as 'means to pleasure' (ibid.: p. 59). Scitovsky (1976: pp. 107–10), for his part, goes on to examine the link between satiability, comfort and necessity in contrast to the link between insatiability, pleasure and luxury.

While there is here a conceptual distinction of a Hutchesonian sort (not, as he admits, that it is original to him), it is not evident that the *term* 'comfort' has to be understood as an ineliminable constituent of one half of this divide. Certainly such a restriction is historically untenable. Like 'luxury', 'comfort' is a word with an instructive past. Literally it means 'strengthen', in the sense of support, as in the King James's version of Psalm 23, 'thy rod and thy staff they comfort me'. Its current sense of 'being comfortable' – of physical well-being – was according to Peter Thornton (1978: p. 10) 'invented by the French in the seventeenth century'.

SHELTER

In general (that is unreflective) usage, 'comfort' is found especially in the context of shelter or accommodation, a sphere that is particularly favoured by advertisers when they employ the label 'luxury'. The

history of housing, both with regard to architectural form and
furnished contents, is well-documented. Rybczynski (1988: p. 217) in
his book on the idea of 'The Home' declares unequivocally, in
language that conforms to my thesis, that 'domestic well-being is a
fundamental human need that is deeply rooted in us and must be
satisfied'. Moreover, a motif of the book itself is the relation between
this well-being and the idea of 'comfort'.[2]

Rybczynski lays considerable emphasis on what he calls 'the
feminization of the home' (ibid.: p. 72, cf. p. 223), by which he means
that the initiative and drive to comfort was led by women. He is not
alone in making this link. Thornton had linked the 'invention' of
comfort to the influence of women, Mme de Rambouillet in particular
(ibid.: pp. 9–10), and the general connexion between luxury goods,
physical ease or sensuousness and women was also made by Werner
Sombart (1913). In his explanation he stresses – indeed he calls it his
Grundgedanke – the role played in the development of capitalism by the
accumulation of wealth derived from trade in luxury goods, where
the stimulus for this trade emanated from princely courts at the
behest, most especially, of courtesans or mistresses (ibid.: p. 77).

What is interesting about these observations is that, in the classical
critique, *luxuria* was almost invariably linked with its supposed
'softness'. This was the object of criticism because, as we shall discuss
at some length in Part II, such softness was indicative of effeminacy,
the effect of which was to undermine the masculine qualities of *virtus*.
Nor has this connexion between the feminine and the luxurious
completely disappeared. A spokesman for Dunhill's (a company that
openly proclaims itself a purveyor of luxury goods) remarked that the
company recognised that 70 per cent of all purchasing power in
luxury goods was at the discretion of women (*Sunday Times* 3/4/88).

We can now pursue more systematically this link between comfort
and shelter. The basic need for shelter is to offer protection against the
elements. Included in this category are all those activities which are
thus protected, that is, those activities which are undertaken to meet
'daily needs' (Rybczynski's 'domestic well-being'). This inclusiveness
means that the scope for luxury-refinement of shelter is correspondingly
extensive. This is supported by the literature. 'Luxurious' dwellings
for the Romans related to such items as furniture and draperies as well
as room number and size. And in contemporary society a 'luxury

[2] Cf. Le Corbusier (1975: p. 29) who follows his notorious remark that a house is a 'machine à
habiter' by the remark that it is 'une machine diligente et prévenante pour satisfaire aux
exigences du corps: confort'.

home' possesses structural features such as double-glazing, central heating and what one company (Commercial Business Installations) advertises as 'drive-in luxury' that is, remotely-controlled garage doors (illustrated with a picture of a Porsche). More compendiously, this home will possess luxury carpets, furnishings and furniture, while no self-respecting 'luxury apartment' is complete without its 'luxury kitchen' and its 'luxury bathroom'. The latter typically refers to refinements such as jacuzzis and saunas, while the chief attribute of the former is its gadgetry and general labour-saving quality. I will have more to say about gadgetry in a moment but first wish to comment briefly upon the bathroom.

It could be argued that the bathroom serves the bodily needs for cleanliness and excretion and that these constitute a separate category. Such an argument is defensible, and to accept it would not damage this analysis in its essentials. However, I wish to resist it. Aside from a desire for organisational economy, and thus a reluctance to multiply categories, my chief reason for this resistance is that any human habitation makes provision to meet these needs. Of course, this provision does not have to be incorporated into the fabric of the shelter (such an incorporation was a refinement that became one of the distinctive hallmarks of luxury) for it to be reasonably included in that category. The needs served by the bathroom are thus to be understood as being accommodated within the inclusiveness of the need for shelter.

This same categorical inclusiveness enables 'shelter' to encompass the gamut of 'household needs'. We can elaborate this by picking up the reference to gadgets. To describe luxury household items as gadgets is to acknowledge their instrumental status. A knife, for example, has the function (meets the need) of cutting and any qualitative refinement of that function/need will bear most directly on its sharpness and its suitability to the particular task at hand and, less directly, on the amount of effort involved. In the light of these two criteria and in line with the above analysis we can now predict that a 'luxury knife' would be electric with interchangeable blades. However, since the knife is an instrument, it means that it can be subsumed within the four basic or generic categories. A knife is something needed for day-to-day living and such living occurs within a 'shelter'. Accordingly one would expect to see listed in the inventory of a luxury dwelling an electric knife with interchangeable blades; it is the presence of the knife that helps to identify the dwelling as 'luxurious'.

We must, however, be on our guard. The example of the knife as a gadget, as an instrumental need, might seem to imply that the process of 'refinement' in the guise of increasing specificity is reducible to the more efficient development of an instrument's function. That this implication is misleading will become apparent later when we discuss the general relationship between luxury, necessity and superfluity. But it will not be out of place at this juncture to examine another popular usage, namely, luxury travel.

LUXURY TRAVEL

The popularity of this usage means that I have a prima facie obligation to accommodate it to my framework. At first blush its relationship to the four basic categories might appear problematic. In a manner akin to the relationship between bathrooms and excretory needs it could be argued that, in some circumstances at least, mobility and carriage possess a stringency such that travel may be regarded as a basic need. But it is possible to push back the need to travel to the more basic purpose of obtaining food and materials for accommodation or clothing or 'joy-riding' (apt phrase). A vehicle is thus like a knife – an instrumental good. For this reason, on balance I am not inclined to see travel, any more than kitchen utensils, as a separate category of luxury goods.

More precisely, again like the knife, a case can be made to treat it as a subset of that already elastic category of shelter. This case is also worth developing because it enables us to introduce a further relevant consideration. The case proceeds as follows. When a car, for example, is described as a 'luxury model' what is typically denoted thereby is its possession of such features as central locking, computer-controlled instruments, electronic sun-roof, leather upholstery, ample leg-room and the like. These features make for a pleasant, relaxing, that is, 'comfortable' journey, and it is because these are widely-desired features that cars with these features are typically marketed as 'luxury' vehicles. We can interpolate here that the requirement that the car provide protection from the elements is no longer regarded as a 'luxury' feature. Cars are, in this sense, mobile shelters and some of them are, indeed, called 'mobile homes' (with scope for luxury gadgets). Recalling the earlier remark that it is misleading to reduce 'refinement' of instrumental needs to questions of efficiency, it is noteworthy that these features are not narrowly utilitarian aspects. The function of the car is to transport one from A to B. The luxury refinement of this is not speed; cars that are designed purely for speed are not designed for comfort.

There is scope for an area of indeterminacy here. Certainly compared to a Rolls-Royce, a Formula One racing car is not a luxury car, while an Italian sports car is perhaps less clearly categorised. Nevertheless the more the sports car emphasises power and speed the less scope there is for the standard luxury fittings. This difference is reflected in the practice of referring to those vehicles that stress speed as 'performance' cars. A more direct piece of evidence that supports that conclusion is provided by the testimony of an owner of a Ferrari F40. The owner stated that this car, which cost £165,000, had 'pullwire on the doors and plastic sliding windows' and 'no carpets, interior light or radio,' but what it did have in abundance was power, so that within seconds of ignition 'the car is into the hundreds' (Peter Inston, 'Me and My Car', *Sunday Times* 21/8/88). We can also observe, in passing, that this particular example illustrates that expensiveness is not a sufficient condition to determine a good's luxury status. Nonetheless it makes sense to call a Rolls-Royce a luxury car because it makes travelling in this vehicle (instrument) a positive pleasure.

Of course it is open to any individual to regard, as Peter Inston clearly does, a car's speed as the source of 'pleasure' and vehicles can be desired for that reason. At the close of this chapter we will consider directly the individual dimension to the identification of luxury but the apparent fact of the matter is that, in popular standard usage as reflected in the language of marketing, the luxury refinement of cars relates to non-functional attributes rather than to issues of increased efficiency. Nonetheless, just as the luxury knife still cuts, so a luxury car is still a means of transport. Thus while on the one hand it is misleading to reduce the knife's 'luxury' to its increased efficiency so, on the other, it is misleading to neglect the fact that all luxuries 'relate' to basic satisfactions. It is important in a consideration of luxury not to identify it with redundancy or uselessness, a point we shall meet again.

THE TRANSIENCE OF LUXURY

Though we have stressed that desires are by their nature specific, we have also, in the context of luxury goods, understood them as falling into four general categories. As we have seen, the category of shelter includes an array of subsidiary instrumental needs and a 'luxury dwelling' is one where the most refined goods or gadgets are to be found. These gadgets are positively pleasing because they make domestic life easier. It is quite simply more pleasant to let others, or machines, perform tasks which are, to you, no more than chores. So widely shared is this disposition that it is one of the areas of the greatest convergence in human desires. (Note the implicit naturalism here.) Thanks to this particular convergence, household chores have been one of the areas of most rapid development and greatest refinements. The percentage of households with vacuum cleaners, washing-machines, gas or electric heating is so high that simple possession of these no longer ranks as a luxury. We shall return to this point, but one implication can be taken up immediately.

Implicit here is the transient status of luxury goods. A luxury is not something static, it is dynamic; it is subject to development as the desires, and necessarily attendant beliefs, are met and then fuelled with further qualitative modifications or refinements. Hence, for example, 'simple possession' of a television is not (now) a luxury. We can discern here a 'drag-effect'. As goods come to be widely available and become cemented into daily life, then possession of, or access to, such goods means they can lose their luxury status. But more than that, they can be thought to be socially necessary. One particularly instructive case is sanitation arrangements. It provides perhaps the best example of how a one-time luxury – interior water-closets – has become a legally enforceable requirement. Characteristically this works both ways so that those who live in an unsanitary dwelling may be said to possess the 'right' to have their dwelling conform to the socially necessary standards.[3]

If we reflect on this case of transience then two important implications can be identified. The first is that a desire appears to have turned into a need. We have to analyse this appearance with some care. In so far as basic needs are at issue, then this can be only an appearance since these needs are categories and not principles of action. There is a conceptual or logical 'gap' here that cannot be bridged. The needs at issue must be some sort of instrumental or volitional need. These needs, as the example of my need for the pen

---

[3] If 'rights' are tied to goods or services that are deemed social necessities and these same goods were one-time luxuries, then this class of 'rights' too must also be understood as fluid, rather than, say, as 'natural' or simply 'human'. One consequence is that there can be no right to a luxury (cf. Raphael, 1967: p. 64).

mentioned above illustrates, do not in principle stand in conceptual opposition to desires. The crucial point in this case is not, therefore, that some transformation of desire into need has occurred but that 'our' society has invested certain instrumental needs with a special status, namely, that of being social necessities. This constitutes the first implication and reinforces the earlier comment that luxuries are not a superadded category. There is, as it were, a continuum in any society from desires which are deemed social necessities to those deemed luxuries. I will return to this.

The second implication concerns this special status. By virtue of their status as social necessities goods can, in context, establish a prima facie claim on the public purse. Think here of the argument that pensioners should be exempted from paying the television licence-fee on the grounds that, like their exemption from prescription charges, we are here dealing with a non-luxury item. (The British Labour Party, in Opposition, committed itself to that policy – see *The Times*, 28/8/90). This is not, however, all one way. The effective spread of private ownership of washing-machines has produced the demise of publicly funded washhouses.[4]

POLITICAL MORALITY

This last point broaches an issue of more general significance. If we confine ourselves to contemporary capitalist societies, then this association between the transience of luxury goods and the dynamism of desire can be linked to another. This second, linked association, is that between the commercially assumed innocence of luxury goods and the legitimacy of private desire.

As we have seen, the direction of the luxury 'refinements' in shelter is, in broad terms, toward the increasing 'privatisation' of such goods. This fact goes a long way to explaining why the 'home' is such a focus for advertisers proclaiming their goods as 'luxuries'. The rapid dissemination of televisions, and then videos, is further testament to these pre-eminent 'leisure goods' being valued because they can be enjoyed 'at home'. And while 'eating out' has, if anything, increased, thus providing counter-evidence, the labour-saving aspect of this does have its privatised dimension in the form of the 'carry-out'. This

[4] Cf. Gershuny (1983) on the growth of 'self-servicing' as a consequence of the spread of consumer durables, a process which he judges as equalising access to services as between the rich and the poor.

privatising or domesticating tendency is in accordance historically with the emergence of 'comfort'. This initially expressed itself within the closets or private rooms of the great houses, where the aptly-named 'easy chairs' or *fauteuils de commodité* were located, before pervading the more formal public rooms (cf. Thornton, 1978: pp. 10, 302).

Looked at in this light we can see that in this process of privatisation some basic questions in political morality are at stake. Indeed, from its inception in Greek thought, 'luxury' was a political concept. In classical, as well as in Christian and early modern thought, 'luxuries' were subject to moral criticism. As we have already noted, they were condemned because they fostered effeminacy and thus undermined virtue and corrupted both the individual and his *patria*. While this line of criticism never completely died out, it lost its edge.

Whereas the pre-modern view, to be canvassed in Part II, saw a threat to liberty in the boundless uncontrollability of human bodily desires, modern thought values the liberty manifest in individuals pursuing their own desires, a task in which every human partakes and for which every human is qualified, and regarding which every human is his or her own best judge. The elitism and sexism of classical thought, whereby only the sage or independent male citizen was free, is transformed. It is, of course, liberalism that best embodies such a transformation with its understanding of what is decisively different about the modern world. It is, therefore, no surprise to find historically that it was liberals, like Adam Smith, who defended luxury or opulence against, among many others, the neo-classical critique of Rousseau or conventional moralising of John Brown's *Estimate* (see Chapter 6). However, it is also no surprise that this liberal picture fails to command universal assent. What we find is that the 'privatisation' associated with, and the innocence of, luxury goods are not immune from criticism from those who wish to dispute the political morality of liberalism. Unlike the classical critique which indicted luxury because it undermined virtue, the modern critique focuses upon the obligation to meet needs.

One of the hallmarks of socialism is that it invokes the morality of meeting needs to indict the immorality of a society that supports the ability to acquire luxuries ahead of the responsibility of ensuring that needs are met. Needs possess, as we noted earlier, a seemingly even more basic universalism than desires. But, as the above-mentioned 'drag-effect' implies, a one-time luxury can become a social necessity, which is to say that there has been a shift in the understanding of what is required to participate effectively in society. It is indeed this very fluidity that accounts for the developments in theories of needs. The recourse to 'need' has been able to retain its popularity and potency in social criticism because, by being extended to encompass notions of autonomy and the like, it has been made applicable to conditions where more than minimal physical survival is at stake. It is this same fluidity that is fundamental to the debates over the 'relative' as opposed to the 'absolute' character of poverty. We shall deal with this question in Chapter 8.

The crucial premise in this socialist critique is a postulated connexion between the failure to meet needs and the suffering of harm. From this is typically generated a principle such that meeting needs ought to have precedence over satisfying desires (see Chapter 8). Accordingly, from this perspective, it is wrong if some individuals in a society are able to indulge or wallow in luxury while other members are in a needy state. One popular expression of this was an indictment of the conspicuous lifestyle of Porsche-owning 'yuppies' living in luxurious dockland flats alongside the original and socially-deprived denizens of the same area. It should be acknowledged that the general thrust of this critique has not been confined to socialists. For example, the World Bank – an institution not usually thought of as socialist – stated that capital aid would not be forthcoming to African regimes if they financed, *inter alia*, 'luxurious consumption' (*Sub-Saharan Africa*, World Bank Report, quoted in *The Times* 22/11/89).

That issue, along with the role played by needs in definitions of poverty, and social criticism more generally, will be addressed in Part IV. It will, however, at this point be appropriate to take up my earlier remark concerning the relationships between 'health goods' and luxury.

HEALTH GOODS

Medical treatment is generally seen as a need, the sufficient and necessary condition of which is ill-health. This generates a moral argument to the effect that any system in which treatment is a function of ability-to-pay is unacceptable because that ability illicitly replaces need as a sufficient condition. It might now seem that this argument could be extended to 'luxury'; any society in which access to health care is a 'luxury' is to be indicted. Such an argument is misdirected. This is so on two fronts. First, it conflates expensiveness and luxury – as we saw with the Ferrari F40 sports car this is not a necessary connexion. Second, and more directly, it is quite literally a category mistake – provision of medical treatment falls outside the four categories of luxury goods.

Where luxury does figure in this context is in the guise of 'plush private rooms with videos, fridges, telephones and special menus' and so on. (This list is from an article in *The Observer* 1/7/90 entitled 'Luxury on the NHS'.) These features all fall within my categories of shelter and sustenance. Presumably, it is features such as these that are being invoked when the *Norwich Union* declares in an advertisement that its scheme will make 'Personal healthcare. No longer an expensive luxury'. I think that this presumption is warranted by the considerations that have been put forward and so this advertisement does not stand as a counter-example to my argument. What is also worthy of note about this advertisement is the locution 'expensive luxury', which, at least, suggests that the two terms are not synonymous. Advertising language is, of course, notorious for its disregard of grammatical niceties but this locution is not pleonastic and is perfectly intelligible. One random example comes from Simon Barnes's column in which, referring to American Football, he writes, 'It is a good idea to have cover for your top man; but a stable of quarterbacks can be an expensive luxury' (*The Times* 5/1/91).

That those with more money can more easily buy treatment may be criticised by denying that there should be a 'market' in such matters, but such a criticism is not conterminous with claiming that mere differential ability-to-pay constitutes a 'luxury'. To receive medical attention because one suffers from (say) a diseased spleen is truly a 'need'. In Hutcheson's terms, the 'desire' to have the spleen removed is not a positive 'pleasure' but the removal of pain. And while, unlike autonomy, 'health' is a basic bodily (widely understood) need, its confinement to the sphere of pain removal or negative desire means it lacks the conceptual capacity to become a genuine 'luxury'.

In the light of the earlier argument this last point perhaps warrants some clarification. There is a difference between the removal of a diseased spleen and the possession of an automatic washing-machine. It is the difference between restoration and improvement. The former restores the body to a *status quo ante* and the desire is negative because it wants to undo what has transpired (sickness). The latter embodies a positive desire to establish a new condition – a less onerous chore. Hence while the washing-machine diminishes the drudgery, to which as a matter of natural fact individuals are averse,[5] the desire to possess that machine is not a negative desire but a positive pleasure because it assists in the execution of a continuing task.

Perhaps the best indicator of the relationship between luxury and health goods is the case of cosmetic surgery. This surgery can be a health need, like treatment for the spleen, when it is performed to ameliorate some psychologically troubling disfigurement. Health can be 'restored' to some socially acceptable norm if a nose (say) is surgically altered. Indeed in this case the operation could be financed from public funds (as it is in the British NHS). Cosmetic surgery can also be elective in the sense that an individual positively desires (say) a more attractive nose. *Ex hypothesi*, this surgery is not determined by considerations of health and it can accordingly, without inconsistency, be regarded as a luxury good (in the category of clothing – see later). Moreover this surgery is appropriately paid for from private funds.

This example brings out a further point. As technology develops so the scope for surgery increases. These developments may mean that a previously permanent disfigurement can be removed – a 'sickness' can be cured, health restored. But, and this is the important point, in this case we have *not* got an example of a luxury becoming a need. What has happened is that a previously unmet need can now be met. This is so even if the same development could be used to realise a positive pleasure. The conceptual distinction between restoration and improvement remains, and is not affected by the possibility that the technology is employed to realise a luxury good before a health good. It bears repeating that to deny that *medical* treatment/attention is amenable to 'luxury' good status is a separate question from whether or not a society should increase public monies to meet health needs by, for example, levying taxes upon 'luxury goods'. That question will occupy us in Part IV and we shall, later in this chapter, make some observations upon the general relationship between needs and desires as an indication of a society's conception of political order.

SUPERFLUITY

That health is not a luxury is the conclusion we would expect from the seemingly obvious 'fact' that luxuries are not needed. While perhaps 'obvious' it nonetheless bears further scrutiny. This we can undertake

---

[5] No claim is being made to the effect that the avoidance of labour is 'natural', a charge that Marx levelled against Smith. The operative word is 'drudgery'.

by exploring the idea of a luxury good as a superfluous item. It is clear that the ideas of luxury and superfluity are commonly associated. Mandeville, for example, as part of his subversive intent, held that the only tenable definition of luxury was as something that is 'not immediately necessary to make Man subsist as he is a living Creature' (*Fable*: I, 107). Sombart (1913: p. 71) followed suit by defining luxury as expenditure that goes beyond what is necessary (*der über das Notwendige hinausgeht*). On a popular level, this association is evident when those cast away on BBC Radio's 'Desert Island Discs' with their eight records and three books are also allowed a 'luxury'. The seeming definition of this is that it must be of no conceivable use in abetting an 'escape' from the island. On a philosophical level, Garret Thomson (1987: p. 96, cf. p. 108) says luxuries are enjoyable items that are 'by definition' superfluous.

Thomson goes on to say that luxuries are 'neither beneficial nor useful'. This is not, however, a necessary consequence of superfluity. While all luxuries are superfluous, the converse does not hold. The crux is the sense in which 'superfluous' is understood. Two senses can be distinguished. It can mean the redundant or it can mean the easily substitutable. The former meaning accords most clearly with the ideas of quotas or fixed quantities. If it takes six screws to secure a shelf then more than that number are superfluous *qua* redundant: a seventh screw is not a 'refined' luxury good. A luxury good as such is not a redundancy – the Rolls-Royce gets one from A to B. As six screws secure the shelf so six slices of bread fill the stomach, also making any more superfluous *qua* redundant. This last example is chosen to evoke Seneca's argument about 'luxurious excess'. But in that argument, it will be recalled, the issue was not so much the number of slices as the relative freshness of the bread – the crucial issue being that luxury is a question of qualitative refinement rather than quantity. Once this distinction between quantity and quality is heeded then we can begin to see why it is potentially misleading to assimilate the notions of luxury and superfluity without some further specification of the latter.

This same conclusion can be reinforced by noting the connexion between luxury and 'pleasure', since the latter is absent when the superfluous-*qua*-redundant is involved. But it should not be thought that we are dealing with two hermetically distinct notions. The concept of Diminishing Marginal Utility provides an illustration as to why this is the case. Conceivably a doughnut can be a luxury and even two or perhaps three doughnuts can still constitute qualitative refinements on bread rolls. However, the fourth doughnut can be a redundantly superfluous confection – it is no longer desired as a pleasing pastry.

Nevertheless, luxury and superfluity do intersect conceptually. The superfluousness of a luxury stems from its negative status – it is something we can do without, it is not needed. We need a certain quantum of fluid intake but don't need a glass of Château-Lafite, even if by some bizarre set of circumstances it should transpire that a glass of Lafite is the quantum of liquid that is needed. In line with the earlier argument regarding the abstract nature of needs then any potable fluid, even urine *in extremis*, can serve to satisfy the need to drink. Château-Lafite is at this abstract level on a par with a glass of water and, as a consequence, as long as we have water then the Lafite can be forgone without harm. But the same could be said equally of forgoing water as long as there is a glass of claret.

Where then does the difference between water and Lafite lie such that standardly (i.e. non-bizarrely) only the latter qualifies as a luxury good? To answer that we need to recall that luxury goods represent the increasing development of specific desires within categories established by certain basic generic needs. They constitute qualitative refinements. As refinements they can always be substituted for a less refined product; if the 'four-star' hotel is fully booked, or too expensive, then a three-star will do.

It is, accordingly, the second meaning of superfluous – the easily substitutable – that supplies the appropriate sense in which luxuries are superfluous. The substitutable is not the redundant even though both can be judged non-necessary and thus both be deemed superfluous. However, it is important to tread carefully. Substitutability itself seems most obviously to apply to needs of the basic categorical sort. The explanation for this lies in the very abstractness of these needs. As our discussion of liquid intake bore out, because anything deemed potable will suffice to meet the need then any one drinkable item is substitutable for another. Simmel, implicitly following Kant (*Groundwork*, tr. Paton: p. 102), made this point when he stated that, 'so long as objects are merely useful they are interchangeable and everything can be replaced by anything else that performs the same service' (Simmel, 1990: p. 74). What this analysis fails to bring out is, of course, the element of necessity in needs-satisfaction. King Midas starved to death because a golden apple is no substitute for a Golden Delicious.

To account for the connexion between luxuries and substitutability we have to heed the earlier distinction between the expansiveness and intensity of desire. We have seen that, in contrast to the abstract universality of basic needs, the language of desire is that of concrete specificity. One aspect of this is that the more specific and concrete a desire is, say for a first edition of *De Cive*, then the less expansive yet more intense that desire is, so that the less a substitute is acceptable. Given this we are now able, in a preliminary fashion, to locate luxuries: it is a hallmark of a luxury that it is something not intensely desired. As we shall explore in more detail later, a luxury is something it would be nice to have, while at the same time not having it would cause no particular pain. Because of this it is very likely that a luxury will be relatively easily substituted; the three-star hotel is perfectly acceptable. This conclusion, at least, accords with an aspect of both received and academic wisdom.

From the point of view of mainstream economists a luxury good is a good or service that enjoys high income elasticity of demand. In their technical language/notation a good is a luxury good when income elasticity is greater than unity ($e > 1$) and a 'necessity' when it is less than unity ($e < 1$) (there are also 'inferior goods' which, after a certain point, are not desired at all ($e < 0$)) (cf., e.g., Lancaster, 1971: p. 68). Economists have also developed their own technical discussion of 'substitutability'. Where, in theory, there exist virtually perfect substitutes, then the very high price elasticity that is definitive of luxuries will be found (Deaton & Muellbauer, 1980: p. 79). Accordingly, should there be, for example, a fall in the price of Château-Latour, then (for the same vintage) one can expect a drop in sales of Lafite as oenophiles (and investors) switch (substitute) chateaux. In a similar fashion, should there be a fall in income then, because luxury goods are substitutable for less refined items (water for Lafite in my earlier – deliberately stark – example), expenditure upon them will decline. This understanding also accords with the apparently common-sense view (as exemplified by Hamish Fraser whom I quoted toward the beginning of this chapter) that expenditure is directed first at what is needed and then, only if there is a surplus, will this be directed toward 'luxuries'. There is also empirical support for this in as much as food retailers have retained their profit margins in a high-interest rate economy like Great Britain in 1989–90 (see, e.g., comments by the deputy chairman of Sainsbury's, *Observer* 19/9/90). Conversely, in 1988 at the time of tax-cuts, there was, in the words of one sub-editor, a 'Boom in luxuries predicted' (see *The Times*, 16/4/88).

Notwithstanding this convergence, it paints too simple a picture.

There is ample evidence that individuals are prepared to sacrifice consumption of supposedly 'basic needs' in order to maintain social status or prosecute a personal 'plan of life'. Even economists recognise the 'demonstration effect' (Duesenberry, 1949: p. 27) and the phenomenon of non-functional demand. In an influential analysis of that phenomenon, Leibenstein (1950) identified three aspects – the 'Bandwagon effect' where demand increases due to the fact that others are consuming the product as, for example, in the case of what is fashionable; the 'Snob effect' where demand decreases due to the fact that others are consuming a particular product, and the 'Veblen effect' where demand increases when the price is higher rather than lower.

If we apply this analysis to our opening paradox, then we can identify as one aim of the rhetoric of luxury in advertising that it is attempting to stimulate a bandwagon effect. Yet the transient quality of the status 'luxury' necessarily means that a particular 'luxury good' will move to the snob effect. This means that self-styled purveyors of luxury goods must always be on their guard to maintain the cachet of 'exclusiveness'.

CLOTHING

The clothing industry provides a good illustration of this and we can perhaps best appreciate this and other related points by means of a more general discussion of the category of clothing as a luxury good. There are, on the one hand, the fashion leaders and practitioners of *haute couture* and, on the other, the mass-market ready-to-wear manufacturers. The latter can advertise a 'luxury' silk blouse to be obtained via mail order, while the former rely on stylistic innovation, inherent quality of raw materials and expertise in cutting and stitching, together with the status of a 'name'.

At one level clothing is seemingly akin to shelter in that it provides protection against the elements. However, since no animal wears clothes this need seems straightforwardly to be a human need. Indeed, despite their reference to physical satisfactions, each of the needs which categorically establish luxuries are *human* needs. While the category of 'leisure' most obviously seems to be a human need the same also applies to food and shelter, as well as to clothing. The identification of these needs as human accommodates the indisputable fact that they exist only as embedded in cultures.

The implications of this embedment have now, if only at this point, in a preliminary way, to be addressed. Not only do no animals wear clothes but the wearing of apparel is no simple functional act. Indeed there is no universal correlation between cold climate and quantity of clothing, as Charles Darwin observed on the Beagle voyage upon seeing the near-naked inhabitants of Tierra del Fuego (*Voyage of the 'Beagle'*: pp. 212–13). What clothing the Fuegians did possess was some covering of the genital area. Nor is the explanation for that self-evident. The least plausible explanation is sexual modesty. This lacks explanatory weight because the trans-cultural tendency is for clothing to attract rather than distract attention. In Madge Garland's words, 'a history of the way people dress is concerned with man's first and most faithful addiction – his intense preoccupation with his own body' (Garland, 1975: p. 7) and, as another historian of fashion has pointed out, the most frequent tendency in the history of costume has been a striving for an increase in stature (Kybalova, 1968: p. 15). Sexual modesty is not the thought that comes to mind when, for example, the elaborate cod-pieces on Elizabethan male costumes are observed.

If sexual modesty thus looks an unlikely explanation for genital covering, then the practical use of such garments to protect the organs necessary for reproduction is perhaps a better bet. But that too is not the whole answer. The protective function does not explain the universal presence of decoration on clothes as well as on humans themselves. Darwin's Fuegians, even when quite naked were nonetheless 'bedaubed with white paint' (*Voyage*: p. 213) and the elective cosmetic surgery mentioned above can be understood as a further example. Once again it is sexual attraction that seems better placed to account for this ubiquity. This raises an issue that goes deep into the territory of morality. We must be content with making an observation from the perimeter, though in Chapter 9 a brief exploration will be undertaken.

What is quintessential to human societies is that the so-called natural processes, such as, pre-eminently, sex along with birth and death, are overlaid with conventions, with ritual and ceremony which are invested with deep symbolic meaning. The effect of this investment is to render over-simple any explanation of human apparel that assimilates it too directly to the functionalism possessed by the tail-feathers of the peacock. And while it is unwise to look for monocausality in this area, the most promising general explanation of the human need for clothes is this link with their symbolic character. It is this character that best accounts for the apparently non-functional aspect of clothing.

ORNAMENT

The fact that the earliest known examples of human clothing are the skins of the animals that are hunted is not simply a case of *faute de mieux* but is indicative of the symbolic dimension. At its baldest the argument is that there is a mythopoeic connexion between wearing the skins and a successful hunt; it is a form of sympathetic magic. It is this same general principle that accounts for ornamentation, the wearing of which 'identified the wearer with animals, gods, heroes or other men' (Boucher, n.d.: p. 10). For example, it is, from this perspective, significant that in the *Iliad* (III, p. 64) when Paris, somewhat uncharacteristically, steps forward and offers combat he is described as wearing a panther's skin. Certainly the remains of the earliest civilisations provide evidence of the perceived indispensability of ornaments and jewellery through their presence in tombs.

So ubiquitous is this human concern to decorate that some writers explain it by invoking a distinct human need to that effect. For example, the nineteenth-century historian of luxury, Henri Baudrillart referred to *l'instinct de parure* (*Histoire du Luxe Privé*: 1, p. 166) and, from a very different perspective, Ernest Mandel (1968: p. 660) refers to decoration as one of the (six) basic needs. However, this is an unnecessary complication. The human need for clothing is itself inseparable from its symbolic role and it is that which is typically manifest in ornamentation, for the 'truly natural state of the adult human is dressed and decorated' (Hollander, 1988: p. 84). Or, as Carlyle put it, 'the first purpose of Clothes . . . was not warmth or decency but ornament' (*Sartor Resartus*: p. 30).

If ornamentation is coeval with clothing, then it means luxury clothing is not to be understood as ornamentation superadded on to some simple utilitarian function. This conclusion has a wider bearing. The 'luxury knife' referred to earlier would not be luxurious *because* it was gold-plated; gold-plating would be another refinement not different in kind from it being electrically powered. Nor is there any necessary order of priority; clearly in this case gold-plating ante-dates the refinement of power. Furthermore, to regard gold-plating as the essence of luxury is to confuse, once again, the redundant with the substitutable – a Trabant can substitute for a Rolls-Royce but the latter is still a means of transport.

The fact that clothing has symbolic significance means that the human need for clothing only exists within a concrete cultural setting. Certainly in Western culture the most frequent symbolic use of clothing has been to maintain social status and social differences. A clear-cut expression of this connexion between clothing and status is the evidence of sumptuary laws. For example, the 1363 Act of Apparel of Edward III spoke in its preamble of the 'contagious and excessive apparel of divers people, against their estate and degree' (in Harte, 1976: p. 138). All such legislation, which we shall examine in some detail in Chapter 3, typically specified in minute detail what each of the various ranks was permitted and (more often) forbidden to wear. It is here that luxury most obviously and pejoratively makes its appearance.

From the perspective of the framers of these laws, 'luxury' represents, in the guise of the desire for sumptuous apparel, the subversion of proper social stratification. But in contemporary society, where luxury is regarded as an essentially innocent desire, it still applies to clothing and the 'meaning' conveyed thereby. Hence modern luxury clothes are distinguished by the exquisite workmanship and quality material found in the Saville Row suit and the Lagerfeld dress worn with jewels from Cartier and perfume from Chanel (and maybe also the effects of elective cosmetic surgery). The above-noted association between luxury and privatisation of consumption is encapsulated in *haute couture* and bespoke tailoring (and choice of nose). Ownership of such goods conveys the meaning of exclusivity and its associated qualities of power, wealth and taste. But whereas in Roman and medieval societies 'luxury' was a threat to exclusivity by representing the subversiveness of private desire, in modern societies the 'message' reinforces the legitimacy of such desire.

CONSPICUOUS CONSUMPTION

Once again we must proceed with due care. It is unacceptable to assimilate without remainder – as might here seem to be implied – conspicuous consumption and expenditure on luxuries. Indeed just as ornamentation is not the same as luxury nor is ostentation. Conspicuous consumption is consumption, the satisfaction of which derives from audience reaction (cf. Mason, 1981). In its purest form, as identified by Veblen, conspicuous consumption is consumption of the totally useless. But this is not to say that such consumption is pointless. Indeed we can detect, perhaps paradoxically, an element of 'necessity' here (cf. Kyrk, 1976: p. 241n), an element that precludes the assimilation of these two types of expenditure.

Conspicuous consumption has to be understood in terms of social perception. To consume conspicuously is to consume these goods that non-consumers are presumed to perceive as (*inter alia*) luxuries. However, from the consumer's perspective this consumption is instrumental/necessary to the maintenance of that very (presumed) perception and thence to the maintenance of their social status (cf. Simmel, 1964: p. 338). *Pace* Dwight Robinson (1961: p. 398), the motivation for luxury is not the pursuit of demonstrable rarity for its own sake; it is for the sake of social perception. Indeed the rationale underlying sumptuary laws was to reserve particular fabrics and ornamentation for certain social orders in order to distinguish them and uphold the social hierarchy. Moreover since any social hierarchy reposes on a configuration of power, and attendant belief, this sumptuary distinctiveness was designed to manifest that configuration. Of Elizabeth I, for example, McKendrick (1983: p. 76) remarks that the extravagance of her wardrobe 'fulfilled a very political need. It was the visible external proof of her divinity; it buttressed her political power; and her courtiers were expected to buttress it further with a spectacular display of satellite finery.'[6]

I shall have more to say about what McKendrick here calls 'political need' in the context of sumptuary legislation in Chapter 3 but the general point is of wider application. The social practice of potlatch and purchases from Asprey's Gift Catalogue can both be understood as instrumental to the maintenance of self-perceived 'position' in society. This self-perception is itself, at least partially, constituted by the presumption that others perceive their consumption as conspicuous in this manner. It also fits this picture that in contemporary societies once the perception changes, that is once the bandwagon rolls so that 'luxury goods' become widely attainable, then they cease to become items to consume conspicuously; they no longer mark out 'distance' (cf. Bourdieu, 1979)[7] – to be the first in your street to own a video means something, a meaning that is lost when every other household possesses one.

---

[6] Cf. Simmel (1964: p. 343) who in his brief essay on 'Adornment' remarks *à propos* of sumptuary law that adornment is the means by which 'social power or dignity is transformed into visible, personal excellence'.

[7] The crux of Bourdieu's (1979: p. 58) argument is that, 'le pouvoir économique est d'abord un pouvoir de mettre la nécessité économique à distance; c'est pourquoi il s'affirme universellement par le destruction de richesses, le dépense ostentatoire, le gaspillage et toutes les formes de luxe gratuit'. Note the universality here, for its significance see text *infra*.

SOCIAL MEANING

A radical implication can be drawn from these remarks. To appreciate this we can return to the connexion between luxury and rarity. Earlier I said that rarity was not a sufficient condition of a good being a luxury and cited, as an example, the limited appeal of a first edition of _De Cive_. What is required is not that the good in question is of limited supply but that _many_ desire it when there are only a few in existence; for example, an internal water-closet could be said to have been a 'luxury good' in the 1900s.

Thus far we have attempted to explain this by reference to the abstract categorical status of 'needs'. An alternative explanation, the 'radical implication', would displace this reference and have recourse solely to the 'social meaning' of a luxury as a rare item. This alternative is part of a more general conceptualisation of consumption as a 'system of meaning' or signs (cf. Baudrillard, 1988: p. 46). According to this account, to possess (consume) rare but widely-desired objects is to enjoy a luxury. Xenos (1989: pp. 94–5) goes as far as saying that 'it is not the scarcity of certain objects that determines their status as luxury items; it is their status as luxury items that renders them scarce objects'. In terminology current in late nineteenth-century France it is, on this understanding, conceptually impossible to 'democratise' luxury (cf. Williams, 1982: pp. 94–104 _et passim_). Luxuries are _by definition_ always out of reach of mass consumption.

A variant of this argument is one aspect of Fred Hirsch's notion of 'positional goods'. These goods are socially scarce in such a way that an increase in their availability changes their character so that they yield less satisfaction (Hirsch, 1977: p. 20). Hirsch adopts the economist's definition of 'luxury' (high income elasticity of demand) and then notes that as the general standard of living rises so the demand for luxuries is diffused (ibid.: p. 66). But this diffusion, he claims, changes the character of the good. Car ownership is an example. When cars are widely owned not only (as in the video example) is the symbolic cachet lost but also the actual enjoyment of the good is offset by such consequences as traffic jams, parking restrictions and inferior public transport (ibid.: p. 167). This analysis does, however, neglect the fact that the good itself has changed as well as its diffusion. In functional terms the cars now mass produced are, on most meaningful criteria – reliability, safety, energy efficiency – far superior to earlier models. The fact that, when first introduced, these early models were themselves superior to horse-drawn conveyances was central to their appeal. They were not centrally or essentially 'snob goods'. By conceptually tying 'luxury' so tightly to the social meaning of rarity/exclusivity the inherent quality of the good, and the reasons for wanting it, are downplayed.

This is not to say that social meaning is irrelevant and I shall myself exploit one dimension of this account later, when I discuss the relationship between the 'grammar' of societies and the identification of goods as necessities or luxuries. However, as I have already suggested, I do not wish to travel all the way down this road. Two considerations underlie my reluctance.

INDIVIDUAL MEANING

The first consideration stems from any earlier caution against assimilating luxury goods to those consumed conspicuously. There is an element of particularity or individuality which exclusive emphasis upon *social* meaning or perception runs the risk of obscuring. The crux of the matter is the 'relativity' of luxury; one person's luxury can be another's necessity. This can, indeed, as we have seen, provide an explanation of the necessity to consume luxuries conspicuously in order to maintain social esteem. However, it is consistent also with another, more individual, aspect of relativity. I might regard the ownership of a word-processor as a luxury but to the professional writer it can be a necessity. Although this is a difference between individuals it is not without possible social significance. The professional writer, for example, might well be able to claim the cost of the processor against tax, thus indicating a societal recognition of this necessity. More importantly, it is not the case here that my identification of this good as a luxury is dependent on the fact that only a few 'consume' it. That identification stems from its place within *my* schedule of desires. This reinforces the earlier conclusion that there is no necessary connexion between luxury and rarity. The corollary of this is that it is not definitionally true that luxuries cannot be widely consumed. I will return to individual meaning at the end of the chapter.

NEEDS AND NATURALISM

The second, broader, consideration that makes me reluctant to follow in its entirety the approach of Baudrillard and others is based on an unwillingness to jettison the naturalism that underlies my four categories. The source of my reluctance can be conveyed by looking more closely at the 'movement' of goods from being rare to being commonplace. It is undeniable that this is the context historically of many instances of 'luxury goods'. As an example let me cite the work of Fernand Braudel. He writes,

Sugar, for example, was a luxury before the sixteenth century; pepper was still a luxury in the closing years of the seventeenth; so were alcohol and the first 'aperitifs' at the time of Catherine de Medici, or the swansdown beds and silver cups of the Russian boyars before Peter the Great. The first flat plates, which Francis I ordered from a goldsmith in Antwerp in 1538, were also a luxury. (Braudel, 1981: p. 183)

And throughout the treasure-trove of minutiae with which his writings abound, we find goods (coffee, chocolate, tobacco and table forks are further examples) the consumption of which was initially limited to a few, referred to as luxuries.[8]

What those who wish to jettison any naturalistic talk of needs do not explain is why such goods did not remain confined to a 'few'. Why did cars come to be mass-produced? Why was the owner of the first video in the street joined by others shortly thereafter? The broad outlines of an explanation are discernible in the above discussion. There is a movement from the 'few' to the 'many' in the case of cars and videos (or sugar or forks) because such a movement expresses the general incidence of the desire for these goods. (Of course this is no guarantee of success; think of the respective fates of videos and the Sinclair C5 'motor-vehicle'.)

And this incidence is general *because* these desires 'relate' to 'universal satisfactions'. The causal element should not be overlooked. It is misleadingly oversimple to attribute this diffusion to the 'totalitarian' compass or 'omnipotence' of advertising (Baudrillard, 1988: pp. 19, 10).[9] The 'naturalism' to which I refer is constituted by the universality of satisfactions. The necessary connexion between luxury and pleasure is similarly significant. The history of fashion counsels against too facile a reading of that connexion; women (especially) have suffered physical discomfort in order to be 'in vogue' and luxury clothing in its guise as 'trend-setter' is no exception.

[8] There is support for Braudel's list and labelling. Erasmus in 1516 lists as *luxum ac delicias* and whose consumption is confined to the rich, 'cotton, silk, dyed cloth, pepper, spices, ointments, jewels' (*Institutio*: p. 262, tr. p. 192).
[9] Baudrillard (1988: p. 42) is later critical of Galbraith (1985) for assuming too much passivity on the part of the consumer and now declares that 'we know that advertising is not omnipotent'.

Nonetheless no amount of advertising can make sugar other than
sweet, and the very fact that large sums of money are spent on
informing consumers of the dangers to health of its overconsumption
is itself testament to the force of the 'natural' connexion. Advertising,
in other words, has to rely for its potency on certain givens, and
central to these givens are the universality of satisfactions enjoyed by
humans. Seen in this light it is no surprise to find sexual attractiveness
used so often to sell anything from clothing to soft furnishings (shelter)
to chocolates (sustenance) to holidays (leisure); as well as 'subsumable'
items such as lawn-mowers and car-tyres. The very ubiquity and
frequency of this marketing strategy itself overlays the fact that goods
of these types are widely desired *because* they 'relate' to these
'naturally' experienced satisfactions.

My recourse to naturalism here should not be misconstrued.
Baudrillard (1981: p. 80) explicitly attacks a naturalistic account of
needs, where that is understood to refer to a 'vital anthropological
minimum'. This minimum, he declares, is a residuum, not a *sine qua
non* point of departure. Societies give priority (variously) to the
'divine or sacrificial share, sumptuous discharge, economic profit'
and only once these have been determined is the 'survival threshold'
identified; it is 'this pre-dedication of luxury that negatively determines
the level of survival, and not the reverse' (ibid.). But I am not arguing
for the 'brute-ness' of these satisfactions (needs). (Indeed in Chapter 9
I shall reinvoke the notion of 'pre-dedication'.) Rather, in line with
my understanding of needs as abstract categories, these needs are
never experienced other than as elements of social/cultural practice
or 'forms of life' in the Wittgensteinian sense. This is why I am not
committed to 'brute-ness' or what Baudrillard (1981: p. 71) calls
'naive factuality'.[10]

Yet neither does it follow from this that 'needs' are simply reducible

[10] Baudrillard's whole 'problematic' is Marxian. Much of the animus of his writing is directed
against the centrality assumed by 'use-value' and 'production' in Marxist theory. Nonetheless,
like others (e.g. Prétèceille & Terrail, 1985) he is (or was, since his position has changed)
concerned to explode the ideological character of needs, where this is understood in terms of
their place in individualistic political economy. Rather, needs are to be understood as
productive forces required by the economic system, that is, as 'a function induced (in the
individual) by the internal logic of the system' (Baudrillard, 1988: p. 82). As an illustrative
example Baudrillard imagines the requirement, sanctioned by law, to change cars every two
years. Although he is critical of Galbraith for having a simplistic view of needs (cf.
Baudrillard, 1988: pp. 38ff.) he is adapting here what Galbraith (1962: ch. 11) called the
'dependence effect'; wants are created by the productive process by which they are satisfied.
When considered outside its problematic it is not easy to see what this Baudrillardian theory
of consumption amounts to. Certainly its preoccupation with the assumptions and practices
of capitalist (and socialist/productivist) economies appears to make it over-specific.

to social constructions. We have distinguished between basic needs that are abstract categories but which nevertheless reflect, in Wiggins's terms, 'the way the world is', and instrumental or volitional needs and, within the latter, have noted that some of them possess the special status of being socially necessary. While the last of these do appear to be socially constructed – a point I shall pick up shortly – it does not mean that this applies to basic needs. It is worth exploring briefly why this is the case.

UNIVERSALISM

Apart from his critique, Baudrillard (1981: pp. 74–6) conceives of consumption in terms of the 'logic of sign-exchange'. It is part of this general 'logic' that needs are social effects and not extra-societal (individual/'natural') causes. In support of his argument, Baudrillard explicitly cites Lévi-Strauss's structuralist anthropology. Just as, according to the latter, the kinship system is not determined 'in the final analysis' by consanguinity and filiation (natural givens) but by 'the arbitrary regulation of classification' so 'the system of consumption is based on a code of signs (objects/signs) and differences, and not on need and pleasure' (Baudrillard, 1988: p. 47). However, Lévi-Strauss's work can be used to show not so much the limitations of Baudrillard's approach as the sense in which my use of needs as abstract categories is 'naturalistic'. The nub issue is universalism. Lévi-Strauss (1968: p. 51) is himself critical of the 'sterile empiricism' of functionalist anthropology with its language of needs (as in Malinowski (1960), for example). Nonetheless there are universal 'forms' that structure each custom and institution; indeed there is 'a single structural scheme existing and operating in different spatial and temporal contexts' (Lévi-Strauss, 1968: p. 21). The earlier discussion of ornament can be usefully re-invoked to clarify the argument.

Different cultures use and value as ornamentation a seemingly infinite array of materials and designs and their 'meaning' is (very often) specific to that culture. It remains possible, however, for those not part of that culture to comprehend that 'meaning' in the sense of appreciating its internal intelligibility. What makes such comprehension possible is the presence of certain 'universals'. Whether these universals are best understood epistemologically or biologically is less important than their presence (cf. Berry: 1986a).

Relatedly, the ubiquity of the phenomenon of ornamentation tells against the inherently implausible claim that it is present within all cultures because each and every culture just so happened to develop this 'practice'. Lévi-Strauss himself provides evidence to this effect. The womenfolk of north American Plains Indians practise embroidery with porcupine quills. This embroidery is 'purely decorative in inspiration' and has 'symbolic significance' (Lévi-Strauss, 1978: p. 249). Lévi-Strauss interprets this significance in terms of the ornamentation reproducing, via the periodicity of the availability of porcupine quills, the periodicity of the major cosmic cycles – including those of female physiology (ibid.: p. 386). The accuracy or otherwise of this account is not here at issue. My point is that Lévi-Strauss is, within his approach, implicitly having recourse to certain 'natural' constants in order to explain/comprehend a particular cultural practice (cf. also Lévi-Strauss, 1977: p. 25).

The relevance of this is that the radical implication whereby luxury is understood simply in terms of social meaning does not do full justice to the phenomenon. Hence the reason *why* food, clothing, housing and leisure can be objects of 'luxury', and thus also have, in many cases, a 'meaning' as badges of distinction, is not mere accidental convergence in different societies at different times and in different places. In the Baudrillardian approach the signs lead only to other signs. It is as if signposts pointed not to a destination but simply to other signposts. Lévi-Strauss himself indicates that there is, in principle, something beyond signifiers,

each matrix of meanings refers to another matrix, each myth to other myths. And if it is now asked to what final meaning these mutually significative meanings are referring – since in the last resort and in their totality they must refer to something – the only reply to emerge from this study [*The Raw and the Cooked*] is that myths signify the mind that evolves them by making use of the world of which it itself is a part. (In Sperber, 1985: p. 83)

In my account the 'something' is constituted by those universally experienced satisfactions that embody what I have called naturalism. I repeat that this does not require any commitment to an extra-societal conception of needs/luxury.

SOCIAL GRAMMAR

While I cannot accept the full 'deconstructionist' thrust of the Baudrillardian approach, I do wish to develop one particular aspect of the social meaning of luxury. This development will be discussed more fully in Part IV and here I confine myself to an outline statement. I stated above that one important aspect of the 'drag-effect' that luxury goods possessed was that such goods could become so widespread that they are judged to be socially necessary. This division between goods that are deemed socially necessary and goods that constitute luxuries is part of what we may call the basic grammar of societies. Just as a language's grammar makes communication therein possible, so this division is one way in which a society is made intelligible to its members. The division acts as a marker, an ingredient in an information/communication system (cf. Douglas & Isherwood, 1979) that helps to establish a society's identity.

This intelligibility does not mean consensus but rather a presupposition that enables dispute about what should be in what category to take place. And wherever we have such categorical dispute – or at least the potential for such – then we have entered more explicitly into the realm of the political. For example, in the UK there is a policy to levy no VAT on books but to impose it on cinema tickets (and as a political policy it is open to amendment). We can state the principle that this example aims to illustrate in more general terms. All societies give practical effect, through legal and fiscal measures especially, to the distinction between needs and desires; books are educational and an educated population is a 'socially recognised need'; the cinema is a recreational outlet of which individuals may or may not wish to avail themselves. The underlying principle here can be formulated as a hypothesis: different evaluations of desire and different notions or identifications of need will result in different conceptions of 'good and politic order' as the 1553 Act of Apparel put it. This hypothesis will be examined or 'tested' in later chapters. Placed in this context, the issue of luxury for all its contemporary commonplace commercial usage remains political.

I want to conclude this preliminary survey by exploiting the notion that luxury can be understood as one of the basic categorising components of a society's grammar. I pursue this objective by drawing a conceptual map, or taxonomy, of societal goods as exemplified in contemporary societies.

A TAXONOMY OF SOCIETAL GOODS

1 A good can be deemed necessary. This necessity is the product of a particular society identifying particular goods as especially important.

The criteria of importance will not only reflect cultural norms and standards but also heed the ineluctable requirements of any human existence. It is through heeding these requirements that whatever is deemed socially necessary makes concrete the abstractness of basic needs. Goods that are given the status of 'social necessity' can be treated as possessing the objective (belief-independent) qualities of basic needs. Hence, to re-use the example of sanitation, regardless of an individual's own thoughts about hygiene any newly-constructed dwelling must, to accord with the law, serve to meet his or her needs in that regard.

2 A good can be needed as an instrumental means to an end. As noted above, this instrumentalist sense is, perhaps, the predominant use of the word 'need'. Accordingly this category of goods encompasses the requirements of day-to-day living – the toothbrush, the tin-opener, the shopping bag, the frying-pan, the pen and so on and on. Nevertheless there remains, even while allowing for substitutability (you can clean your teeth with dental floss or an appropriately shaped twig), an element of necessity. We can see how by means of an example. If what I want to do is cross the Atlantic in the shortest time possible, then I, as a civilian, have no alternative but to go by Concorde. But, if that is indeed the case, then flying by Concorde has become an instrumental necessity. It is desired simply as a necessary means to the realisation of a specific end and is not desired for itself or for any intrinsic reason.

3 A good can be coveted or desired fervently; it is the realisation of a specific objective for its own sake or because it is especially valued. If I have a fervent or settled desire (if I 'really want' (cf. Gosling, 1969: pp. 107–9) to fly supersonically and I direct my energies to accumulating the fare by forgoing other expenditures then flying by a 747 is not an option. Fervency of desire is, in this regard, thus assimilable to instrumental necessity. Similarly, if the book-collector intensely wants or covets a first edition of *De Cive* then no other edition is acceptable.

4 A good can be cherished. There is no requirement that such a good be widely cherished; certain goods have a 'sentimental value' that is particular to an individual. That particularity is immune to the perceptions of others. It is also immune to the relative penetration of goods of that type, simply because it is not a good of a *type* but a good the value of which lies precisely in its non-reproducibility, in its specific associations.

5 A good can be a luxury. We can identify such goods negatively by

their not being goods that are deemed socially necessary; nor utilitarian instruments, necessary means to an end; nor objects of fervent desire; nor cherished possessions. What then, positively, is a luxury?

A luxury good is an indulgence. It is a good that is thought desirable or pleasing by an individual. By extension it is a good that is assumed by advertisers and the manufacturers of consumer goods to be desirable or pleasing to the generality of individuals. As we have seen the category or *taxis* of luxury within this taxonomy itself encompasses four (sub)categories. Within these categories of sustenance, shelter, clothing and leisure, a luxury good is a good that it would be nice to have or experience – the special quality of which is precisely that it does not fall into the other taxonomical categories that have just been identified. On an individual level this encompasses how small, relatively inexpensive goods can be thought of as luxuries – for example, hiring a baby-sitter and going to the cinema. This falls into the leisure-class of luxury goods: it is not (1) a social necessity, unlike swimming-pools there are no public funds to meet this leisure activity; not (2) an instrumental necessity, the parents are not incipient baby-bashers for whom a night-out is therapy; not (3) something necessarily planned for, any film would do and its expense is relatively slight; not (4) a cherished habitual pastime; rather, (5) it is a treat, a positively pleasant experience and all of this is consistent with the parents being happy to stay at home.

It should be apparent from this last example that this taxonomy must be understood three-dimensionally – our map is a relief map. The goods referred to in this taxonomy are particulars. And any one particular good can fall into any *taxis* 2–5 depending on the particular desires of a particular agent. Hence a Rolls-Royce can be an instrumental necessity; it is a means of demonstrating municipal dignity or company prosperity or personal status. It can be an object of fervent desire, a vehicle for which one would plan for either by long-term saving or by systematic 'trading-up'. Or again, it can be a prized personal possession. And, of course, it can be a luxury. It is worth pointing out another apparent paradox. All the manufacturer cares about is selling the car, and the advertiser believes calling it a 'luxury automobile' is a selling point. But, on my account, some, perhaps indeed many, of the purchasers are not treating it as a luxury. Those who buy a Rolls as a *luxury* are, it follows from this analysis, perhaps best characterised by the pools-winner or the equivalent. In my strict sense, therefore, a luxury good, though desired, is not a goal at which 'action' is directed.[11] In sum, *luxuries are those goods that admit of easy and painless substitution because the desire for them lacks fervency.*

The fact that a Rolls can in this way fall into any of these four taxonomical categories accords with our initial remark that luxury goods were not a separate category superadded to a fixed determinate set of basic necessities. This fact also explains why it is intelligible that one person's luxury can be another's (instrumental) necessity. I should also add that from a particular individual's point of view any number of social goods can be a matter of complete indifference – hence to someone who is neither a mayor nor a company chairman, who cannot, and will not learn to drive, and has no wish to be driven, a Rolls-Royce would be redundant. However, if my account is right (or, more modestly, is along the right lines) then such an individual would not be puzzled by a Rolls-Royce being described as a 'luxury'.

It is this interpersonal relativity that provoked Mandeville's stringent definition of luxury as something not absolutely necessary, for, as he went on to maintain, once a less stringent criterion is adopted, and since 'the wants of Men are innumerable, then what ought to supply them has no bounds; what is call'd superfluous to some degree of People will be thought requisite to those of higher Quality'. In the light of this, Mandeville further claimed that once a less stringent definition is employed then 'there is no Luxury at all' (*Fable*: 1, 137).

However, on my analysis, while I have agreed with Mandeville's comments as to the indefiniteness of luxury (non-stringently identified), I have demurred from his conclusion that 'luxury' is therefore indefinable or unidentifiable. Let me now recapitulate my analysis to explain this.

In abstract terms, the assumption in contemporary commercial usage is that a luxury good is a widely desired (because not yet generally attained) good that is believed to be 'pleasing', and the general desirability of which is explained by it being a specific refinement, or qualitative aspect, of some universal generic need. These refinements, as products of desire, reflect the differences between individuals: I want coffee, you want tea, he wants lemonade,

---

[11] Cf. Gosling (1969: p. 108) 'It may be allowed that the person would be glad if x were to be handed him on a plate, and perhaps even hopes that this will happen, but he will not himself stir a finger to bring it about.'

she wants whisky. These differences nonetheless have a common focus because of their root in common need: we all need a drink. I have identified four chief categories of luxury goods corresponding to four basic needs – sustenance, shelter, clothing and leisure. Thus it is that we typically regard caviar, a palace, a Dior gown and a weekend in a certain Lake District hotel as luxuries.

The 'we' in question here are the members of late twentieth-century industrial societies. Those who lived in earlier, different, societies would have specified the content of these categories differently but the same four categories would have been identifiable. What would have been different is the social values placed on these goods. In Parts II and III I investigate the changes in valuation that have occurred.

PART II

The classical paradigm

CHAPTER 2

The Platonic prelude

The concept of luxury has had an eventful history. Its contemporary usage in the rhetoric of advertising is far removed from the opprobrium to which it was subjected by Cato the Elder. We shall discuss Cato's position and that of subsequent generations of Roman moralists in Chapter 3. While it is the Roman usage that achieved paradigmatic status for future thought, that usage itself was not without precedent. In this chapter I examine in some detail perhaps the most notable precedent – Plato's account in Book II of the *Republic*.

Before proceeding I should explain the relative lack of attention that Aristotle will receive. The simple explanation is that Aristotle in fact says very little about luxury. This is not to say, however, that his contribution to the topic is slight. This contribution lies not in a specific discussion but in the general teleological cast of his philosophy. As we shall see it is the assumptions of that approach which underpin the discussion of luxury up until the seventeenth century. It is testament to this fact that the overturning of those assumptions heralded, not coincidentally, the first moves away from the negative and toward a positive assessment of luxury. It is the very diffuseness and generality of Aristotle's contribution that makes it appropriate to treat him sparingly in this chapter. This exiguous treatment is, however, offset by the fact that the pervasiveness of his contribution will require us to make frequent references to him in the chapters that follow.

NEEDS AND THE POLIS

Plato broaches the subject of luxury in the context of his celebrated proposal to study the nature of justice and injustice in the individual by examining justice and injustice in the polis (*Politeia*: 368e). The proposed method is a thought-experiment that will focus on the polis as it comes into being (369a). The origin of the polis is to be found in

common needs (*chreia*). Three basic common needs are identified –
food, dwelling and clothing (369c). As we intimated in Chapter 1, this
trio was to remain the standard definition of basic needs. Still in line
with the discussion in Chapter 1, and importantly for the subsequent
argument, these needs are identified by Plato as pertaining explicitly
to the 'body' (*sôma*). But though these needs apply to the individual's
body, this fact goes hand in hand with the further fact that no one
individual is self-sufficient (*ouk autarkês*) (369b). To meet these
common needs necessitates some degree of co-operative interdependence. This co-operative interdependence is, says Plato, called a
'polis'. The polis thus has its origins in necessity.

The polis at its barest, the necessary polis (*anagkaiotatê polis*), will
consist of four or five men (369d). Even this polis will, however,
practise the division of labour. Since the division of labour constitutes
one of the major motifs in the whole work it is in keeping with its
importance that Plato introduces it at this fundamental level. He
states that the three needs will each require a corresponding *technê* –
farming, building, weaving – and since individuals are *by nature*
diverse, the result is that each 'craft' is best done by those who are best
fitted by nature to execute it. Through each utilising their natural
bent or functioning *kata phusin* (370c), the outcome is more and better
goods.

However, it is probable that this minimal polis is intended merely
as an illustration of the principle of the diversity of natural aptitudes.
The initial definition of the polis had in fact referred to 'us' having
'many needs' that require 'many persons' to help us meet them
(369c). In line with this definition Plato proceeds to depict the scope
of these 'many needs' and the concomitantly many tasks required to
satisfy them. It is important to note what Plato here includes. There
will be a wide range of artisans since the farmer, for example, will not
make his own plough nor will he raise his own beasts of burden and
similarly the builder and weaver will not make their own tools.
There will also be an import and export trade, which implies further
that there will be money and markets and thus the polis will have
within it sundry financial and commercial occupations. The scope of
the market is such as to include that of labour, though Plato makes
no reference to slaves, talking instead of hired servants (*misthôtoi*)
(371e).[1]

---

[1] Calvert (1987) cites this passage to counter Vlastos's arguments (1940; 1968) that Plato
would not have objected to Aristotle's argument in defence of natural slavery.

Having obtained Adeimantus' agreement that this depiction completes the growth of the polis, Socrates moves to a consideration of its way of life (372a). This turns out to relate to clothing and diet, both of which will be simple. The clothing is strictly functional since it will only be needed in the colder winter months and the diet will be vegetarian. Socrates summarises that life in this polis will be convivial and peaceful. More particularly there will be neither poverty nor war (372b). The reasons for this can be inferred from the earlier description though Plato does explicitly mention that these citizens will apportion the size of their families to their means.[2] However, the more general explanation of the lack of poverty and war is that human interactions are geared to the meeting of needs.

What underlies this explanation is the postulate that these needs have fixed limits. This postulate will be of the utmost importance not only for Plato but also for all subsequent accounts that link luxury and corruption. As we shall shortly indicate, it is here, too, that Aristotle's teleological approach has its greatest impact. The postulate underpins the explanation because, since these needs are fixed, then when they are met there is no purpose to be served by wanting more. Further, since these needs are easily met then all the polis-members will be satisfied. Two additional factors will ensure that this satisfied life will endure. The control of population will keep the numbers of those in need in bounds so that relative scarcity, whence the possibility of general poverty, will be forestalled. Secondly, the division of labour to meet these definite needs constitutes a consensual bond so that there is here no source for dissensus or conflict. I shall consider this argument in more detail later.

THE CITY OF PIGS

Glaucon now famously interrupts to declare that this description would fit a 'city of pigs' (372d). Socrates inquires as to what is missing and Glaucon replies by citing furniture (couches and tables) and what Lee (1955) translates as 'normal civilized food' or what Jowett (1895) renders more ponderously, if more literally, as 'dainties and desserts in the modern fashion'. Socrates now interprets this reply as a request for something different; what Glaucon is asking about is a

---

[2] Sex does not figure in lists of basic needs. In Plato's case Chanteur (1980: p. 23) conjectures that its absence is due to the fact that unlike food, clothing and shelter its satisfaction does not depend on labour. Her point would perhaps be less ambiguous if she referred to the absence of a particular *techné*, as she had herself earlier suggested (ibid.: p. 15).

luxurious (*truphôsan*) polis (372e). Socrates also immediately characterises this as a fevered or an inflamed (*phlegmainousan*) polis. This alternative description has obvious medical connotations. Indeed Socrates explicitly contrasts the fevered condition of this polis to the 'true' (*alêthinês*) and 'healthy' (*hugiês*) city that had been described thus far.

We will return to this contrast between the healthy and the luxurious city, but next we should note what the contents and consequences of this latter city are. This city is thought by some commentators (e.g. Mossé, 1979: p. 355) to refer to contemporary Athens. (Pseudo) Xenophon, in fact, remarks that in Athens, due to its dependence on naval power and thus on the need to crew warships, slaves lived in luxury (*truphan*) (*Ath. Gov't*: 1, 11). Building upon Glaucon's references to furniture and foods, Socrates elaborates by saying that we should not now be limited by the necessities that characterised the earlier or 'first' city. For example, painters and embroiderers will have a place. Presumably they will decorate the existing houses and clothes but to do so they will require additional materials such as gold and ivory. A physical extension of the city will now be required to accommodate the multitude of occupations which will be called into existence once the standpoint of necessity has been passed (373b). Socrates produces a list of what he has in mind. This includes poets, dancers and musicians, which tells us that the first city, devoted as it is to the meeting of necessary needs, will contain shopkeepers but not 'artists'. Also on the list are many more craftsmen to make the wider range of utensils and clothing now in use. This particularly applies to women since the city will now contain courtesans (*hetairai*). In addition to the craftsmen there will be an increase in servants who will perform such tasks as barbering, nursing and cooking. The latter will now include meat dishes, for Plato is explicit that swineherds will be needed to maintain sufficient beasts for consumption. Implicitly picking up the medical sub-theme, Socrates also says that the luxurious city will have a greater need for physicians (cf. 405d).

The most significant consequence of the city's luxurious condition is that it will generate warfare. This will transpire because the increase in number and scale of activities means that more territory will be needed. This extra land will have to be appropriated from a neighbour. But if our neighbours are also committed to a life of luxury then they, on their part, are liable to threaten to annex us. The next step in Plato's exposition is of pivotal importance for our perspective. This step is his identification of the source of this conflict. He simply states, that is he does not provide an argument, that this conflict and territorial aggrandisement is consequent upon the pursuit of unlimited wealth (*epi chrêmatôn apeiron*), which itself stems from forsaking the limits of necessity (373e). This source for the cause of war is also said by Plato to be the cause of almost all the evils, both private and public, in the polis. Before returning to the causes of this evil we can follow Plato's account of its effects.

Indeed, having introduced warfare Plato is now able to broach his next major theme, the consequent necessity for the polis to possess warriors. These are individuals who, by nature, are fitted to the task of protecting the city. But, and this is, of course, a point of great significance, this is no mere quantitative extension; it constitutes a qualitative change. What these warriors possess *kata phusin* is that quality of spirit, spunk or perhaps even machismo that translates as *thumos*.

To thumoeidês is one of the three elements of the human soul and is embodied in Plato's ideal city in these warriors (later termed 'auxiliaries'). Since the rational element (*to logistikon*) in the soul is embodied in the 'guardians', it means that the first and the luxurious city must both, as 'economic' associations, embody the residual element of appetite (*to epithumêtikon*). This in fact pinpoints more exactly the difference between these two cities. The difference is that between 'desire' understood as fixed appetite, what Plato calls 'need', and 'desire' as insatiable appetite. The *truphêros polis* embodies the latter and it is this understanding of appetite that remains operative. In confirmation of this last point, Plato later, when explicitly talking of the parts of the soul, refers to appetite in terms of its natural insatiability (*phusei aplêstotaton*) and its devotion to bodily pleasures (*sôma hedonôn*) (442a). He makes the same point elsewhere. In the *Phaedo* (66c) he states that war and conflict originate in the 'body and its desires (*epithumiai*)' and love of money; but money itself, he goes on, has to be acquired for the sake of the body.

HEALTHY NEEDS AND INFLAMED DESIRES

Before dealing with the significance of the conjoined emergence of warriors and *thumos*, we need to elaborate upon some of the assumptions in Plato's account thus far. The first one to consider is the link between the peacefulness of the healthy city and the fact that it is given over to the meeting of necessary needs. Why should there be this link? We can begin to answer that question by picking up a strand of the analysis in Chapter 1. For Plato, needs are universal: *all* need food, clothing and shelter and this universality supplies a commonality of interest or consensus. Plato presents this commonality as a bond because each individual requires assistance to meet his needs. This lack of self-sufficiency prompts exchanges on the principle of *quid pro quo*, where each has his own benefit in view (369c). This principle operates successfully because, according to Plato, the division of labour is based on natural ability. The 'natural' farmer will grow food enough for all which, saving sufficient for his own need, will be exchanged for the woven clothes and constructed shelter produced by the 'natural' weaver and builder. Since this picture refers to the illustrative absolute minimal city of just four or five 'men' it seems Plato thinks the principle will apply equally to the enlarged 'economy' of markets, external trade and money.

Since it is this city of many tasks to meet many needs into which luxury is introduced we are able to identify by contrast what it is that Plato assumes about luxury. Luxuries, as Socrates defines them, still pertain to the body (food, clothing and housing) but they are no longer restricted to meeting these 'natural' needs. Accordingly, the inflamed city experiences 'fancy' food (dainties), 'fancy' clothes (embroidered) and 'fancy' dwellings (with gold and ivory) and 'fancy' women, the latter implying perhaps sex as a desire independent of the 'need' to have a controlled number of children. (As we shall see in Chapter 4, it was central to the 'Christian contribution' to establish a link between luxury and lechery.)

A point of some general significance is lurking here. The luxurious city represents an expansion of what, in Chapter 1, we called 'qualitative desires'. Humans get pleasure from, for example, embroidered clothes, that is, from the very fact that they are embroidered and not just a functional protective covering. Similarly they derive pleasure from decorative surroundings and elaborately prepared food. These qualitative dimensions are also responsible for the presence in this city of the attributes of 'culture' or 'civilisation' – artists, poets and the like. Plato implies that these qualitative aspects mark a move beyond 'need' *qua* simple, quantitatively fixed desire. Later, indeed, he seems to make this explicit when he argues that the need (*epithumia*) for a drink (thirst) is properly a need for a drink pure and simple (unqualified) and not for a cold or hot or large or small drink (437d–e). *Pace* Barker (1959),[3] what Plato is thus seemingly committed to is the denial that humans possess a *need* for adornment or 'culture'.

This denial can be given both a narrow and a broad reading. Narrowly, it is a rejection of the argument subscribed to by Mandel (1968) and Baudrillart (*Histoire*) (see also Chapter 1) that there is a distinctive human need for decoration. For Plato, as we shall see in more detail later, nothing distinctively human can be located at the somatic level of need satisfaction. Broadly, it signifies a rejection of the basis of my claim that 'leisure' constitutes generically a category of luxury goods. Recall how Plato had implicitly distinguished the shopkeeper and the artist and nowhere in this account of the first city is there an acknowledgement of 'play'. However, as my interpretation of Plato's account will aim to demonstrate, the central element of his own argument is to explain the *development* of the human *psuche*, so that, at this point, his presentation is necessarily incomplete.

For Plato, once appetite goes beyond what is necessary to meet fixed bodily needs, it will develop out of control (in our terms, it is always possible to qualify further any existing qualitative aspects). More pointedly, peaceful *quid pro quo* exchange gives way to competitive desires and conflict as, for example, the quality of the embroidery on the clothes or the tenderness of the meat or the opulence of the furnishings give rise to invidious comparison, envy and dispute. The division of labour, no longer being tied to meeting finite needs and thus no longer underwriting consensus, now facilitates dissensus by allowing infinite desires to express themselves. The city becomes inflamed in the sense of being unbalanced or disharmonious, where, in typical Greek fashion, balance and harmony are characteristics of health (cf. Andersson, 1971: p. 94). In the inflamed condition, the original commonality of mutual need satisfaction is replaced by the pursuit of unlimited wealth (373d).

In the text we are given no independent argument as to why this should happen. It appears to follow definitionally: unbalanced desires are, as such, insatiable. These desires are an indelible mark of

---

[3] Barker (1959: p. 107) calls 'pictures and poetry, music and dress "needs of mankind"', but then immediately follows this with the less perspicuous statement that 'men need satisfaction of the desires for refinement'.

intemperance.[4] What is currently important is that this transition
from mutual need satisfaction to insatiability is, for Plato, a necessary
development; the 'necessity' in question lying within the requirements
of his own argument. There are two dimensions to this.

The first dimension relates to the very *raison d'être* of the discussion
in the first place, that is, the search for justice. Plato quite explicitly
uses the introduction of the luxurious city positively in order to see
where justice and injustice occur. The important implication is that
in the first city 'justice' has no place precisely because of its simplicity
and singularity. Justice is a relationship between classes in the polis
and these are the model for the elements in the soul. But, as we have
seen, in the first city there is only one class – that of artisan/tradesman
and only one element, the appetite. In Hegelian terms this city is, in
its lack of qualitative differentiation, a simple unity; it is only a city
'in-itself' it is not yet 'for-itself'. Hence the necessity for development.
We can only have justice in the sense of harmony (keeping to one's
place) if there is the possibility of disharmony. Just as, to exploit Hegel
once more, we can only know what is right when wrong has
occurred.[5] It is this possibility of disharmony that the introduction of
the luxurious city realises. The root of the disharmony (the fever) is
the collapse of the need-based economy and its replacement by one
driven by luxurious desire. Yet if this is to be genuinely a development,
it must be generated from within and not from some contingent
external source.

The second dimension relates to this inner development. It is true
that Socrates supposes that there will be some dissatisfaction with the
simple life of the first city (373a). But this dissatisfaction is contingently
superimposed upon the description thus far given and cannot provide
the requisite development. Rather, as we have already discussed, the
decisive event, or qualitative shift, is the calling into play, by the
warfare engendered by the luxurious city, of those spirited elements in
the human soul. Since these elements are indeed part of the soul, their
emergence can truly be called an 'inner' development. Similarly, the

---

[4] In the *Gorgias* (492c), Plato has Callicles link intemperance with luxury and licence (*truphê kai akolasia*) as part of his (Callicles') argument that the best life is one that allows 'desires (*epithumias*) to wax to the utmost' (491e).
[5] Cf. Irwin (1991: p. 204), who invokes Hume's view that 'when goods are in plentiful supply there is no place for justice' but immediately states that 'in the city of pigs people are not exactly more just than in swollen city, but they are less unjust'. Leaving aside the consistency of this statement alongside the attributed Humean view, Hegel is, I think, more informative than Hume here precisely because he does incorporate the necessary element of immanental development – in Hume it is (fittingly) a contingent matter.

first polis is too confined, because it cannot accommodate what are, in fact, the definitively human elements of courage and reason. It is thus a mistake to talk, as Melling (1987: p. 81) does, of the first (what he calls the 'Basic') city as a 'sharing community of rational persons'.

THE TRANSCENDENCE OF ANIMALITY

Glaucon called the first city a city of pigs, a label that Socrates does not contradict. The reference to 'pigs' signals a further assumption. This city is one where need satisfaction and satiable appetite prevail because its activities are designed to meet bodily or physical or animalistic requirements. Even with the allowance that the diet of bread can be supplemented with fruit and vegetables – with what Socrates refers to generically as *ophon* (which Lee, unfortunately and misleadingly for the argument, translates as 'luxuries') – there is nothing distinctively human here. The source of the human lies preconditionally in the introduction of luxury and insatiable appetite into this city but effectively, and for Plato decisively, in the generation of warfare by the circumstances of luxury.

Against the backcloth of the city of *pigs* we can see that *humanity* is characterised by the transcendence of that city's exclusive concern with self-interest/need-satisfaction and of the luxurious city's preoc-cupation with bodily pleasures. As we shall see, this distinction is not only basic to the 'classical' perspective (as we may be permitted to call it) but also sets the benchmark in terms of which luxury can be condemned. In Plato's case this transcendence is truly achieved in the case of 'reason'. It is through reason that the true reality of the Forms is apprehended. The Forms are necessarily immutable, and to know them cannot be the attribute of selves whose lives serve their own particular and mutable interests. This transcendence can, however, also, though to a necessarily lesser extent, be achieved by exhibiting 'courage'. And, given its close connexion with luxury, this mode of transcendence merits further discussion. However, we can at this point relevantly indicate the nature of Aristotle's contribution.

ARISTOTLE'S CONTRIBUTION

In his *Politics* Aristotle declares that in the best form of polis mechanics (*banausoi*) will not be made citizens (1278a). The justification for this exclusion is that their physical fitness as well as their *psuche* is adversely

adversely affected by their way of life (1337b). In this same general category Aristotle also includes those who are involved in the pursuit of gain. The explanation of this contrast between citizenship, or political matters, and mechanical or commercial occupations rests on Aristotle's teleological framework. It is this framework that pervades all subsequent discussions of luxury.

At the risk of caricature, we can summarise Aristotle's argument as follows. For Aristotle the polis is not the product of contingent agreement or of some human artifice like the 'social contract' of sixteenth- and seventeenth-century thought. Rather, the polis is natural. Aristotle uses the term 'natural' in a special and distinctive sense: the nature of anything is its essence (*Metaphysics*: D. 4). This essence, however, has in itself a principle of motion or generation whereby inherent potential is actualised or realised. The nature of X is thus expressible as the potential when actualised, as its end, goal or purpose (*telos*). The polis is a species of the genus community. The essence of the genus is the achievement of some good. The specific essence of the polis, its end, is to sustain the 'good life' (*eu zên*) (*Pol.*: 1252b). The good life can formally be identified as a self-sufficient life, that is, a life that is led for its own sake and not instrumentally for the sake of something else. The substance of the good life, for Aristotle, thus consists in intrinsically worthwhile activities. While contemplation – the expression of wisdom to comprehend what must be, what is beyond human control – is perhaps the most self-sufficient activity, the activity of politics also has a non-instrumental, intrinsically worthwhile character. It is this character that lies behind Aristotle's famous definition of man as a being intended by nature to live in a polis (*anthropôs phusei politikon zôon*) (1253a).

However, the polis is not the sole sort or species of community and its nature is only to be grasped in its full significance when two other species are identified. First, there is the family or household (*oikos*). The nature of the household, the end it serves, is the satisfaction of what Barker translates as 'daily recurrent needs' (1252b; 1946: p. 4). Second, there is the village (*kômê*) – a collection of households – the end of which is the satisfaction of more than daily recurrent needs (*chrêseôs*). Aristotle effectively assimilates these two communities when he says that these associations have 'mere life' as their end, in contrast to the 'good life' of the polis proper.

There is obviously a resemblance between this picture of communities based on need in contrast to a community that goes beyond need and Plato's contrast between the 'first city' and that which transcends it by exhibiting truly human qualities. What distinguishes Aristotle's version is the openly teleological relationship he establishes between the communities. Directly referring to Plato's account in *Republic*, Book II he criticises him for implying that cities are formed for necessities and not to realise the good (*kalon*) (1291a). For Aristotle, the household/village is an instrumental means to the attainment of the intrinsically valuable political (good) life. The household and village thus exist for the sake of something other than themselves.

Because of this fundamental difference in nature between the good life of politics and the merely instrumental – and thus subordinate – economic life it is *para phusin* to confuse them. Nowhere is this confusion more likely than in the case of money-making (*chrêmatistikê*). The household's task (*oikonomikê*) is to gather such goods as are necessary to its function. This is a finite task and the limits are definable *kata phusin* (1256b). Aristotle declares that it is – again like the practice in Plato's first city – in line with this natural purposive order for exchange/commerce to take place. Hence a shoe may be exchanged *kata phusin* for food so long as the recipient uses it as a shoe (meets the need with it) and so long as it was not produced for the purpose of exchange (rather than need) (1257a).[6] Still within *oikonomikê*, money can play a legitimate role by facilitating such exchanges. But with money there comes into existence *chrêmatistikê* and, although its origins are legitimate and it has a proper role to play, what concerns Aristotle is that those (*kapeloi*) who spend their lives exchanging will come to regard money(making) improperly as an end in itself, rather than as a facilitating means. This reaches its own consistent conclusion in the practice of usury (*tokos*). Usury is *para phusin* because it uses money not for its proper purpose (facilitating need-based exchanges) but to multiply itself (1258b). Once separated from its true, natural function, therefore, money-making becomes limitless (1257b). This separation is a perversion. It is corrupt because money-makers are now preoccupied with the subordinate concerns of 'life' rather than the nobler, human concerns of the 'good life'. And this preoccupation is limitless because their desire for life (bodily enjoyments) is unlimited (1258a). Although Aristotle does not here

---

[6] Cf. Meikle (1979) for Aristotle's articulation of the difference between use- and exchange-value.

refer to luxury,[7] this contrast between the natural good life and a perverse or corrupt life given over to bodily pleasures and unlimited accumulation (*pleonexia*) is one that will come to underwrite the notion that a life of luxury is an unworthy life.

COURAGE AND THE WARRIORS

During this discussion Aristotle remarks that those who make *chrêmatistikê* their object treat everything – including medical and military matters – as sources of wealth. The reference here to the military we can take as a cue to rejoin our discussion of Plato. Military men or warriors manifest their transcendence of the appetitive life by displaying courage: courage is their appropriate virtue. Warriors in the city do not, as we saw, simply constitute another type of artisan, like the embroiderer (or doctor, *pace* Melling (1987: p. 79)), called forth by the unlimited demands of luxury. The difference lies precisely in the fact that the duty of the warrior is to fight and hence risk death (cf. 386a). To engage in that task, to fulfil such a duty, requires the presence of 'spirit' and that possession signifies a capacity to transcend the self-interestedness of appetite, of a mere 'economic life'. Plato makes plain that those who lead this life (artisans, tradesmen and the like) lack this element; they will not be fearless (375a), they are incapable *kata phusin* of defending themselves (374a). Even in the first city the retailers (*kapeloi*), those who buy and sell in the market – a task for which *ex hypothesi* they are *naturally* suited – are those who are weakest in bodily strength (371c). This depreciation of economic life, implicit in Aristotle as we have already seen, is one of the persistent ingredients in the classical conception of luxury and a re-evaluation of it one of the hallmarks of the modern conception. What fuels this negative assessment is that if the economic life should

---

[7] In Book IV (1291a), when cataloguing the parts of a polis, Aristotle includes within the *banauson* order those whose *technai* are necessary (*anagkês*) and those who contribute to luxury or living the good life (*truphên ê to kalôs zên*). It would be contrary to the standard usage if the 'or' was conjunctive (linking luxury and good together) rather than disjunctive (making them alternatives) but the text is ambiguous. Less equivocally, in a discussion inspired by Phaleas' scheme for equal holdings of property in an ideal polis, Aristotle (1266b) remarks that the size of the holdings (rather than their equality) is crucial, since if too large they promote luxury (*truphan*). Not only is this reference redolent of Aristotle's doctrine of the 'mean' (for equal holdings can also be too small) but reflects the judgment that luxury is a misuse of the proper end of property. Moreover, on the issue of equality what is more important than holdings is an equalisation of desires (*epithumias*) by means of a legally enforced educational system (*paidenomenois*); an argument close to Plato's in the *Laws*. The few other explicit references to luxury in the *Politics* concern oligarchies – see text below.

trespass its boundaries then it will corrupt the entire community, as when the military life is looked upon as a source of wealth.

In general terms Plato guards against this corruption of treating everything in terms of wealth by a strict differentiation of function accompanied by a rigorous educational regime. In the case of the warriors, who are, to repeat, our main point of focus, this means that their ability (*kata phusin*) to overcome the life of appetite has, nonetheless, to be nurtured. Their education is of two sorts; gymnastics for the body and music for the soul, with the latter first on the curriculum. The thrust of Plato's comments here is that only simple as opposed to complex music is suitable (just as only literature that will ennoble and strengthen and not corrupt and undermine the warrior is appropriate) (cf. Nettleship, 1962: p. 109). In the midst of this discussion, Socrates is suddenly made to exclaim that through making these educational proposals they have unbeknown (*lelêthamen*) purged the polis of its luxury (399e). The explicit reference to 'purging' (*kathairômen*) connects up with the medical theme and the identification of the luxurious with the inflamed city. The warriors need to be purged so that their war-like natures will indeed exhibit aggression to enemies yet gentleness to their friends (375b).

Plato in fact likens this dual-capacity to the behaviour of a well-bred guard dog. On the face of it this analogy weakens the force of the contrast between truly human and animal behaviour. Courage is not the sole prerogative of humans; Plato attributes it to horses or indeed 'any other animal' as well as dogs. Moreover, the dog (*kunis*) is said to discriminate between friend or foe on the basis of knowledge which is to say with a love of knowledge (*philosophon*) (376b). It is very likely that Plato is making a play on words. As Adam (1965: 1, 108) notes, there is a possible allusion to the doctrine of the Cynics. Aside from that possibility we should note that this is not Plato's last word on courage.

Despite this seeming assimilation of human and canine courage, Plato later dissimilates them. When summarising the warriors' education he states that its positive purpose has been to instil in them the ability to make correct judgments about danger. It is the exercise of this ability that he now says he will call 'courage'. Not only does this imply that the earlier assimilatory discussion was thus provisional but also he has Glaucon comment (with Socrates' assent) that this proper use of courage is to be distinguished from the 'mere uninstructed' behaviour of a beast or slave (430b). Indeed this is underlined by its description in the very next paragraph as political courage (*politikê andreia*), and Plato's later considered view is certainly typical of 'classical' thinking. Aristotle, for example, distinguishes courage as spirited action generated by 'a right and noble motive', which only humans can perform, from the behaviour of animals when they are in pain, as when they charge those who have wounded them (*Nic. Eth.*: 1115b–6b).

THE MEANING OF 'LUXURY'

We can now take up the postponed theme of the relationship between the healthy and the inflamed city. Luxury needs to be purged because it is unhealthy. The nature of the disease can be discerned from the range of meanings that the term *truphê* carried. This range also indicates more generally the contexts where the pejorativeness of 'luxury' was thought applicable. As a verb it conveyed the meaning of living softly and feasting sumptuously. It is indicative of this meaning that Glaucon is stimulated to interject after the description of the diet in the first city. This is no mere quirk because diet was a constant matter of concern in Greek medical writing. In addition, the connexion with feasting was to persist, becoming a major ingredient in the various sumptuary laws passed in the Roman Republic to restrict banqueting excesses (see Chapter 3).

As an adjective applied to persons, *truphêros* conveyed voluptuousness and effeminacy. It is the latter sense, in conjunction with 'softness', that is perhaps the most telling. Before elaborating upon this it is perhaps worth noting that Plato's usage is not remarkable. Aristotle, to give just one example, places luxuriousness (*trupherotês*) at one extreme from hardiness (*karteria*) with endurance (*kakopatheia*) as the appropriate mean in the illustrative catalogue of emotions that he provides in the *Eudemian Ethics* (1221a). The luxurious man is thus one who is so 'soft' that he can endure no pain. Indeed in the *Nichomachean Ethics*, Aristotle explicitly identified luxury as a type of softness (*malakia*) (1150b).

We here broach what is perhaps the decisive reason for the negative evaluation of luxury in classical thought. In Plato's case, it accounts for the lengths to which he goes to educate the warrior class. Those individuals whose lives are given over to a soft, luxurious life are, as we have seen, incapable of defending themselves; they are naturally unfit to be auxiliaries. They are effeminate because it is of the essence not of humanity but rather of masculinity to fight, to risk death. It is not without relevance in this context that the word for courage (*andreia*) and the word for man (*anêr/andra*) are connected: to be courageous or brave is to act like a man. The same etymological link is made in Latin between *vir* and *virtus*. This connexion also underwrites that common prejudice against artisans and traders since such individuals are thought to be signally lacking in courage, and thus in proper manly attributes. Xenophon provides convenient testament to this train of associations when he links the practice of handicrafts (*banausikia*) to weak, effeminate bodies and feeble minds such that these practitioners are unsuitable as defenders of their city (*Econ.*: 4, 2–3). The crucial link is echoed by Aristotle when he cites the case of King Astyages whose luxury had so weakened him that he was attacked by Cyrus (*Pol.*: 1312a).

Men who live a life of luxury thus become emasculated. Plato himself gives a striking confirmation of this association of ideas later in the *Republic* (590b). There Socrates remarks, in such a way as to indicate that he is stating a commonplace, that 'luxury and softness' (Jowett) or 'effeminacy' (Lee and Cornford) (*truphê de kai malakia*) are censured because they make us cowardly. The effect of this upon the warrior class should now be obvious since cowardice is self-evidently the most damaging factor in a warrior. Hence, too, the need to educate him so as to purge him of any exposure to luxury. This also explains why music is such a central part of this education since, on Plato's understanding, too much of the wrong sort of music produces softness (*malakôteron*) (410d) and a soul that is out of harmony will be cowardly (411a).

It is significant testimony to the salience of this militaristic context that it is in writings on 'trade' (what Montesquieu, among others, revealingly called *doux commerce*) that the first moves are made to look upon luxury more positively (see Chapter 5). In a closely related manner, as we shall note in Chapter 6, Hume and Smith, as part of their vindication of commerce, take it upon themselves to demote the virtue 'courage' because it is no longer appropriate to the 'modern' world. And when it is recalled that humanity/masculinity and the exercise of courage were intimately connected, then this displacement of courage is no minor adjustment; it is integral to a general re-assessment of human nature or human self-understanding. For example, humans come to understand themselves as properly motivated by private sentiments, not public commitments, and one consequence of this shift is to regard as perfectly legitimate the aspiration to enjoy luxuries.

For all the significance of the connexion between luxury and softness for the education of warriors, in Plato, this connexion also affects the traders and artisans; it affects not merely the 'lion' or spirited element in the soul but also the 'dragon' or desirous/appetitive element. The 'crafts' of the artisan have multiplied with the fever of luxury and we may thus speculate (for here Plato is unforthcoming) on the appropriate treatment for them. The point of this speculation is to bring out an important relationship between desire and need. The artisan class in the ideal Platonic city will, of course, be firmly controlled and, by sticking to their tasks, they will be part of the just order. Their appropriate virtue is temperance or moderation (*sôphrosunê*), for the possession of this will enable them both to be obedient and to perform their *technai* well. The crux, therefore, is the moderating or tempering of their desires (ibid.: 389d–e). Recall how the notion of inflammation meant the unbalancing of desires so that they become insatiable and, as such, an indelible mark of intemperance.

In Book iv, Socrates remarks that the *technai* themselves, as well as their practitioners, are liable to become corrupt through either wealth or poverty. The former produces luxury and indolence (*truphên kai arkian*) (cf. *Laws*: 900) while the latter generates meanness (422a). If we apply this commonplace (Adeimantus answers immediately that these causal links are 'very true') to the earlier account of the two cities we can note that the harmony of the first city is characterised by absence of poverty (explicitly) and wealth. These extremes are thus produced by the expansion of the city into the production of luxury goods. As we have noted, what fuels this expansion is the generation of desires beyond necessity. In the *Laws*, Plato revealingly locates the source of poverty not in lack of property, but in an increase in desires (736c, cf. 870a).

The solution to this is not to extirpate desire/appetite. Such an extirpation would, on Platonic terms, be an impossibility since appetite is a component of the human *psuche*. The Platonic solution is training. But again we can note that the knowledge that this is indeed the solution is only possible after desires have been inflamed with the development of luxury. Similarly, the identification of *sôphrosunê* as the appropriate virtue presupposes that desires require moderation, and such a requirement is absent in the first city, where the 'desire' is satiable, where fixed need is the norm. For training to be an effective solution some guideline is required. This is where the model of the first city based on need satisfaction can be seen to come into its own. Here we have perhaps the first enunciation of the crucial principle that need should be the measure or guideline of desire. The various manifestations and rationale of this principle constitute one of the leitmotifs of this study.

We can see the principle at work in Plato's preliminary discussion to his description of the democratic character. In this discussion, Plato (558–61) distinguishes between necessary and unnecessary desires (*epithumias*). The former are both ineradicable and of benefit to use when they are satisfied. Plato here deliberately associates 'necessity' (*anagkaios*) with 'nature' (*phusis*); it is our nature to satisfy them and that fact makes it appropriate to call them 'necessary'. Although Plato does not, for his own particular reasons, employ the term 'need' here, this characterisation of 'necessary desires' fairly represents what are standardly taken to be basic elements in the notion of 'need'. This interpretation is supported by the example which Plato here gives of a necessary desire. His example is the desire for food, which, of course, was one of the three basic needs that he had identified at the genesis of a polis.

In contrast to necessary desires, unnecessary desires are both eradicable and of no positive good to us. The eradication, however, can only be achieved if it is undertaken deliberately and only, too, if it is begun when young. The example of an unnecessary desire is, revealingly, desire for what both Lee and Cornford translate as 'luxurious diet' (*alloiôn edesmatôn*: Jowett renders this as 'viands of a less simple kind', but recall the basic vegetarian diet of the first city) rather than simple or plain food, which is the proper object of a necessary desire. This example thus repeats, in effect, the one given earlier when the transition from the first to the luxurious city was discussed. It follows from the definition that this unnecessary desire can damage the health of both the body and the soul but that it can be checked by discipline and education (*paideuomenê*).

Lest it be thought a straightforward matter within Plato's account to approve of a life of necessary, and disapprove of a life of unnecessary, desire the context within which this particular discussion is embedded should be acknowledged. Plato is discussing the transition from the oligarchic to the democratic character. The initial reference to 'necessary' desires is to link them with money-making or wealth-producing (*chrêmatistikai*) (559c) and these are characteristic of the oligarch. Because money-making is a desire then it means that the oligarchic character is thus governed by that element in his soul. This means not only is reason subservient to desire but so too is spirit (553d). In the oligarch more particularly, the love of money, as the ruling passion, leads to a neglect of *sôphrosunê*, that is, of the virtue that a life of desire requires, if that life is to be just and harmonious. This lack of moderation results in the oppressive political rule of the rich over the poor and the younger generation of oligarchs leading a life of luxury (*truphôntas*) (556b). (Aristotle makes exactly the same point (*Pol.*: 1310a, cf. 1311a).)

From what we already know, it thus follows that not only is this an idle life but also a soft one, which makes its devotees unable to resist pain or the temptations of pleasure. This combination of oppression and emasculation produces the overthrow of oligarchy by democracy. But the democratic character, because of its inherent lack of discipline, will eventually lapse into the pursuit of unnecessary and useless desires (561a). From there it is but a short step to the pursuit of unlawful or unnatural (*paranomoi*) desires (571b) which characterise the tyrant. And in the tyrannical character we find, in stark terms, the connexion between desires and animality; for when reason is ineffective, then our bestial nature (*thêriôdes te kai akrion*) – with which we are born – is let loose (571e, 572a).

The moral of the story is that if desires are freed from control, either as internally imposed in the form of reason or as externally imposed in the form of law, then we eventually end up with parricide and cannibalism (571c). By inflaming desires, luxury plays a key role in that story. It is a role that will recur. In Plato's version, two aspects stand out as a prelude of what is to come. The first is that luxury represents the dynamism of human desire. This dynamism takes society beyond the confines of mere need-satisfaction. However, it is a further fact about this dynamism that, unlike need, it is boundless or insatiable. The second aspect follows. This insatiability requires some form of control because if left unchecked it will lead to the ruination of both society and its citizens. Since luxury is in this way a threat to social order, it is a basic question of politics to find a way of 'policing' it. In the next chapter we will examine how the Romans, as one case, sought to institutionalise that task.

CHAPTER 3

The Roman response

I argued in Chapter 1 that luxury is a component of political morality and remarked that all societies give practical effect through fiscal and legal measures to the distinction between needs and desires. This suggested the hypothesis that different evaluations of desire and different identifications of need result in different conceptions of political order. This chapter tests this hypothesis by examining one instance of the relationship between these factors – the preoccupation of the Roman moralists and legislators with luxury. (We shall have occasion to return to this hypothesis in later chapters.)

Luxury played a central and distinctive role in both Roman thought and practice. This fact is important, and thus worthy of study, in its own right. It is also important historically because until the eighteenth century it was the Roman response to 'luxury' that attained paradigmatic status in discussions of virtue and corruption. For the Romans, and beyond, luxury was a political question because it signified the presence of the potentially disruptive power of human desire, a power which must be policed. In that police action the Roman 'state' can be seen as enforcing its (negative) evaluation of desire and as underwriting a notion of need that located, or identified it, within a rational or purposive context and in so doing it was – in line with the hypothesis – giving practical effect to its particular conception of political order.

In general, such a conception is implicit but we can have recourse to the more explicit comments on these matters as found in the Roman moralists (chiefly in the form of Stoicism). This interpretative strategy should not be thought of as making any profound statement about the relationship between 'theory' and 'practice'. Luxury is both a standard ingredient in the rhetoric of 'Roman corruption' and a contemporary perception, or awareness, of an increase in opulence and government instability. In this way 'luxury' was a significant component in the repertoire of explanations, justifications and consequent modes of self-understanding that were available to educated Romans. It is a mistake (as it nearly always is) to regard recourse to *luxuria* as 'mere' rhetoric; all the more so since the Romans themselves would never have so regarded it. Hence, luxury has a place in the relatively abstract speculations of the moralists *and* in the concrete political activities of the age. This chapter will aim to encompass these two dimensions of the one 'reality' by examining some aspects of the moralistic speculation as well as some instances of the actual legislation passed.

THE NATURAL LIFE

We can start with the moralists. Epictetus opens his *Manual* by contrasting things that are in our power and things that are not. The former are 'by nature free, not subject to restraint or hindrance'; the latter are 'weak, slavish, subject to restraint, in the power of others' (*Manual*; §1). It is one of the hallmarks of Stoic thought that the man of virtue (the sexism is not incidental) is one who understands this contrast and lives his life accordingly. Conversely, to fail to understand this contrast, to think in particular that things that are naturally slavish are really 'free', is to suffer harm. It is a further characteristic of Stoic thought that it included the body among those things that are naturally slavish. According to Seneca (*Epistle*: 65), the body is 'nothing more or less than a fetter on my freedom' and it is a refusal to be influenced by one's body that 'assures one's freedom'.[1]

Although Seneca does at times utilise the Platonic imagery of the soul imprisoned in the body, the fact that the soul is embodied demands an appropriate acknowledgement. This proper acknowledgement takes the form of 'living according to Nature'. There is a proper limit to meeting the body's requirements because the fulfilment of these requirements is itself naturally limited. Humans have bodily needs, but Nature herself fixes a boundary to their satisfaction. Since 'it is self-evident (*aperta*)' that Nature's requirements are few, small and inexpensive, then it follows that the 'natural life' is also the simple life (Cicero, *Tusc. Disp.*: 5. 35). The Stoic depiction of the simple, free life, where the limited needs of the body are easily met and kept in their proper subordinate place, serves, like Plato's 'first city' vis-à-vis the inflamed luxurious city, as a normative benchmark against which

---

[1] In citing Seneca's *Epistles* (hereafter cited in text as *Ep*. with the relevant number) I draw upon the translations of Campbell (1969), Barker (1932a) and the Loeb Library edition (with text) of Gummere (1932b).

unnatural, unfree or corrupt lives can be assessed. This depiction is one of the basic contexts for the concept of luxury in Roman thought and, given the historical salience of the Roman response, this also became the framework within which luxury was assessed until the late seventeenth century.

Because of its importance, the bearing of this argument on an aspect of our discussion in Chapter 1 is worth analysing. In that chapter it was argued that basic needs were abstract and it is in line with that argument to observe that a life *kata phusin* or *secundum naturam* must necessarily be indeterminate. When Cicero and the Stoics (especially), therefore, recommend the natural life, in contrast to one of luxury and desire, the certitude and fixity of that life, despite their asseverations to that effect, is not self-evident. Their idea of a 'natural life' is precisely that: 'their idea'. The assumptions on which that idea rests we will discuss shortly, but we can bring out the specificity of the idea by noting its divergence from what these Romans took to be the Cynics' conception of a natural life. The story that Diogenes lived part of his life in a barrel (since those without homes had to seek such refuge) is only the best-known application of the Cynical conception (Zeller, 1885: pp. 317ff.).[2]

The Cynics' conception of what was 'natural' offended what Cicero called *decorum*. *Decorum* required, *inter alia*, that one be neither boorish nor over-elaborate in appearance and dress (*Offices*: 1.35).[3] Cicero, in this same passage, even chided the Stoics when they, in his judgment, approximated the Cynical position. But the so-called Middle Stoa also dissociated themselves from Cynical 'excesses'. Hence Seneca, too, advocated sober conformity in attire and cleanliness; the simple, natural life should not be a crude one (*Ep.*: 5). Seneca, of course, was himself immensely wealthy (a condition he defends in 'De Vita Beata': 21–6). Even Epictetus, who was perhaps the most austere of the later Stoics and who cited Diogenes the Cynic favourably on many occasions, nevertheless rejected the interpretation of 'natural' that regarded as 'unnatural', and thus unwarranted, the use of water to wash oneself (*Discourses*: 4.11).

The significance of these remarks is that once this normative role, allotted to nature and need as part of some purposive order, is

---

[2] Seneca (*Ep.*: 90) gave added currency to another well-known story when he reported Diogenes' destroying his (artificial) cup upon seeing a boy taking a drink (naturally) by cupping his hand.

[3] In citing Cicero's *The Offices* I draw on the translations of the Loeb Library edition (with text) of Miller (1913), and also of Cockman (1894) and Atkins (1991).

overturned by a descriptive or 'materialist' interpretation, then the understanding of luxury as an unnatural transgression is also going to be displaced. This displacement, which I shall label 'de-moralisation' (see Chapter 5), sets 'luxury' on the road that will culminate in its widespread and guileless use in the world of contemporary advertising.

If we now return to the Roman notion of a natural life, we discover that one recurrent feature is its supposed frugality. Cicero openly associates *frugalitas* generically with the Greek virtue *sôphrosunê* or self-control and, more specifically, with control of appetite and lust (*Tusc. Disp.*: 3.8). Accordingly, those who keep within the bounds of nature will not experience poverty; rather, poverty is only experienced by those who have exceeded those bounds, who ever desire more (Seneca, 'Ad Helv.': 11.3; cf. *Ep.*: 2). It is the element of desire that is decisive. It is the definitive characteristic of desires that focus on the body, and forsake thereby the natural measure, that they become boundless. It is a criterion of the 'unnatural' that it has no terminus (*Ep.*: 16). Once the 'natural limit' is passed, then there is no other further resting place. Viewed from that perspective, human life will always appear too short. Those who see matters in this way have 'become soft through a life of luxury' and have lost their freedom, because in their desire to prolong life they become frightened of dying (Seneca, *Ep.*: 78; cf. 'De Brevitate Vitae': 1.3).

Life should be under control but to invest it with a value for its own sake and to act purely so as to stay alive is to lose that control. Those who place such a high value on life are failing to see that, as Seneca puts it, there is 'nothing so very great about living'. Seneca immediately supports that observation by remarking that 'all your slaves and all the animals do it' (*Ep.*: 72). The fact that Seneca regards this reference to slaves and animals as a form of support reveals a significant set of associations: an unfree life of luxury given over to the enjoyment of bodily pleasures is no better than an animalistic slavish life.

Cicero makes these associations explicit (cf. *Off*: 1.30). Since brutes can only enjoy bodily pleasures then, if a man should become addicted to sensual pleasure, he is transformed into a 'mere brute'. It is inappropriate for man to seek pleasure, rather he should simply preserve his health and strength. In accord with that criterion it follows that it is unworthy and base to wallow in luxury, softness and effeminacy (*quam sit turpe diffluere luxuria et delicate ac molliter*), and that is is proper and becoming (*honestum*) to lead a frugal life of temperance, austerity and sobriety.

This association between luxury, softness and effeminacy, which, as we saw in Chapter 2, was already present in Plato, rested on the assumption that devotion to easy, soft living emasculates and that this, as a consequence, makes for military weakness. A relatively explicit expression of this connexion is made by the historian Florus. He records that King Antiochus of Syria, having seized the Greek islands then spent his time in *otia et luxus*. But, Florus continues, as a direct consequence of this indulgence, when the Romans took the field against him he succumbed easily. The explanation Florus supplies for his defeat was that he had already been defeated by his own luxury (*History*: 1.24).

Luxury, thus, corrupts; it produces bad cowardly soldiers. They are cowardly because, as Seneca said, they have invested life with value and become, as a consequence, afraid of dying and incapable of acting like men (*Ep.*: 124). The life of luxury is especially debilitating because once the pleasures of the body are sought, they are insatiable. Once the natural limits of need are forsaken then, because human desires lack self-regulation, they will simply feed on themselves: 'the greedy are always in want' (*Semper avarus eget*; Horace, *Ep.*: 1.2), just as the rich are never rich enough, and the pleasure-lover never satisfied.

ROMAN HISTORY

This 'model' of corruption was applied to Rome's own history to explain her own perceived decadence. Sallust provides perhaps the most revealing analysis of this convention, since it is given succinctly as part of a deliberately heightened depiction of Roman corruption as revealed in the Catilinean Conspiracy.

Catiline himself is said by Sallust to have been incited by the corruption of a society plagued by two disastrous vices – love of luxury and love of money (*avaritia*) (*Cat.*: 5, p. 178). When, in that past age of virtue, Rome was frugal, harmony was at a maximum while avarice was at a minimum (*Cat.*: 9). But thanks to external success, and the availability of riches, avarice emerged to destroy 'honour, integrity and every other virtue' (*fidem, probitatem ceterasque artis bonis*) (*Cat.*: 10, p. 181). Ambition, too, is let loose. *Ambitio* is the desire to attain distinction (*gloria*) and power by deceit. Fellow citizens, as a consequence, are treated, not according to their merits, but according to personal advantage (ibid.). While Sallust says ambition made most headway initially (because it is a perversion of the search for glory which is a virtue), avarice is more serious; it is a poison that weakens both body and spirit. Indeed, in language that we have already met,

Sallust declares that avarice emasculates (*virilem effeminat*) (*Cat.*: 11, p. 182). Like all vices that centre on the body it is insatiable. Furthermore, once wealth itself becomes established as the norm then a frugal life (the concomitant of virtue) becomes a disgrace. The cumulative effect of this upon the next generation is that it becomes prey to *luxuria atque avaritia cum superbia* (*Cat.*: 12, p. 183).

Sallust's account of this particular episode reflected, in all its essential ingredients, the standard structure present in all explanations of Rome's decadence or corruption. In origin Rome was virtuous and uncorrupted but she suffered degeneration which, though initially exogenously stimulated, took hold within the polity itself to culminate (variously) in bloody civil war, the death of the Republic and rule by tyrants. In this rhetorical guise, *luxuria* figures as a factor in the causality of decline.

The conception of Rome as a virtuous republic is stated clearly at the very start of Livy's *History*. Its location there is itself testimony to its rhetorical role (especially within the republican tradition) as a benchmark from which Rome's corruption can be traced. Livy writes,

> no republic was ever greater, none more virtuous (*sanctior*) or richer in good examples, none into which luxury and avarice entered so late, or where poverty and frugality were so honoured. For it is true that the less wealth there was, the less desire (*cupiditatis*) there was. More recently, riches have imported avarice and excessive pleasures with a craving for luxury and a wantonness (*per luxum atque libidinem*) to the ruination of ourselves and everything else. (*History*: Preface, 10)[4]

This delay before luxury made an appearance is caused by the presence of two factors – frugality, the simple life of need-satisfaction rather than indulgence in desire, and Rome's struggles against other tribes in Italy. And even when Rome became pre-eminent in the Italian peninsula, she was exposed to rivalries from further afield so that she remained on a war-footing, committed to the manly life of virtue and inured to discipline and hardship.

However, the success that these very qualities produced became responsible for their corruption (evidence of Fortune's capriciousness, according to Sallust). Contact with, and eventual victory over, the East ('Asia') and the Greeks, most especially, meant exposure to luxury: as Juvenal put it in a verse that was to be quoted frequently in subsequent centuries,

[4] In citing Livy's *The History of Rome* I draw on translations derived from Spillan (1854) and the Loeb Library edition (with text) of Sage (1934).

Now all the evils of a long peace are ours;
Luxury, more terrible than hostile powers,
Her baleful influence wide around has hurled
And well avenged the subjugated world.[5]

It is characteristic of all the Roman strictures on luxury that they identify an exogenous source.[6] Since the subject was politically loaded, there was not complete agreement on which source was most to blame.[7] However there is a broad consensus over what is of prime interest to us, namely, the mechanics of corruption.

Valerius Paterculus gives a typical account (*History*: II, 1.1). The absence of an opponent (he cites the defeat of Carthage) leads to a lack of discipline and vigilance, which induces indolence. As soon as there is a relaxation, then the pursuit of arms gives way to the pursuit of pleasure.[8] At first the latter expresses itself in public magnificence

[5] *Nunc patimur longae pacis mala, saevor armis/ luxuria incubuit victumque ulciscitur orbem* (Juvenal, *Satire*: 6 (tr. Gifford)).

[6] Not that this was novel. A fragment of Ion of Chios contrasts Asian luxury with Peloponnesian simplicity (cf. Rawson, 1969: p. 19). It is Plato's determinedly endogenous explanation of the emergence of luxury that is the exception.

[7] One of the favourite sources was the return of Manlius Vulso's troops from 'Asia' in 187 BC. This source was given its greatest currency by Livy who traced to this victorious army the seeds of all future luxury (*History*, Bk 39, chs. 6–7). It is not without significance to the later discussion to note what Livy here explicitly identifies as luxury goods. He mentions furniture, tapestries and an increase in the expense and elaborateness of banquets. In addition, Vulso distributed financial largesse to his troops, which, although not without precedent, was of such a scale as to sow, perhaps, those baleful seeds of future corruption. Polybius regarded the importation of the riches of Macedonia from 168 BC as marking the decisive point because from then Rome's 'universal dominion was unchallenged' (*The Histories*: Bk 31, ch. 25). What resulted from this contact with the Greeks was 'moral laxity' and the display of wealth in both public and private life. That such display featured Greek and eastern luxuries (spices, silks, jewellery, marble and so on) is undeniable (cf. J. Griffin, 1976). These same corrupting effects occasioned by the lack of any rivals are traced by Sallust (*Catiline*: 10) to the destruction of Carthage in 146 BC. Sallust is followed by Velleius Paterculus who remarks that when Rome was freed of the fear of Carthage the way was opened for luxury so that 'the path of virtue was abandoned for that of corruption (*vitia*) not gradually but in headlong course'. (*History of Rome*: Bk II, ch. 1. 1). For comment on why the identification of sources could be 'politically loaded' see A. Lintott (1972). Lintott, however, talks too easily of 'propaganda' in this context and does not appreciate how there has to be a pre-existing conventional association between luxury and corruption so that it could be exploited for propaganda purposes.

[8] Tacitus gives a concrete illustration of these mechanics being deliberately put into use. Agricola knew that in order to pacify the Britons he had to accustom them 'to rest and repose through the charms of luxury (*voluptates*)'. This he achieved first by public works and the provision of a liberal education for the sons of chiefs so that, later, the Britons sought to emulate the Roman ways. The upshot was that 'step by step they were led to things which dispose to vice, the lounge, the bath, the elegant banquet'. In effect though, as Tacitus observes, this transition of the Britons from war-inclined barbarism to civilisation has produced their servitude (*Agricola*: 21, p. 690). Tacitus applied the same moral to Rome, commenting that luxury had undermined ancient discipline and simultaneously undermined Rome herself because her 'power had a surer foundation in valour than in wealth' (*virtute quam pecunia*) (*History*: 2.69, p. 516).

but it is soon followed by a soft effeminate life of private luxury. We will return to this contrast between 'public' and 'private'. Polybius adds a further refinement that helps to expose the assumptions that this account of the mechanics of corruption supposes. Like Plato, he exploits a medical analogy. Just as external causes of bodily injury (fatigue, extreme heat and so on) are more preventable and remediable than abscesses that originate within the body, so the same should be assumed about a city or a state. Polybius immediately proceeds to assert that there is a single rule that applies equally to 'armies, cities and to the body', that is, never allow any of them to remain indolent or inactive especially when they enjoy prosperity and plenty (*Histories*: 11.25).

The moral is that all attempts should be made to guard against the external threat of riches. As we have seen, this must be an external threat because, left to itself, the frugal life, and the self-discipline that goes with it, will not produce luxury. But should the soft, indolent and relaxed luxurious life of bodily pleasure be established within society, then cupidity and other associated desires will also be established. But more than that they will flourish because, as we have also seen, they not only feed insatiably upon themselves, but are also, once established within the 'body politic', almost impossible to extirpate.

PHILOSOPHICAL ANTHROPOLOGY

It is clear that the crucial point about the luxurious life is its uncontrollable character, and it is this fact that is central to the philosophical anthropology that underpins this whole discussion. As we have seen, once men pursue bodily pleasures for their own sake they are operating at a slavish animalistic level. But animals are creatures of instinct. This means that although their lives are governed by the requirements of the body, they are, nonetheless, 'governed'. In humans, on the other hand, the governance of their lives is entrusted to their minds. To seek the differentia between man and beast in the possession of mind or intellect was, of course, standard in the 'classical world'. Should, however, this governance be missing or become relaxed, then the desires of the body will be 'set free'. Accordingly, to live a proper human life, control is necessary.

This control is, however, within human possibility. There is no inherent flaw or vice (no 'original sin' in other words) such that humans are doomed to live corrupt lives. This assumption that

'Nature weds us to no vice' (*Nulli nos vitio natura conciliat*) (Seneca, *Ep.*: 94) explains the emphasis on the dangers of relaxation. The price of Stoic freedom is eternal vigilance. To maintain this vigilance means philosophically, the cultivation of *apatheia*.

We quoted earlier Epictetus on freedom, the essence of which in his view lay in properly judging what things were under our control. To make a faulty judgment in this regard will result in grief and harm. Epictetus, though chronologically part of the final phase of Stoicism, is here (as elsewhere) echoing the argument of the founders of the school. To Zeno, to live according to nature (*kata phusin*) is to live according to reason and that is a life of virtue (Diogenes Laertius, *Life*: p. 25). To attain that life is to attain a state of perfection (*teleiosis*), and a sage is one who is perfect in that manner; he judges correctly between the categories of the good, the bad and the indifferent (*Life*: p. 29). The good consists of the virtues – justice, courage, temperance – and the bad consists of their opposites. The indifferent (*adiaphora*) are those things which are in themselves neither good nor bad. These include life, health, pleasure, beauty, strength, riches, good reputation and their opposites death, disease, poverty and so on. The wise man makes use of these indifferents but does not invest them with value in their own right. To treat life or riches as valuable is to fall into error. All humans are prey to error in this way. Error is a 'disease of the soul' (*Life*: p. 33).

The language here is significant because it is indicative of the monistic psychology of Stoicism. Error produces perturbations (*pathê*) of the soul. Since the natural life is the rational life, then these perturbations are irrational impulses or 'pathological disturbances of the personality' in Rist's felicitous definition (1969: p. 27). The rational life of the sage will be an 'apathetic' life. All the emotions that the sage will experience will be rational, since he will always and necessarily respond in the right way to stimuli (cf. Inwood, 1985: p. 139). The passions of human nature are thus *not* outside human control; to be 'carried away' or 'swept off one's feet' by feelings of fear, rage, lust, greed and so on is to commit an error of judgment. This, as should be obvious, is contrary to the Platonic and the Christian imagery of different parts of the soul battling against each other (the idea of a 'psychomachia' will be discussed in Chapter 4). It is, rather, a question of a lack of harmony, balance or symmetry within the whole that is the human soul. Hence it is that a passionate life is an unnatural life of 'excess' or 'superfluous impulse' (*hormê pleonaxousa*):

the sage will drink but he will not get drunk (*Life*: pp. 32, 34).

It is true that the later Stoics toned down this teaching. We have already noted Seneca's version in 'De Vita Beata' and, generally, there was a shift in emphasis from the perfect sage (*sapiens*) to the *imperfectus*. Corresponding to this shift in emphasis is a less austere interpretation of 'apathy' and the requirements of a life *kata phusin*. Starting from the position of one who has not attained the perfect life of virtue/reason/nature, the stress is on how such an individual can best strive to approximate such a life. The doctrine of a life according to nature is now reformulated as a life in accordance with the starting-points given to us by nature (cf. M. Griffin, 1976: p. 179). Since wealth, health, beauty and fame are 'things indifferent', then if they are put to 'good use' they can acquire some value.[9]

Two comments are in order. First, this reformulation facilitates the pejorative use of 'luxury'. Luxury is the bad or corrupt use of these things. The Aristotelian framework of proper or true ends is applicable. In line with this luxury is the use of wealth for personal or private advantage, not public well-being. This we shall return to. Second, this Roman 'moderation' is indicative of the fact that this control of the *pathê* was for them never merely abstract philosophical speculation, if only because the 'sage' was so exceptional. With regard to the main run of humanity, it was, therefore, necessary to enforce this control. In this way luxury, or the perceived necessity to discipline it, was a practical political question. The 'problem' was that, in notional contrast to *antiqua frugalitas*, Rome appeared to have 'gone soft'. This softness was expressed in diverse ways. Seneca (*Ep.*: 114) summarised the symptoms as follows,

where prosperity has spread luxury over a wide area of society, people start by paying attention to their personal turnout. The next thing that engages people's energies is furniture. Then pains are devoted to the houses themselves, so as to have them running out over broad expanses of territory, to have the walls glowing with marble shipped from overseas and the ceilings picked out in gold, to have the floors shining with a lustre matching the panels overhead. Splendour then moves on to the table.

As we would expect, the common feature in these symptoms is their application to the 'body'. What they represent is an unnatural extension of a life 'according to nature' designed to meet Plato's basic

---

[9] Cf. Cicero's remark that *more communi* hold *honores, divitiae, voluptates cetera* to be goods (*Tusc. Disp.*: 31).

set of needs – clothing, shelter, food. Though Seneca mentions 'the table' last this was in fact the most conspicuous context where the Romans did attempt to regulate desire. In fact one of the most frequent of all the contexts where luxury is invoked is banqueting and feasting.

Banquets were an important and prominent item on the Roman scene. They provided an outlet for social prestige. In particular, and as we shall see this is a fact of some moment, wealthy benefactors paid for public feasts. These feasts were a central element in the practice of 'evergetism', which Veyne (1976: p. 20) defines as '*les libéralités privées en faveur de public*'. The practice involved praetors, aediles or other 'public' officers spending lavishly from their own pockets to put on public spectacles (what Juvenal was later to deprecate as *panem et circensis*). There are indeed records of vast sums spent on banqueting and feasting. Balsdon (1969: p. 37) notes that an inaugural priestly dinner in the early Empire might cost a million sesterces when it was possible to live comfortably on 3,000 sesterces a month. Not surprisingly, such extravagance attracted the scorn of satirists like Juvenal and Horace.

But beneath the scorn lay that same philosophical anthropology. Given that the stomach's capacity is limited, then porridge, bread and water will suffice to meet the need for sustenance. In the light of the discussion in Chapter 1, we can discern two crucial assumptions at work here. The first is a functional or teleological perspective which asks why food is needed – the answer being, to keep the (human) organism alive. The corollary to this is that this need can be met with a definite quantum of sustenance because 'naturally' the stomach can only hold so much food. The second assumption is that qualitative factors are non-functional or contrary to the natural telos: all that Nature demands is that the belly be filled, not flattered (Seneca, *Ep.*: 119). This means that, despite the attempt at a quantitative increase by means of vomiting part way through a banquet, this 'luxurious excess' expressed itself qualitatively. This comes out clearly in Epictetus' example of the shoe. The measure of a shoe is the foot, its purpose is protection but once that necessary task is exceeded, once 'the shoe is gilded, then of a purple colour, then embroidered', there is no limit (*Manual*: §39).

For the Romans, luxury signified fine, or qualitative, distinctions where in Nature there are none. This is the context of Seneca's example of bread that we cited in Chapter 1. Hunger will make stale bread seem soft and wheaty and to insist always on fresh bread, and to refuse to eat stale, is to allow the stomach, that is bodily desire, to hold sway. As Seneca himself put it, 'a stomach firmly under control . . . marks a considerable step towards independence' (*Ep.*: 123). He is explicit that it is in accord with the *vivendi iura* that we should exist in well-being, not in luxury (*ut salvi essemus, non ut delicati*) (*Ep.*: 119).

CATO, CENSORSHIP AND SUMPTUARY LAWS

While these 'laws of life' to which Seneca refers emanate from the 'creator of the universe' and not from men, it was, throughout the Republican period in particular, thought to be the proper task of the public authorities to oversee the personal conduct of the citizens. We shall look in a moment at one particular aspect of how on a practical level this task was carried out, but first it is worth taking note of a wider, more general, point. At the level of philosophical assumption, what underlies this concern with personal conduct is the importance attached to the virtues of character.

We can detect this assumption in Sallust's judgment that once wealth had driven out frugality it was the succeeding generation that fell prey to luxury. This same judgment was, as we saw in Chapter 2, made by Plato in his account of how it was the sons of oligarchs who were softened by luxury. What lies behind these judgments is the idea that a virtuous character is an interactive product of the social environment. Once again, Aristotle's articulation of this idea is definitive. Virtue is an activity the practice of which is attained by means of a process of habituation; a process of character-formation whereby a natural disposition is developed and given expression. So important is this process that it is a matter of public concern; it is, Aristotle affirms, the intention of every polis that its 'legislators make their citizens good by habituation [by training them]' (*nomothetai tous politas ethizontes poioustin agathous*) (*Nic. Eth.*: 1103b). Politics proceeds pedagogically. This explains the great emphasis throughout the 'classical world', and its recurrence in the Renaissance, on education as a moulder of character and personality.

It is true that post-Aristotelian philosophy did tend to emphasise how an individual can attain virtue through self-discipline and, speaking as philosophers, both Seneca and Epictetus, for example, continue to stress how the individual, through practising discipline, can attain mastery of wayward desires. However, in Rome the value and crucial importance of the right social conditions were once again appreciated. What made luxury so pernicious was that it was both a symptom and a cause. It was symptomatic of a society of riches and easy-living where bodily desires were given their head. But since character was not an extra-social given, but the outcome of a set of dispositions that had been shaped by their environment, then a 'luxurious' environment produced a weak character. A society of weak characters is a society that cannot defend itself against either external enemies or internal conflict.

This close relationship between individual character and social well-being meant that concern with the former was a proper matter of public business. Indeed if an individual should, in a private capacity, restrain the young from the pursuit of money and luxury and instil virtue in them then he will have performed a public service (cf. Seneca, *De Tranq. Animi*: 3.4). And because this concern with character was properly a political question, there could be no qualms in investing public authorities with an obligation to maintain the 'morals' of its citizens. The most important such authority was the office of Censor. Originally concerned with assessing the property of citizens and putting them into the various social/political divisions of tribes, classes and centuries, the Censorship extended into a concern with the manner of life being led (cf. Abbott, 1963: p. 73).

The most celebrated holder of the office of Censor was Cato the Elder. The chief (if not the only) source of his fame was his stand against the evils of luxury. Cato's career became in fact authoritative as subsequent writers reported and built upon his actions.[10] Cato was elected to the Censorship in 184 BC and he gave notice that, if elected, his *lustrum*, or purification, would not be the ritualistic perfunctory business that had become the established practice. Rather he would, in Plutarch's account (*Life*: 16), make it his task to eradicate the hydra-like 'luxury and effeminacy' (*truphê kai malakian*) of his contemporary society.[11]

---

[10] For example, for Cicero, Cato was a model of the active, virtuous life because he put mere theoretical considerations of virtue into practice (*De Republica*: Bk 1. 1). For Sallust's participation in this appropriation of Cato see Earl (1961: pp. 45, 101).

[11] Plutarch, *Life of Cato* (§16). Livy records his actual measures as follows, 'Jewels and women's dresses and vehicles which were worth more than 15,000 asses he directed the assessors to list at ten times more than their actual value; likewise slaves less than twenty years old, who had been bought since the previous lustrum for 10,000 asses or more, he directed to be assessed at ten times more than their actual cost, and he ordered that on all these articles a tax of three asses per thousand should be imposed' (*History*, 39.44). (Plutarch's account omits the reference to slaves but includes household furniture (§18)). Since the customary rate of tax

But, perhaps, even more than the office of Censor, with its remit over personal life, the most direct evidence of the deliberate concern by the Romans to regulate desire is provided by their various sumptuary laws. Throughout the last two centuries BC down to the reign of the Emperor Tiberius, the Romans passed several laws regulating consumption. These laws are worth considering in some detail, not only because of the insight they throw on the 'practical' dimension of the Roman conception of luxury, but also because, more generally, sumptuary legislation reveals much about a society's system of values and basic identity. Furthermore, the gradual atrophying of that legislation in the modern period is indicative of the change in evaluation that luxury underwent; a change we shall examine in Chapters 5 and 6.

In 195 BC, Cato opposed the repeal of the *lex Oppia*. This law, which had been enacted in 215 BC, included in its scope that no woman should possess more than half an ounce of gold, nor should she wear a coloured robe (in particular one trimmed with purple), nor ride in a carriage inside the city. Livy reports that women lobbied for this law to be repealed, and he produces a speech that he attributes to Cato (though it is very unlikely to be what he said) where Cato takes particular exception to this 'mobbing' by women of senators (*Hist.*: 34.3). Women are 'untamed creatures' with 'uncontrollable natures'

was one as per thousand then there is perhaps justification for Livy's description of these measures as 'stern and harsh'. The reason why Cato should have acted in this way has inevitably generated scholarly debate. Scullard (1951: p. 154) largely follows Plutarch and interprets Cato's efforts as the 'last real attempt of old-fashioned Romans to re-establish a more austere life in the face of social and moral decline resulting from Rome's expansion in the Mediterranean and contacts with the East'. Kienast (1954: p. 134), however, thinks that this is an exaggeration and A. Astin (1978: p. 99) thinks it is misleading to stress the backward-looking element in Cato's censorship. Nevertheless Astin does accept Plutarch's account of the association between the spread of luxury and the enervation of the moral strength of the people. He believes that this was indeed a matter of contemporary relevance because there is 'no denying that corruption, extortion and personal extravagance all occurred on an enormous scale' (Astin, 1978: pp. 97, 101). While Kienast (1954: pp. 77–9) sees a pressing need for funds to pay for the *cloaca maxima* lying behind Cato's extraordinary levy, Astin (1978: p. 95) attributes Cato's policy to his view of the proper conduct of public service in the light of which 'indulgence in expensive luxuries was a major stimulus to avarice, and that avarice led to corruption, to extortion and to the personal appropriation of booty or other wealth that should properly have passed to the state or the rank and file soldiers'. Astin's reference here to 'soldiers' does echo the earlier comments about both the softening effects of luxury on the military virtues and the source of luxury in imports from Asia. In similar fashion, Scullard explains the reference to slaves in Cato's list as a desire to limit the influx of Greeks, with their harmful habits, into Roman households. N. Forde (1975: p. 204) thinks the youthfulness of the slaves more to the point, and Polybius does report a speech of Cato's wherein he said that when 'pretty boys' fetch more than fields it is the surest sign of deterioration (again the context is the infection of Rome by Greek laxity) (*Histories*, 31.25).

who want no restrictions on their spending and luxury. Cato prophesied that if the law was repealed there would be great competition and rivalry among the wives, each wishing to outdo the other in conspicuousness (the process that Veblen was to address at the end of the nineteenth century). This rivalry would be even worse since it would occur *after* a period of restraint and, in a revealing image, Livy has Cato declare that 'luxury', like a wild beast, is rendered angry by its fetters and will do more harm if let loose than if it had never been captured in the first place.

This imagery is to be expected given the associations between a luxurious life and one devoted to a life of bodily satisfaction, a mode of being characteristic of beasts. It is also not surprising to see luxury being associated with women since its 'softness' is what emasculates. Pliny (*Nat. Hist.*: 12.41), in a typical aside, laments the costs incurred by our luxuries (*deliciae*) and our women, while Juvenal's *Satires* (see especially *Satire* 6) are notorious for drawing out a misogynous association of the wantonness and irresponsibility of women with a society given over to wealth and luxury. On a more general level, these connexions between women, beasts and uncontrollable, therefore less rational, behaviour do, as feminists point out, reflect the assumption that it is males who embody what is distinctive about humanity.

Cato's declamations, whether genuine or not, were to no avail. But although the law was repealed 'his' sentiments persisted as Rome, at consistent intervals, introduced and reintroduced laws specifically designed to curb consumption. The *lex Orchia* of 182 BC limited the number of guests who could be invited to dinner. Later laws went into detail about costs and menus. It is characteristic of all sumptuary laws that they are forced to go into detail. Thus the *lex Fannia* (161 BC), as reported by Aulus Gellius (*Attic Nights*: 2–24–1), required the leading citizens to take an oath not to spend more than 120 asses on feast days, and restricted expense on other days to ten asses, though thirty asses were allowed on ten days in the month. Also foreign wine should not be served, and the value of the silverware was regulated along with the number of extra-familial guests (five were permitted on feast days and three on other occasions).

The rise in food prices made this law even formally ineffective so that other measures were passed. Hence the *lex Licinia* (c. 103 BC) raised the normal daily limit to thirty asses and fixed the price of wine. Other legislation prohibited the consumption of, for example, shell-fish and imported birds (*lex Aemilia* (78 BC). Both Sulla and Caesar, in their dictatorships, passed sumptuary laws. Cicero remarks that the gourmandising habits of the Romans were equal to the challenge because, since vegetables were exempt from regulation, they used them to produce elaborate and delicious meals (even if one of them gave him severe diarrhoea) (*Ad. Fam.*: 9.15).

If we ask what these determined attempts at legislation signify, then to the Romans themselves they did indicate that something was amiss. Gellius, speaking of the later efforts of the Emperors Augustus and Tiberius, says that the laws were passed so that 'the rising tide of luxury might be restrained' (*Attic Nights*: 2–24–15). The perceived need to re-issue the laws, besides being testament to their ineffectiveness, could also indicate that the corruption was more deep-rooted than ever. Macrobius, writing in the fourth century AD on these various sumptuary laws, put the failure of the *lex Antia* (68 BC) down to the entrenched character of *luxuriae et vitiorum* (*Sat.*: 3–17–3).

At one level, this sumptuary legislation is a straightforward example of political control of the ways that human desires are to be allowed to express themselves. And, as we have seen, the philosophical anthropology of the Roman moralists underwrote this control with its claim that the 'good life' was the simple life that confined consumption to meeting the naturally limited and finite needs that humans, as embodied subjects, possessed. While this is an important part of the story, it is equally clearly not the whole story. We have still not explained why, precisely, luxurious consumption was thought to be so dangerous. As a matter of practical politics, what underlay this legislation?

SUMPTUARY LAWS COMPARED

We can best answer that question if we contrast the Roman sumptuary laws with later examples of such laws. This contrast will also assist the discussion in later chapters when we consider the objections that were raised to this type of legislation. An informative contrast is afforded by the English legislation between the fourteenth and seventeenth centuries. England, it should be noted, was not alone in issuing regulations, though the date of the final Act in 1604 is much earlier than on the continent. (This excludes the requirement of a 1666 Act to bury the dead in a sheet made only of wool.)

Since the first English sumptuary law of 1336 concerned itself with food, there might seem to be little difference between it and the Roman legislation. Hence, like the Roman laws, this Act (10 Edw. III) proclaimed, for example, that no meal should consist of more than two courses (except for certain feast days) and no course should consist of more than two sorts of food without sauce. However, this Act was an exception because, as N.B. Harte (1976: p. 133) observes, compared to the Roman legislation 'the sumptuary legislation of the later Middle Ages and the early modern period was of a significantly different nature . . . it was concerned primarily with dress and with men rather than women'.[12]

Since our aim is comparative, it will suffice to concentrate on one example of the typical English legislation. The second Act designed to 'regulate apparel' was passed in 1363 (37 Edw. III). This Act had seven clauses, which, typically, go into considerable detail (in Strutt, 1832: II, pp. 104–6). The rationale of the clauses is differences in status and/or occupation. Hence, Clause I deals with grooms and servants; Clause II with tradesmen and artificers; Clause III with gentlemen 'under the estate of knighthood' who possess lands whose annual value is under 200 pounds, while Clause V refers to knights whose lands yield above 200 pounds. The final clause refers to 'all labourers and lower classes of the people not possessed of goods and chattels to the amount of 40 shillings'. Corresponding to each class the maximum price of apparel was fixed, and some type of apparel proscribed. Hence the grooms in Clause I could not wear cloth that exceeded more than two marks and were forbidden to wear any gold or silver. The knights of Clause V, on the other hand, could wear apparel up to six marks' value but were forbidden to wear cloth of gold, ermine or jewelled embroidery. The labourers were to wear no cloth but blankets and they had not to exceed twelve pence a yard. To support this last measure, clothiers were commanded to make sufficient quantities of the requisite material at the fixed price.

This last point does indicate an economic motive. The earlier 1336 Act was, in fact, explicit in this regard since it stated that, with the exception of the royal family, nobody was to wear imported cloth (although Wales, Scotland and Ireland were exempted). Such

---

[12] This statement is, of course, a generalisation which admits of exceptions, especially since the special attention to women was reinforced by Christianity (see, in particular, Tertullian's *De Cultu Feminarum* discussed in Chapter 4). Harte (1976: p. 148), himself, quotes a Scottish Law of 1567 which proclaimed 'it be lauchfull to na wemen to weir abone their estait except houris'. From Solon onwards prostitutes were invariably required to differentiate themselves by means of their apparel.

protectionism was common. The 1510 Act, for example, had a clause forbidding foreign woollens and furs (cf. Hooper, 1915: p. 423). There are, indeed, protectionist elements within the Roman laws. Both the *lex Aemilia* and *lex Fannia* forbade certain foreign produce. In the Roman context, this protectionism would also serve more generally to exclude 'luxury' goods, since they came, virtually by definition, from Greece or the 'East' and had thus to be imported.

But notwithstanding these 'economic' motives, which arguably loomed larger in later sumptuary legislation (especially on the continent (cf. Freudenberger, 1963)), the most obvious fact about the 1363 Act (and the other English Acts) is their 'class' character. This is clear from this Act's preamble which complained of the 'contagious and excessive apparel of divers people against their estate and degree' (in Harte, 1976: p. 138). There are two assumptions underlying this complaint. First that society is not only stratified hierarchically, but that it is properly so ordered and, second, that a threat to that hierarchy is a threat to the very constitution of society. It was these assumptions that gave the issue of 'luxury' its political dimension. In England the political dimension is manifest in, for example, the 1553 Act of Apparel which spoke explicitly of the necessity to repress,

the inordinate excess daily more and more used in the sumptuous and costly array and apparel customarily worn in this realm . . . [which is] to the great, manifest and notorious detriment of the common weal, the subversion of good and politic order in knowledge and distinction of people according to their estates, pre-eminences, dignities and degrees. (In Harte, 1976: p. 139)

And in similar fashion the preamble to a French edict of 1644 declared *'Comme il n'y a point de cause plus certaine de la ruine d'un Estat que l'excès d'un luxe déréglé'* (quoted in Galliani, 1989: p. 110).

If we return to the Romans and their legislation, it appears to differ in its scope from the English (and French). Although both contain a protectionist element this is not in either case the chief consideration. Where the Roman legislation seems to differ most strikingly is by not making explicit reference to 'classes'. This is not because Rome was unstratified. The reverse if anything is true and therein *perhaps* lies the clue to the difference.

The Roman legislation was restricted (recall that according to Gellius the *lex Fannia* applied to the *princeps civitatis*), and this accurately represents the 'reality' that politics was the preserve of a self-perpetuating oligarchy. It is because, in the last two centuries of the Republic, this oligarchy was so solid that it had no need to concern itself with the niceties of apparel (the early *lex Oppia* which did regulate female garments was repealed in 195 BC). This is not to say that there was unanimity, but even the division between the *Optimates* and the *Populares* was a division *within* the nobility (cf., e.g., Scullard, 1982: p. 7; Earl, 1967: p. 12). This suggests that typical medieval and early modern sumptuary laws bespeak a fluidity of social or class relations and it is only because there is this fluidity (together with the perception that it is increasing) that sumptuousness of dress could appear as a threat to the social order. One striking illustration of this is the institution by the Venetian republic of three *provveditori delle pompe*, whose task it was to ensure that the sumptuary laws were adhered to, especially among the leading families (cf. Davis, 1973: p. 69). Certainly those most affected by sumptuary legislation were not the labouring classes but the middling ranks and gentry (cf. Marly, 1985: p. 21). Such a suggestion would accord with Quentin Bell's (1976: pp. 113–15) theory that 'fashion' depends on the presence of a class beneath the ruling order with the financial power to vie with that above it, and with, accordingly, the wherewithal to emulate its dress and thus defy its sumptuary laws.

This is only a 'suggestion' and should not be overstated, since apparent exceptions quickly present themselves. For example, in ancient Athens, Solon had passed a law (594 BC) restricting the number of garments women could wear and, in the Roman Empire, laws were passed restricting the colours of clothing according to rank (cf. Ribeiro, 1986: pp. 21–2). Nevertheless, if suitably guarded, the generalisation holds. Even the force of those two exceptions can be mitigated. Solon's regulations were part of a deliberate reform and, though this is extremely speculative, it could be argued that the Empire, in its early years, was more conscious of its divisions when seen against the light of the relative political equality of the Republic. In addition, this suggested relationship between the imposition of sumptuary laws on apparel and a conception of political inequality helps to explain both the minutiae and frequency of laws on apparel.

It is because the social order exhibits fluidity that new social distinctions occur, and new ways of expressing these distinctions are made possible. Hence Henry VIII repealed all existing legislation and enacted new (hence presumably more appropriate) minutely detailed regulations. This awareness of fluidity can be discerned even in the 1363 Act. This Act had to accommodate, by means of a

separate clause, 'merchants, citizens, burgesses' who possessed goods
to the value of 500 pounds. Such individuals were entitled to the same
apparel as 'esquires and gentlemen' whose estates yielded a hundred
pounds (and merchants worth a thousand pounds were in the same
category as esquires worth 200 pounds). This accommodation lends
weight to the view that the demise of all sumptuary legislation by the
eighteenth century was due in no small part to the disintegration of
sharp divisions. Galliani (1989: ch. 4), in his survey of the French laws
emphasises (indeed it is his dominant theme) their intended role in
preserving *la distinction des rangs*. Certainly, the blurring of divisions
was the contemporary perception in England (admittedly the most
'advanced' economy) as N. Forster (1767) testifies, 'In England the
several ranks of men slide into each other almost imperceptibly . . .
hence . . . the perpetual restless ambition in each of the inferior ranks
to raise themselves to the level of those immediately above them. In
such a state as this fashion must have uncontrolled sway. And a
fashionable luxury must spread through it like a contagion' (quoted
in McKendrick, 1983: p. 11). As we shall see in Chapters 5 and 6, this
disintegration (and the symptomatic role played by 'fashion') was
viewed with alarm by many others in addition to Forster.

The example of the Tokugawa period (1603–1868) in Japan helps
per contra to make the same point. The sumptuary laws of that era have
been called 'the strictest . . . the world has ever seen' (Hurlock, 1965:
p. 297). These laws specified 'exactly how men, women and children
were required to work, build their houses, dress, stand, walk, sit,
speak, eat, drink and smile. They even specified the kind and value of
toys that parents were allowed to give their children' (Edgerton,
1985: p. 174). Japanese society was rigidly stratified into four main
classes – soldier, farmer, artisan, merchant – but each was itself
minutely sub-divided and class membership was hereditary (cf.
Fitzgerald, 1974: p. 194). Though it is always prudent to be wary of
very sweeping 'explanations', it would seem plausible to account, in
part, for the scale and rigour of this legislation by referring to the fact
that the Tokugawa shogunate came to power after a period of civil
war. This suggests that an important factor in accounting for the very
detail of these rules was that they were an attempt to establish fixity
and to forestall fluidity.

If the subject-matter of the Roman laws does not therefore parallel
these standard cases of sumptuary legislation, what role do their laws
play? Despite its differences from the other legislation, it is still

possible to detect in Rome the same connexion in principle between luxury (and hence sumptuary laws) and an idea of 'good and politic order', as the 1553 Act put it; a connexion the tracing and explicating of which is an enduring concern of this study.

The key factor about the Roman laws is that they apply to food rather than clothes and, ostensibly, that is because of the central role that banquets played in electoral politics. Hence the *lex Antia* (68 BC), which forbade magistrates, or magistrates-elect, to accept invitations to dinner in private houses, was an attempt to control corruption in office. This law, like the earlier *lex Orchia*, was 'clearly intended to restrict canvassing for office' (Lintott, 1972: p. 631; cf. Williams, 1962). Similarly, Ronald Syme (1963: p. 59) thinks the *lex Antia* 'looks like an attack on intrigue no less than luxury'.

It remains necessary, however, to retain some interpretative caution. On one count these concerns should not be judged from some modern standpoint of political rectitude. The Romans held no sharp division between public finances and personal wealth. Bribery was the norm. The candidates for the various magistracies vied with each other in paying for games and extravagant feasts. These feasts or banquets were frequently given under the pretext of some familial occasion, especially funerary. That these were a pretext is evident from the fact that candidates would delay the 'celebration' until politically convenient. Caesar, for example, boosted his aedileship by distributing largesse in memory of his father who had died twenty years previously (cf. Gelzer, 1968: p. 37). From this perspective, the sumptuary laws could thus be connected with the various laws that were passed against bribery and corruption (*leges de ambitu*). Veyne (1976: p. 426) explains the presence of this legislation, and its multiplication in the last century of the Republic, as an attempt, welcomed by the candidates, to offset the ruinous costs that such 'evergetism' was entailing.

That being accepted, we still need to be on our interpretative guard. For all their provenance in the power-plays among the ruling elite, these laws do, nonetheless, represent a conception of 'good and politic order'. They cannot be dismissed completely as *la façade légaliste* (Veyne, 1976: p. 426) because they are trading on conventions which are not arbitrary but do signal a particular conception of 'politic order'. For the Romans of the Republic this 'order' rested on the proper relationship between private and public life. Given our concerns, Cicero neatly encapsulated the key point when he remarked that 'the Roman people loathe private luxury but they love public splendour' (*Odit populus Romanus privatem luxuriam, publicam magnificentiam diligit (Pro Murena*: §76)).[13] This remark was made in the context of defending a client against a charge of electoral malpractice or *ambitu*, which provides some justification for utilising the principle implicit within in to explore the connexion between politic order and luxury and, thereby, eliciting why the Romans thought the latter so dangerous.

The way to achieve *gloria* and *dignitas* had always been through public office (cf. Adcock: 1964). Since such an achievement redounded on the whole family, there was no sharp division between pursuing the public interest and furthering self/familial interest. Hence, to be successful in a military campaign not only affirmed one's personal *virtus* and one's familial *gloria* but also, in fact, helped establish and maintain Rome's political hegemony. But as Rome grew in power this ideal fusion broke down. Integral to this collapse was the effect of the wealth that accompanied this military success. Ideally this wealth was properly utilised for the public good. Cicero uses Paulus Aemilius as an example. After the conquest of Macedonia, Paulus brought back so much booty that the need for a property tax was superseded, but he brought nothing to his own house except 'the eternal memory of his name'. Paulus (like his son – Scipio Africanus – after him, with the spoils from Carthage, or Lucius Mummius, with the booty from Corinth) preferred to adorn not his own house, but Italy; yet in so doing 'his own house was, as it seems to me, adorned all the more' (*Off.*: 2.22).

It is significant that we have come across these same examples in the different context of the corruption that they engendered. It is against the backcloth of the Ciceronic ideal on the one hand, and the corruption of foreign wealth on the other, that we can most accurately identify the place of 'luxury' in Roman thought.

ROMAN LUXURY

Luxury represented the use of wealth to serve private satisfactions. These satisfactions could take three main, inter-related forms, each betraying a socially-injurious defective character. First, private luxury could mean self-indulgence. This could express itself in (as Valerius (*History*: II, 33.4) said of the admittedly notorious Lucullus)

---

[13] Incidentally in the course of his defence Cicero bears further witness to the convention that Asia is to be associated with *luxuriae* when he gives as evidence of his client's probity the fact that he left his sojourn there *avaritia neque luxuriae vestigium* (§§ 11, 20).

'extravagance (*luxuriae*) in building, in banquets and in furnishings'. But its most serious expression was its emasculation of *virtus*; as Cicero asked rhetorically, 'What is more vile or disgraceful than an effeminate man?' (*Tusc. Disp.*: 3.17). As we have seen, this effeminacy has its source in finding satisfaction in bodily pleasures with the consequence that men become unable and unwilling to act for the public good when that might involve risk, or even death. The military context of 'virtue' present among the Greeks is retained and will, thanks to the salience of the Roman response, be passed on to later thought through Machiavelli and others.

Second, private luxury could mean greed or *avaritia*. In the past, when the Republic was virtuous, which is also to say when its citizens were frugal, any 'surplus' was spent, as Cicero remarked, on public splendour (*Pro Flacco*: 28). But once wealth and riches became desirable for private consumption, the ideal of public service was corrupted; giving precedence to private over public interest (*communis utilitatis*) was as worthy of condemnation as an act of treachery (cf. 'Cato' as represented by Cicero (*De Finibus*: 3.64)). As we noted earlier, Sallust regarded avarice as a poison engendering every kind of evil. Prominent among those evils was *imperi cupido* and, in similar vein, Cicero pronounced avarice the worst of vices, especially in political leaders (*Off.*: 2.12). The corruption that private luxury in the form of avarice brings about is that identified by Aristotle (and influentially pursued by Polybius) whereby aristocratic government degenerates into oligarchic rule. For Aristotle, 'aristocracy' was rule by a 'few' – the best (*aristoi*) – with a view to the public good or what is best (*ariston*) for the polis, while 'oligarchy' was rule by the rich few in their own interest (*Pol.*: 1279a).

Third, private luxury could mean *ambitio*. This could take the form of personal wealth being used to establish a body of dependent men (such as soldiers who are loyal to an individual rather than to Rome) as a personal power base. Hence the powerful republican and 'civic humanist' (see Chapter 6) tradition that is famously encapsulated in M. Antony's speech that 'Caesar was an ambitious man'. But, as Polybius argued, ambition could also be dangerous because it 'stirred up the people'. This is corrupting because, while 'oligarchy' has given way ostensibly to 'democracy', it has in reality degenerated into 'the worst kind of state' – mob-rule or ochlocracy (*Hist.*: 6.57). In this way, Polybius articulated a concern – as in the medieval sumptuary laws – for the proper maintenance of a proper hierarchy.

In each of these forms, luxury perverts the good and politic order.

What these three forms have in common is that they are species of desire. These desires, when they have been stimulated, are capable of perverting good order because they all place a premium upon self-gratification. The more such 'selfish' pleasures are indulged, the less responsibility and commitment to the public good will be exhibited. Since it is the proper business of any state to uphold some conception of public good, then it will attempt to regulate such desires as it judges would be detrimental to that good.

For the Roman theorists, this regulation was guided by invoking the natural grounding of need. This, in principle, provided a fixed point. But, of course, in practice this theoretical natural fixity had to be underwritten by political action – by acts of censorship and by sumptuary laws, that is, by 'police' as that term was understood in early modern Europe (cf. Oestreich, 1982). These measures aimed to control the tendency of human desire to go beyond what was needed. It was this tendency that was encapsulated by the notion of luxury. Once luxury emerged then civic virtue (in the republican tradition) or a proper ordering of ranks (in the aristocratic tradition) would be undermined.

Ideally, therefore, the Roman 'state', in principle, had a firm understanding of what its citizens needed and, concomitantly, it judged expressions of desire for bodily satisfactions to be inimical to its proper functioning. However, once desire is understood as the effective 'mover' in human nature then this Roman position is overturned. Hence, too, once needs themselves are conceptualised as not fixed; once, that is, the teleological naturalism of classical thought which sustains this directly normative conception of fixed needs is superseded, then – and this is characteristic of contemporary thought – this indeterminacy makes the political definition of 'need' more apparent. These are points we shall pursue in later chapters. But we conclude this chapter by affirming that these relationships between desire, need and political order in the Roman position exemplify our starting-point and hypothesis.

CHAPTER 4

The Christian contribution

In the *OED*, the first meaning of 'luxury' is lust or lasciviousness and a line from Chaucer's *Man of Law Tale* – 'O foule lusts of luxurie' – is cited. If, however, that line is looked up in the Penguin edition, it is given as 'Foul lust of lechery'. Since the latter is a modernised edition, this says something about the meaning of 'luxury' in the fourteenth century. It is this meaning, the interchangeability of 'luxury' and 'lechery', that I wish briefly to examine. In French, the connexion is more evident with *luxure* remaining the standard translation of 'lechery' or 'lewdness' (Chaucer's own usage is itself probably indicative of the relative closeness of the two languages at that time). In part, this examination serves to illustrate the breadth of meaning possessed by the term in pre-modern discourse.[1] This meaning goes back far beyond Chaucer. It has its roots, as we would expect, in Roman usage but it is in the early Christian era that these roots bear this distinctive fruit. It is, accordingly, the chief purpose of this examination to acknowledge the 'Christian contribution'.

This acknowledgement has its place not simply to fill a gap (even in this study which is not designed as a comprehensive historical survey) but also because without it the fact that late seventeenth- and eighteenth-century theorists had to struggle intellectually to articulate a more neutral view of luxury would seem hard to comprehend. While after the Renaissance an element of the Roman response – in the guise of civic humanism – was important, this itself was, notwithstanding its doubtful compatibility, most typically subsumed under orthodox Christianity. The intellectual culture, we might say, did not make a nice distinction between sin and vice.[2]

---

[1] For example, Sekora (1977: p. 46) in his survey, provides several instances in Shakespeare where 'luxury' conveys the meaning of lust.

[2] Cf. Goldsmith (1985: ch. 1) for a discussion of the conflation of pagan and Christian attitudes to public and private virtue; also Burtt (1992: esp. chs. 2 and 3).

A characteristic of our contemporary usage is that there would seem to be little or no connexion between luxury and the notion of the 'seven deadly sins' (themselves – and this in itself is indicative – a shibboleth). At best there is a vestige that can perhaps be discerned in some advertising campaigns. I am thinking especially of the promotion (NB!) of cream as wicked or sinful, that is, seemingly, as a threat, an indulgence – a luxury. Despite such playful possibilities, the lack of any straightforward connexion between luxury and sin constitutes the theme of this brief discussion. While 'lust' would be included in any current list of 'sins', the early Christian enumerations would have *luxuria*.

In Christian writings of the early centuries AD, the close conceptual link between luxury and corruption that the Roman moralists had drawn was retained. What Christian writers added was the identification of vices as sins. Luxury came to take its place as a sin in opposition to sobriety and chastity. These latter virtues were not a major concern of classical/pagan thinkers but it is their heightened position in the Christian picture that enables luxury to become identified with lechery.

Many complex and involved historical questions are at stake here which I shall not tackle. What I shall do, simply, is confine my examination to two issues. The first of these attempts to develop an analysis that will enable a connexion between lust and luxury to be, in principle, maintained. This analysis will focus on St Augustine. His work, especially the *City of God*, has been chosen because it is historically definitive and, also, because of the particular importance he attaches therein to the place of lust in fallen human nature. The second issue selects an especially influential historical theme, namely, the figurative 'battle' of the virtues and vices in Prudentius' *Psychomachia*. This will in turn lead us to a consideration of luxury/lust's place in a list of sins.

I

In Chapter 3 I discussed the roles played by *luxuria* in Roman moralism and, though originally part of the republican vocabulary of corruption, it persisted into the Age of Empire with a corresponding shift from public to private concerns. The 'feminine' softness of luxury was associated with indulgence and lack of self-control so that, within this usage, the term *luxuria* was able to combine lasciviousness and luxury (cf. Veyne, 1987: p. 178). In the light of this combination, the Christian contribution can appear to be derivative. However, while not originating with Christianity, the combination did attain its salience with Christianity's eventual triumph. In addition, Christianity was able to accentuate, in the form of Eve tempting or, on some glosses, seducing Adam into sin (cf. Prusak, 1974: p. 94), the longstanding connexion between luxury and women. Tertullian, in the opening chapter of *De Cultu Feminarum* (p. 304), proclaimed women to be 'the devil's gateway'. Tertullian's discussion of female dress, like Clement of Alexander's discussion of feasting, reiterated Stoic language on the necessity of control and the dangers of luxurious excess.[3]

The story of the relationship between Christianity and sexuality is a story both of the relationship between the body (flesh) and soul and also of the proper place of marriage (and hence virginity and celibacy) in a Christian life. As a matter of historical fact it is Augustine's version of this story that triumphed in the Latin 'West'. This triumph had less to do with the greater intellectual cogency of his arguments (see Pagels, 1990: chs. 5 and 6 for a scathing critique) than with the establishment of the hegemony and authority of the Bishop of Rome.

The *City of God* was written after the fall of Rome in AD 410 to strip away the divine significance of the event. This was partly a response to those pagans who blamed the fall on the christianisation of the Empire consequent upon Constantine's conversion in AD 312. In addition, it was a disavowal of those Christian writers, like Eusebius, but also his own teacher, Ambrose, and, indeed, the poet Prudentius (cf. Berry, 1977), who had seen God's hand in the conjunction of universal empire and recognition of the one true religion. One obvious tactic against the pagans was to demonstrate that Rome was weak *before* the conversion. And that demonstration would carry added rhetorical force if Roman authors could be cited decrying that weakness. To that end the moralistic lament against *luxuria* was tailor-made for Augustine's purposes. Accordingly we find him, for example, citing Scipio's worries about the effect of the defeat of Carthage on Roman virtue (*City of God*: 1.30, 31). Again he has no compunction in using Sallust's account of the corruptions of luxury and avarice that fuelled the ambitions of Catiline (cf. 2.18, 19). Even

---

[3] For Tertullian as Stoic see Brown (1989: p. 77); for Clement see Chadwick (1966: pp. 41–2, 60).

if these citations are argumentative ploys they do, nonetheless, reveal Augustine's familiarity with this vocabulary. This is substantiated later in less polemical parts of the book. Two examples will suffice. In one passage he refers to Nero's luxury being so great that there seemed no grounds to fear any manly (*virile*) act (5.19). In another he refers to the vice of *luxuria* as the pursuit of bodily delights (*corporeas voluptates*) (12.8). (Interestingly Healey, in his 1620 translation, renders this as 'lust' while Dods, in his 1871 version, gives 'luxury'.) Augustine, of course, is not alone in his use of this vocabulary and, on a wider footing, the Stoic support for a frugal, simple life had long chimed in with the asceticism of the early Christians.

Tertullian's *De Cultu Feminarum* is a good example. We have already noted that he refers to woman as *diaboli ianua* and he believes, along with many other Church Fathers, that female physicality literally embodies a threat to the soul. Anything that serves to enhance, or even simply accept, that physicality is thus dangerous and must be controlled. It is to this end that in this treatise he inveighed against *cultus* and *ornatus* (1. 4, p. 309).[4] The former referred to garments of gold, silver and gems, which bespeak ambition, and the latter, which referred to hair and skin-care, bespeak prostitution. Of course, here echoing the Stoic disavowal of Cynical excesses, women should not appear dishevelled and slovenly but they should heed 'the limit and norm and just measure' (*modo et cardine et iustitia*) of personal cultivation. That measure, which is pleasing to God, is determined by the confinement of desires to simple and sufficient refinements (*quam simplices et sufficientes munditiae*) (ibid.: II. 5, p. 320). To go beyond is to indulge in *luxuria* – the desire to please others by means of finery and cosmetics.[5] In view of his similarity to the Stoics it comes as no surprise that Tertullian, in the course of reproving these affronts to Christian modesty (*pudicitia*), remarks that these 'delicacies' tend 'by their softness and effeminacy to unman the manliness of faith' (*deliciae, quarum mollitia et fluxu fidei virtus effeminari potest*) (II. 13, p. 331).

---

[4] Ruether (1974: p. 161) points out the connexion between the Patristic attitude to woman's 'nature' and their 'obsession with blotting out the female bodily image' as manifest in their concern with 'questions of female dress, adornment and physical appearance'.

[5] Cf. similarly Clement of Alexander, who regards 'excess' in all things as an evil, thinks natural desires are 'bounded by sufficiency' and looks upon those who want more either quantitatively or qualitatively (as in the love of ornament) as 'pompous, luxurious and effeminate' (*Writings* (*Paedogogus*): pp. 194, 197, 269). Nor does Clement shy away from using pagan examples. He quotes Euripides on how Sparta was corrupted by clothes and luxury (p. 282). Throughout, the effeminacy of luxury is harked upon.

It is not, however, in the context of an advocacy of a 'simple' (Christian) life that Augustine demonstrates decisively the saliency of sexual desire in human life. This demonstration is, rather, the crux of his investigation of sin. When Adam sinned all mankind became justly condemned. The root of this sin is pride. The essence of pride is mankind's belief that it is self-sufficient (*City of God*: 14.13); the very belief that lies at the heart of Stoicism. The consequence was that instead of being their own masters humans were condemned to live in wretched bondage. One mark of that servitude was that Man became irretrievably *mente carnalis*. Augustine remarks that this carnality is usually called 'lust' (*libido*) although that term itself is a general name for all desires (*cupiditates*) (14.15). Nonetheless, in its usual sense, it pertains to physical sexual excitement (*obscenae corporis partes excitantur*) (14.16). It is the particular gloss that Augustine puts on this that is decisive, and it is this gloss that I wish to utilise.

Augustine imbues sexual lust with an unparalleled potency. The key factor is control. Human emotions/desires are controllable by the will. To give one of his own examples, we raise our hand when, in anger, we wish to strike someone but whether a blow is actually struck or not depends on an exercise of will, and not on the power of the desire itself. The particular potency of sexual lust is that it constitutes a special case. Whereas raising one's hand can mean hitting out in a rage, it can also mean many other things – in this sense Augustine's analysis is in line with A.I. Melden's (1961) well-known contemporary account that 'meaning' is distinct from physical behaviour. But the nub of Augustine's case is that lust is exceptional; an erect penis or moist vagina means but one thing. The sexual organs have, so to speak, an independent mind of their own; they are not the outcome of will, but are wilful. It is upon this independence and wilfulness that Augustine seizes.

Properly, in accordance with Man's special status in Creation, the soul should rule the body; but the power of lust over the sexual organs demonstrates how mankind has fallen away irretrievably from this proper arrangement. In a state of sexual arousal the body is liable to evade that rule for no act of will need be involved to excite the sexual organs – even the most pious can experience penile erection (cf. *Contra Julianum*: 3.13, cited in Pagels, 1990: p. 141). The solution to this – and one that had its advocates and practitioners (cf. Rousselle, 1988) – in the form of castration, is in fact no solution, since, as Augustine insists, it is part of the Divine economy that mankind propagate itself

(Adam and Eve were enjoined to increase and multiply). Such drastic attempts at control are, in fact, still further evidence of the unruly power of sexual desire. So independent is this desire that no matter how much intercourse is willed if lust is absent then that will cannot of itself command obedience – the spirit may be willing but the flesh weak (14.19).

This independence and rebelliousness of lust is to be contrasted with a putative pre-lapsarian condition. As we have seen, it is no part of Augustine's argument (unlike that of some early Christians who, convinced of the imminence of the eschaton, saw no need to propagate new souls) to reject all sexual activity. Indeed he wrote a treatise (*De Bono Conjugali*) in defence of married life and was careful to note that the censuring of lust (*libido carnalis*) should not be confused with a condemnation of marriage (cf. *De Nuptiis et Concupiscentia*: 1.6). Nonetheless, he has to argue that *originally* Adam and Eve's participation in that activity was distinctively different. Though his views on this much-debated question oscillated (cf. Ranke-Heinemann, 1991: pp. 87ff.), there are two related ways in which this difference manifested itself.

Firstly, pre-lapsarian sex took place without lust; at that time the sexual organs were under control and responsive to will (*voluntate motis, non libidine concitatis*) (*City of God*: 14.24). In our fallen state, however, all sexual activity, even that between husband and wife, is associated with carnal concupiscence. Secondly, as sex for the propagation of children was then willed behaviour, it was undertaken without shame, whereas now, on the contrary, mankind is ashamed. It is a mark of that shame that everywhere (even in India) the genitals are covered and intercourse itself takes place away from public view. Augustine uses this argument to indicate a further difference between lust and anger. It is proof that anger is still a matter of will since, despite it being a vicious emotion, its expression is not hidden, while it is because of the very wilfulness of lust that we shamefacedly avoid spectators. Indeed this is now so much a part of human nature that even when a married couple properly have intercourse this is done privately. Furthermore they would rather be seen acting unjustly through anger in public than copulating licitly in the open (*City of God*: 14.19).

For Augustine it is especially fitting that the state of sin, in which all humanity now exists, is manifest in sexual lust, since all come into existence as a consequence of its exercise (15.1; 13.14; cf. *De Nup. et*

Con.: 1.25 where Augustine refers to the *peccati vinculum* that concupiscence passes on via birth). This physical fact underpinned Augustine's version of how it was possible to regard the newly-born as already marked by sin and justly condemned. Christ, of course, was not so conceived and He alone was born without sin.

If we step back analytically from Augustine's own concerns, we can see how his account of lust is assimilable to the general understanding of luxury held by Greek and Roman thinkers. In their thought, luxury meant the exceeding of proper limits. These limits were established by Nature so that, for example, one ate because one was hungry and ate until one was satisfied. To that end it mattered not whether the bread was stale or fresh. It was a mark of luxury if that distinction was made to matter – if stale bread was spurned. Such discrimination meant illicitly substituting bodily delight (the taste of freshly baked bread) for a judgment as to the proper function of consumption. This substitution treats a purely instrumental means as being of some inherent value, as being something that is desired for its own sake or in its own terms.

Sex fits this 'model' perfectly once it is allowed that it has a proper purpose. For Augustine this purpose is the propagation of children, and that is a valuable activity given God's injunction to increase and multiply, even if that has indeed lost some of its imperativeness since the days of the Patriarchs (cf. *De Nup. et Con.*: 1.14). If, however, sex is engaged upon because it gives pleasure, or because of a pressing urge, then this is lechery. Accordingly, to take an example that is commonplace among the Stoics as well as the Christian Fathers, to have sex with a pregnant woman is, for both male and female, to go beyond the proper purpose; it is a lecherous indulgence in carnal delights. That this also applies to women is significant. Indeed it is even more shocking if a pregnant woman should desire sex; by definition she is already fulfilling her proper purpose. Alas the inherent 'softness' of women predisposes them to 'luxurious' behaviour; as Clement observed they have 'dangerous appetites' within them (*Paedogogus*: II.2; tr. p. 209).

Of course, that a formal, analytic link can be discerned between lechery and luxury does not demonstrate that these two terms are interchangeable. The historical but contingent fact that this synonymity did occur can only be accounted for by the provision of a narrative to that effect. This narrative has yet to be written and I am not here in a position even to approximate that task. Rather, still keeping to an analytical mode, it is possible to speculate about what, in principle, would be consistent with the story that such a narrative would relate.

From the perspective of this book, what Augustine has done is re-articulate the Roman indictment of *luxuria*. Taking *luxuria* as a shorthand for the complex of avarice, ambition and sensual indulgence, Augustine made it the indelible character of humanity. Hence, unregenerate humankind is indefeasibly bound to pursue avarice (*libido habendi pecuniam*), glory (*libido gloriandi*) and power (*libido dominandi*). In terms of Augustine's own argument, this re-articulation enabled him to regard the Christian solution/response/explanation of this 'fact' about humanity as infinitely superior to the Roman reliance on human ('all too human') virtue. Furthermore this indelibility was constituted by the necessary facts of conception. Since for Augustine there was an ineradicable conjunction between lust and these facts, this meant that concupiscence was able to attain a salience hitherto absent. Having established that sexual lust is a given of the human condition and is characterised by a rule-trespassing wilfulness (lechery), it became perfectly apt to adopt the term *luxuria*, as its meaning had been developed, to identify this phenomenon.

II

One consequence of the Augustinian attack on the tenability of pagan moralism as an effective counter to the vices of *luxuria* was that it represented a radical break with the pervasive Aristotelian tradition of virtue as a mean. We recall that, for Aristotle, *trupherotês* as a vice was counterposed to *karteria*, with *kakopatheia* as the appropriate mean. Augustine here is simply stating, if more thoughtfully and, it must be said, disingenuously, the long-standing Christian claim that Athens has nothing to do with Jerusalem. It is one aspect of that claim, or of its implications, that it licenses an understanding of the relationship between virtue and vice as one of implacable opposition – there is no conceptual space for mediation. Moreover this opposition is no static stand-off, but is rather a question of conflict; a conflict that occurs within the soul of each individual. Prudentius' poem *Psychomachia* (c. AD 400) graphically depicts that conflict.

This poem merits a brief discussion because it is in its own right a revealing indication of the place of luxury in Christian thought at a less rarified level than Augustinian theology. Additionally, and perhaps more importantly in our context, this poem became one of the chief inspirations of medieval imagery and it is in that imagery, and the associated notion of seven (or eight) cardinal sins, that the identification of luxury and lechery is most evident. Although, as we shall see, the identification is not overtly made by Prudentius himself.

It goes without saying that Prudentius is not breaking new ground. Mâle (1958: p. 98), following Puech, cites Tertullian's *De Spectaculis* as the first to talk of a battle (*pugilatus*) between virtues and vices.[6] Lewis (1936: pp. 56–68) also cites Puech, though he thinks the *Psychomachia* was the outcome of a general intellectual 'drift' toward allegory, associated with changes in religious and moral belief. Bloomfield (1952: p. 65) cites Lewis and identifies Philo as the ultimate source of the allegory, though admits there is no evidence of direct borrowing. All three agree, however, that Prudentius' significance lies not in his originality but in his legacy.

There is no need to rehearse Prudentius' 'argument' in any detail. The poem describes a series of confrontations – Faith against the old gods (*Veterum Cultura Deorum*); Chastity (*Pudicitia*) against Lust (*Sodomita Libido*) who is depicted as a whore; Patience against Anger; Pride against Humility. It is upon the defeat of Pride that *Luxuria* enters (*Psychomachia*: ll. 310–44). The structure of the poem means she is clearly distinct from Lust. Prudentius emphasises her general sensuality; she is a voluptuary rather than an erotomane (Thomson translates the vice as Indulgence, as does Mâle). Her hair is perfumed and she has so given herself over to voluptuousness (*deliciis*) and pleasure (*voluptas*) that her spirit (*anima*) is softened and her understanding (*sensus*) is weakened. Although listless (unlike the energy associated with Lust) she is nonetheless a formidable adversary.

She appears on the scene riding a beautiful chariot made of gold and encrusted with jewels. So wonder-full is this vehicle that it disarms the Virtues, whose stupefaction is increased by *Luxuria*'s weaponry of violets and roses. The terminology used by Prudentius here is revealing. One indication of the conception with which he is working is provided by the seven attendant vices he gives to *Luxuria*, namely, *Iocus, Petulantia, Amor, Pompa, Venustatis, Discordia, Voluptas*. The agonistic context of his work means that the 'classical' concern that luxury will instil cowardice and undermine *virtus* can be exploited. Hence *Luxuria* is a venom which weakens resolve, softens strength, and saps courage. The over-all effect of this is to insinuate

---

[6] Tertullian pairs off *impudicitam* against *castitate*; *perfidem* and *fide*; *saevitiam* and *misericordia*; *petulantiam* and *modestia* (*De Spectaculis*: 29).

into the Virtues a desire to surrender, to enslave themselves willingly to *Luxuria*'s rule. It is the power of the seductress, not the rapist. On this reading, while we can appreciate a significant difference between luxury and lust, we can also discern how the two can come to share a common thematic meaning – the powerful appeal of sex.

This reading also makes it difficult to accept entirely either of Lewis's (and Bloomfield's who directly follows him (1952: p. 65)) comments upon this passage. First, Lewis (1936: p. 70) claims that '*Luxuria*, in the medieval sense, does not appear at all' (that is, presumably, *qua* lechery). And, second, he goes on to say that Prudentius' luxury is 'a kind of blend of *Gula* [gluttony] and *Superbia*. She is, in fact, something very like "luxury" in the modern meaning of the word – the sin of the profiteer.' This last sentence says, I think, rather more about Lewis than Prudentius. It is true that in one place Prudentius describes *Luxuria* as 'gluttonous' (*edax*) and refers to her feasting and drunkenness, but the overall discussion tells against this reading. Hence, although Lewis thinks *Amor* (strong desire) an insignificant attendant, others in Prudentius' list (*Venustatis* – beauteous charm or allurement in Thomson's version) and *Voluptas* support the reading that allies Prudentius' *Luxuria* with seductive sexuality; indeed he calls her *malesuada* at one point.

Despite the potency of her charms, *Luxuria* does not triumph. Temperance (*Sobrietas*) enters the fray (*Psychomachia*: ll.345–454). The other Virtues are upbraided at length for submitting to this pleasant sin (*dulce malum*) and betraying God. Then Temperance overturns *Luxuria*'s chariot by holding a cross in front of the horses, causing them to rear; *Luxuria* herself is mangled (given in gory detail) by her own chariot's precious wheels before Temperance dispatches her. For the sake of completion we can note that after *Luxuria*'s demise, *Avaritia* appears to snaffle up the gems scattered by *Luxuria* but she in turn is overthrown by the combined forces of Reason (*Ratio*) and Beneficence or good works (*Operatio*), who distribute Greed's bounty to the needy. The final confrontation is between Concord and Heresy, with Faith reappearing to ensure the downfall of the latter.

As we have observed, it is the development of this notion of a battle between virtues and vices in later centuries that gives Prudentius' poem its status. It is in that development too that the conflation of luxury and lechery is achieved. This process would seem largely to be the fruit of the mingling of the idea of a psychomachia with an enumeration of cardinal sins. The sins varied slightly in content, as well as in order of presentation and in number between eight and seven. The former number was proposed by Evagirus of Pontus (d. AD 400), whom Bloomfield (on whose standard account I draw) nevertheless dubs 'the father of the seven cardinal sins' (Bloomfield, 1952: p. 57). Eight sins were also identified by Evagirus' pupil Cassian, whose list, again according to Bloomfield, is of 'great significance' (ibid.: p. 60). Evagirus' list includes *porneia* and Cassian's *fornicatio*, as its Latin equivalent.[7] Cassian's context is the requirements of, and regulations for, a monastic life. And the sin of fornication, which includes masturbation and sexual fantasising, is stressed (there are twenty-three chapters in the book devoted to it (*De institutis coenobiorum*: Bk 6) along with *gastrimargia* (gluttony) as a particular threat to that life.

However, throughout that book the word *luxuria* does not appear. The word does feature in Gregory the Great's version. This is significant in as much as it was his version that became standard and which, thereby, fixed the number of sins as seven (Bloomfield, 1952: p. 72). In Gregory's list *luxuria* is substituted (in seventh place) for *fornicatio*. Given the historical impact of Gregory's account this substitution now establishes itself. In Gregory *luxuria* has a wide remit. It incorporates moral blindness and self-love as well as hatred of God; indeed a little earlier it is said to destroy all virtues (*Moralia*: 21.12).

Like Cassian before him, Gregory closely associates lust (*fornicatio/luxuria*) with gluttony (*ventri ingluvies*) (cf. 31.45, 89).[8] Aquinas in his largely critical gloss of Gregory, provides some instructive comment on this linkage. Aquinas enumerates three kinds of goods of man – of the soul, of the body and of externals. The second of these is subdivided into self-preservation and preservation of the race. Corresponding to these two subdivided goods are two evils; gluttony (*gula*) is the excess of the first and *luxuria* of the second (*coitus*) (*Summa*: I–II, 84.4).

As the context of Aquinas' discussion illustrates, luxury has taken

---

[7] This same convention is found in Paul's list of the 'sins of the flesh' in Galatians (5.19) which includes *moicheia*, *akatharsia*, *aselgeia* and *porneia* and which the Vulgate renders (respectively) as *impudicita*, *immunditia*, *luxuria* and *fornicatio*. St Augustine quotes this passage (14.2). Revealingly, the Authorised Version gives (respectively) adultery, uncleanness, lasciviousness and fornication.

[8] There is in fact an etymological link with 'lechery'. Since its root is 'lick', a 'lecher' could mean one devoted to eating.

on the meaning of lechery in the sense of the sin of valuing bodily – chiefly sexual – enjoyments. By the time of Spenser, as Tuve (1966: p. 119) points out the meaning of luxury as an embodiment of concupiscence was 'perfectly habitual'. It would be superfluous, as well as tedious, to attempt to catalogue references to 'luxury'. As an example, by drawing principally on the work of Mâle, I shall confine myself to the imagery in French cathedrals. Following illustrations of Prudentius' poem, the masons of various Romanesque churches depicted the virtues and vices, frequently as opposed pairs; including as at Aulnay and Laon, *Luxuria* and *Castitas* (Mâle, 1958: pp. 102–5). Somewhat later, when Prudentius' influence was less direct, and the conventions had been well established, the great cathedrals of Notre-Dame Paris, Chartres and Auxerre all pair luxury and chastity. In the rose window of Notre-Dame, luxury is represented as a woman titivating herself in front of a mirror (ibid.: p. 117).

But this is a considerable refinement from earlier versions, and even at Amiens, of a slightly later date, 'luxury' is represented by an embracing couple. Of the earlier representations, that found in the Porch at Moissac (1115–30) is perhaps the most uncompromising. Here *Luxuria* is paired with *Avaritia*, each having their accompanying demon. These two are set alongside the parable of Lazarus and Dives and symbolise the two cravings of the latter – for worldly gain and carnal pleasure (cf. Cohn, 1970: p. 101). *Avaritia* is a man with a devil sitting on his shoulders, *Luxuria* is a naked woman. But this is no simple nude. Although the masonry around the head is mutilated, the contours and surface are, in Schapiro's (1985: p. 124) judgment, 'unforgettably expressive'. It is, however, the depiction of her punishment that conveys the unequivocal message: her sexual organs are being devoured by toads while two serpents are suckling her breasts. It requires little hermeneutical skill to 'read' this 'sign'.

While there is, of course, a great gap between a twelfth-century piece of French masonry and the *Faerie Queen*, it is yet a mark of the depth of impact of the Christian contribution to the idea of luxury that a clear family resemblance can be detected. However, when we read that sincere Christian Dr Johnson's remark in 1778 that 'you cannot spend money in luxury without doing good to the poor' (Boswell, *Life*: p. 342), we cannot but be aware that a sea-change has occurred. That change is the subject of Part III.

The transition to modernity

CHAPTER 5

The de-moralisation of luxury

As we have seen, 'luxury' was a stock ingredient in the moral vocabulary of the 'pre-modern' period. There is a generally accepted story about the characteristic features of the modern world-view and of its emergence from the earlier period. Of course there are many differing strands in this story, each of which is individually open to question and dispute (frequently taking the form of inquiring just how 'modern' a particular representative figure like, say, Descartes or Galileo or Grotius 'really' is). Even more contentiously, there are differing and competing explanations offered to account for this emergence. The change in esteem enjoyed by luxury can itself be seen as another strand in the general story. I do not wish to tell this story in its entirety but wish instead, and in keeping with the selective approach adopted, to highlight a crucial episode.

The episode covered in this chapter sees the separation of what was contemporaneously called 'political' luxury from an overtly moralistic discourse. This non-moral usage is aptly called 'political', or sometimes 'civil', in so much as it concerns the well-being of the political nation or 'state', as it came to be called. The decisive break is not the political focus, for the moralistic language of luxury had always had that focus, but the understanding of this 'well-being' in terms of economic prosperity. It is in the context of 'trade' that we can discern a significant shift in the meaning of luxury. It is that 'shift' that is the concern of this chapter.

There are, so to speak, two dimensions to this concern. First, there is the need to acknowledge that changes in evaluations or normative discourse are to be plotted with care. Conceptual shifts usually take the form of exploiting existing 'meanings', in particular exploiting ambiguities. This exercise, again usually, is undertaken for limited and specific, perhaps even argumentatively tactical, purposes. Hence, to take an example from the present topic, to defend the East India Company – to defend the business in which it was engaged – required deflecting the attack that this business was (*inter alia*) a harmful purveyor of luxuries. This first dimension thus involves detailed particularistic historical investigation. The second dimension – in no way opposed to the first – relates to the general significance of the particular shifts in argument. The criterion of 'significance' here is supplied by hindsight in the way that Hegel said comprehension is only to be attained after the event – the owl of Minerva takes flight at dusk. 'We' now know that in its common apprehension 'luxury' is attached innocently to objects that are widely desired. It is because we are in possession of a *terminus ad quem* that we are able to identify what in the 'then' produced as a matter of contingent but historical 'fact' our 'now'. Such identification does not commit the sin of anachronism; it serves, rather, as a necessary principle of selection.

In the light of the opening remarks about the emergence of 'the' early modern world-view, it is in the seventeenth century that we would expect to see the articulation of a de-moralised idea of luxury. Aside from the particular preoccupations with contemporary circumstances, there is evidence that at least some of the discussions were undertaken in a self-consciously 'modern spirit'. Perhaps the most striking of these is the Preface to Dudley North's *Discourses upon Trade* [1691]. The author of that Preface (who may be Dudley's brother, Roger (cf. Letwin, 1963)) refers to the fact that in the Discourse itself trade is treated 'philosophically'. This treatment is explicitly identified as Cartesian or 'mechanical', and this in turn is characterised as being 'built upon clear and evident Truths'; a 'Method of Reasoning' that has been introduced by the 'new Philosophy' (in McCulloch, 1952: pp. 500–1).

I

THE BALANCE OF TRADE

North's was only one of many tracts and pamphlets that discussed 'trade'. The aspect of these discussions that is most pertinent is the debate over the 'balance of trade'. The most significant early text (or at least that upon which most commentators remark) is Thomas Mun's *England's Treasure by Forreign Trade* published in 1664 but written some thirty or more years earlier.[1] At the beginning of his

---

[1] See Supple (1954) for the germ of Mun's arguments, being present in 1622–3 in memos to the Commissioners of Trade. For the importance of that period see Hinton (1955).

second chapter Mun states the guiding principle, 'the ordinary means
. . . to increase our wealth and treasure is by Forreign Trade wherein
wee must ever observe this rule; to sell more to strangers yearly than
wee consume of theirs in value' (in McCulloch, 1952: p. 125).

The underlying conception is of trade as a zero-sum game. The
very imagery of a 'balance' suggests that a nation can only prosper, be
'up', if others are 'down'. The traditional, moralistic, understanding
of luxury fitted this conception almost perfectly. Silks (to take a token
example) have to be imported. However, as even Davenant, as a
defender of the East India Company, admitted, they serve 'luxury'
(*Essay on East India Trade*, in *Works*: 1,90) and, as such, they are not
only superfluous but also pernicious in that they stimulate vanity and
an illimitable desire for their possession. Since, moreover, there is no
market for British goods in the Orient, these luxuries must be paid for
by bullion (the East India Company was licensed to export a fixed
amount of 'treasure'). The balance is, therefore, 'down', which means
Britain is in debt. This was the crux of the so-called 'bullionist'
argument. Debt would produce, variously, unemployment, a fall in
land-values and a consequent upsurge in vagrancy with all its
associated moral ills. Given this 'fit' between the economic and the
moral argument we can anticipate how a shift in the understanding of
trade could serve to 'decouple' the economic from the moral.

THOMAS MUN

We can pursue this relationship initially by looking more closely at
Mun. Mun wished to defend the East India trade (he himself was a
director of the East India Company). He rejected the bullionist
argument and advocated the idea of a general, rather than a specific
country-by-country, balance (cf. Thomas, 1926: p. 12). There are, of
course, two ways to tip the balance in your favour – either increase
exports or decrease imports. The latter can be attained by providing
at home what is otherwise imported, and here Mun recommends the
cultivation of waste ground so as to preclude the need to import
hemp, flax, cordage and even tobacco (p. 127). This decrease can also
be attained, and this is the particular point of most interest to this
inquiry, if

we soberly refrain from excessive consumption of forreign wares in our diet
and rayment, with such often change of fashions as is used, so much the more
to encrease the waste and charge; which vices at this present age are more
notorious amongst us than in former ages. (Ibid.: p. 127)

Later in his pamphlet, Mun elaborates upon these present-day vices. Our current behaviour is a 'general leprosie' of

Piping, Potting, Feasting, Fashions, and mis-spending of our time in Idleness and Pleasure (contrary to the Law of God, and the use of other Nations) [which] hath made us effeminate in our bodies, weak in our knowledg, poor in our Treasure, declined in our Valour, unfortunate in our Enterprises, and contemned by our Enemies. (Ibid.: p. 193)

Although Mun does not refer to luxury in these passages – indeed in the entire treatise luxury by name scarcely figures – it is plainly no distortion to see many of the traditional themes implicit within them. Given that the context is a concern to curtail imports, one such theme is the charge, central to Livy's account for example, that the import of 'foreign luxury' has been integral to, perhaps even causative of, the deterioration of standards from an earlier, more virtuous, era. It is a mark of this deterioration brought on by luxury that we have become effeminate and possessed of less valour. It is reasonable to suppose, further, that the 'diet' and 'rayment' in question are not the basic stuffs required to meet basic needs; Mun refers to 'Silks, Sugars and Spices' as 'unnecessary wants' (p. 192). These 'wants' are luxurious refinements and the 'needs' that they serve can perfectly well be supplied by domestic production. Mun's references to 'fashion' are further evidence of the presence of the traditional understanding (elsewhere (p. 192) he refers explicitly to 'monstrous fashion'). As we shall see, this context will change as 'luxury' becomes 'de-moralised'. Similarly, the implicit acceptance of fixed limits in Mun's reference to 'excessive' in contrast to 'sober' (that is, duly proportioned) consumption will also be circumvented as the argument comes to be made that luxury and fashion are acceptable because they stimulate consumption, which in turn generates trade and employment and thence produces greater overall well-being (cf. Sombart, 1913: pp. 138–41).

Despite Mun's adherence to the standard moralistic understanding of luxury, he does, within this treatise, adumbrate arguments that will subvert this understanding. This is significant in as much as it indicates that it is in the context of 'trade' that this subversion occurs. In outlining his basic principle, Mun is also underwriting the social value of the merchant; it is a noble profession which, when it is properly executed, enables private gain ever to accompany public good (p. 122). Hence it is because Mun is writing an 'economic' treatise and not a straightforward moralistic tract that he says that it is *not* desirable that we become so frugal that we would have little use for foreign goods. Even more pointedly, he declares that 'all kind of Bounty and Pomp is not to be avoided' (p. 180). The reason why Mun does not wholeheartedly endorse frugality as a social principle is precisely because it would make it impossible for us to sell abroad. And if there were no trade, he asks rhetorically, 'what will become of our Ships, Mariners, Munitions, our poor Artificers and many others?' (p. 180). Mun's considered position is the equally classical 'golden mean' – 'it is more safe to run a middle course by spending moderately, which will purchase treasure plentifully' (p. 180).

As the title of his treatise indicates, the balance of trade is measured in 'treasure' by which was meant, principally though not exclusively, gold and silver. I say not exclusively because it was also appreciated that, more indirectly, foreign trade is,

The School of our Arts, The supply of our wants, The employment of our poor, The improvement of our Lands, The Nurcery of our Mariners, The Walls of the Kingdoms, The Means of our Treasure, The Sinnews of our wars, The terror of our enemies. (Ibid.: p. 209)

BALANCE AND REGULATION

According to what we might call its inherent logic, the doctrine of the balance of trade required that trade be controlled. To employ Robert Nozick's terminology, the balance of trade is an 'end-state doctrine'. There is a specific goal that is known in advance and to which, therefore, all 'economic' effort should be directed. Dalby Thomas, in 1690, states the point categorically,

trade is of that nature that it requires frequent pruning, loping and much restraining, as well as cultivating and cherishing, and thrives much better under proper and rightly applied restraints, duties, taxes and excises than in a general looseness. (Quoted in Novak, 1962: p. 17)

Two very general assumptions are present in this connexion between the balance and the regulation of trade. First, it is assumed not only that a balance can be computed (an assumption assailed devastatingly by Barbon and Child), but also, more significantly, that there is an Archimedean point from which this computation can be assessed. This assumed point is the 'general interest'. In the guise of the 'common good', this notion has a long pedigree. The force of the notion depended on the contrast between it and 'self-interest'. In political/constitutional thinking it provided a criterion to distinguish good from bad rule. It also distinguished the properly 'political', that is concern with matters of common interest (*res publicae*), from the 'economic', that is, self-regarding activity within the *oikos* directed to the necessary task of meeting needs.

Given this backcloth, it was relatively easy to criticise any particular trader for enhancing his own (economic) interest at the cost of the public's. Thus a critic of the East India Company was able to argue that since through the importing of foreign textiles the native manufactories suffered while the importer grew rich, the Nation was impoverished (*Great Necessity and Advantage of Preserving our own Manufacturies* by N.C., quoted in Cunningham, 1910: II, 465). So entrenched could this attitude appear that merchants themselves were seemingly forced to disavow any personal interest. Writing in 1648, John Battie declared that like all men the merchant too was 'to employ his utmost endeavour to the general good and not to have the least thought in particular or private ends' (quoted in Gunn, 1969: p. 211). Mun himself, as we have seen, while defending the nobility of the merchant profession also allowed that it was possible that a merchant could flourish while the 'commonwealth' declined (when, that is, 'through Pride and other Excesses' the people consume more in imported goods than 'the wealth of the Kingdom can satisfie'). Mun did observe additionally that the opposite outcome – merchant suffering, commonwealth prospering – was also possible (pp. 147–8).

The second assumption is the well-worn 'classical' motif that corruption is not self-correcting. Once virtue is lost, once frugality has been abandoned, then corruption will feed upon itself without end. There need, therefore, to be either regular purges (the Roman *lustrum*) or persistent regulation such as sumptuary laws. In this way the need to maintain a favourable balance chimed in melodiously with the traditional pro-frugality anti-luxury moralism. But, by the same token, it indicates how the advocacy of 'free trade' was out of tune with this moralism; a point to which we shall return.

THE DUTCH EXAMPLE

In the later seventeenth-century English discussions, what gave particular force to the link between trade regulation and this traditional moralism was the rivalry with the Dutch. As the seventeenth century progressed, the English found their major export, woollen cloths, losing out to Dutch competition. One common explanation was to compare English 'virtue' unfavourably to that practised by the Dutch. Mun had remarked that the Dutch had, in the early seventeenth century, given up the 'swinish vice' of following the pleasures of 'pipe and pot' and, not coincidentally, had also 'taken up our wonted valour' (p. 193). This valour was evidenced in their struggles against their Spanish overlords and, more recently and most unambiguously, in their military success against the English, a success that culminated in the destruction of English shipping in 1667 while it was still in the Medway.

A crucial text in formalising this attitude to the Dutch was Sir William Temple's *Observations upon the United Provinces of the Netherlands* (1668). According to Temple, the Dutch 'furnish infinite luxury which they themselves never practise, and traffic in pleasures which they never taste' (*Works*: 1, 131). This morally commendable abjuration of luxury and pleasure coheres with the practical advantages gained from having a favourable balance of trade. The basic argument is the same as that made by Mun. It is due to their 'general industry and parsimony' that the Dutch export more in value than they import. The former trait increases native commodities, while the latter increases exports and lessens the consumption of both their own as well as of any imported goods (p. 130). Though Temple lays great emphasis on the establishment of these traits through habit and custom, he does remark that the Dutch themselves were forced to enact some sumptuary laws since, in recent years, there has been a 'greater Vie of Luxury and Expence' among the merchants (p. 138).[2]

The obvious moral to be drawn was that the English too would maintain a favourable balance through developing these two traits. But, of course, moral exhortation could hardly be relied upon; the English had perhaps gone too far 'to pot'. Hence, to more effect, there was much support and argument for 'protection'. Andrew Yarranton, for example, in a pamphlet revealingly entitled *England's Improvement by Sea and Land, to Outdo the Dutch without Fighting* ... (1677) advocated protection of the linen industry (cf. Schumpeter, 1954: p. 349). Sir Josiah Child opened his *Brief Observations* (prefixed to his *New Discourse of Trade* [1690]) with a list of fifteen explanations that had been put forward for the 'prodigious increase of the Netherlanders'. One of these explanations is indeed their 'parsimonious and thrifty living' (p. 3). But, to Child, the 'causa causans' is their low rate of

---

[2] Schama (1987: p. 634) points out that these laws were not common and then they were issued at times of crisis. The laws were generally directed against 'unnecessary and sumptuous banquets'. In normal times there is evidence enough that the Dutch did enjoy their prosperity; they had their own moralists to invoke the classical indictment of luxury living (cf. ibid.: pp. 119, 182, 187, 336).

interest, and thus the bulk of his discussion is given over to advocating that England emulate the Dutch rate with the consequence that 'it would in a short time render us as rich and considerable in trade as they are now' (p. 6). Some writers also appreciated that the basis of Dutch strength was profits derived from Amsterdam's role as a entrepôt port and from the freight charges levied by their ships (see John Cary, *Essay on the State of England in relation to its Trade* (1695) in Cunningham, 1910: II,676n).

In due course the very basis for what had become the almost ritualistic citation of Dutch virtues (cf. Bowley, 1973: pp. 27–8) came under scrutiny. Not unexpectedly perhaps, Mandeville (himself a Dutchman) remarked that the Dutch reputation for frugality stemmed from their conflict with Philip II (*Fable*: I,185), that is, not from moral conviction but from necessity. But less expectedly, Sir George Mackenzie, in his resolutely traditional treatise splendidly entitled *The Moral History of Frugality* [1711] comments that the 'Hollanders practised at first Frugality rather through Necessity than Choice' (p. 304). And even Temple himself had argued that it was their unfavourable physical circumstances that had forced them into industry and trade, in contrast to the favourable circumstances and idleness of the Irish (I,119–20).

II

BARBON ON TRADE

I turn now to an examination of Nicholas Barbon's *Discourse of Trade* [1690]. The justification for concentrating on this particular discourse is that within it, more than in any other work at the time, we can discern the crucial assumptions that serve to transform the whole understanding of 'luxury'. I use the verb 'discern' advisedly. Barbon should probably be read with some circumspection. The *Discourse* is a pamphlet and, as such, neither a learned philosophical treatise nor even a sustained argument like Mun's treatise.[3] It is a pamphlet that

---

[3] Barbon was trained as a doctor and appears to have been an entrepreneur in the sense of taking up a variety of tasks from banking, through fire insurance to building (regarding which, not coincidentally, he wrote a pamphlet – *An Apology for the Builder*). A contemporary accused Barbon of writing his anti-Locke pamphlet (*Discourse concerning Coining* (1696)) in order to support the price of guineas to benefit his bank (cf. Kelly, 1991: p. 37), but Barbon himself in the Preface to that work stated openly that if he was to consider his 'private interest' he would be arguing against the view that he here upholds. At least one historian echoes the contemporary judgment. Wilson (1965) is scathing of his activities, calling him a 'crank and a charlatan' (p. 11), a 'rascal' (p. 188) as well as the 'greatest speculative builder of the times' (p. 334).

says a number of arresting things and there is, in consequence, a temptation to read rather more into them than might be there. The chances are that by singling out Barbon in this way I will succumb to that temptation. My anticipatory defence is that I am *using* Barbon's text to encapsulate my theme and I am treating his 'arresting' observations as indicative of certain basic shifts in assumption and evaluation. An additional justificatory factor is that despite 'only' writing pamphlets there is a consistent thread running through them, indeed a portion of his discourse on *Coining* (1696) repeats the argument of the *Discourse of Trade*, and does so, moreover, on those issues that are of most immediate concern to this enquiry.

What appears to give added force to the need for circumspection is that Barbon himself only once uses the term 'luxury' (*pace* Novak, 1962: p. 135). This occurs in the Preface but the context of its use there is, I think, clear testament to Barbon's awareness of the non-traditional character of his *Discourse*. This awareness is apparent in his selection of Livy and Machiavelli alone as examples of writers who have ignored the question of trade. Livy, as we have already discussed, is an important and influential purveyor of the story that luxury is corrupting. Machiavelli, whom Barbon calls 'the best' modern writer, was the seminal figure in the transmission of the civic republicanism of the Romans into early modern thinking; a transmission effected, of course, through his *Discourses on the First Decade of Livy's History of Rome* [1532].[4] We shall discuss in Chapter 6 how Machiavelli's legacy was combated by eighteenth-century writers like Hume and Smith.

Barbon's explanation for the indifference shown to trade by Livy and Machiavelli is historical. It is not until trade is seen to be necessary to 'provide Weapons of War' that it is considered. Prior to that, he remarks, it was always 'thought Prejudicial to the Growth of Empire'. Barbon now openly demonstrates his awareness of the moralistic tradition. He identifies, as the source of this prejudice, the judgment that trade resulted in 'too much softening the People by

---

[4] Machiavelli is also referred to in the *Apology* (p. 22) and in the *Discourse* (p. 28) he remarks that 'free peoples' are more successful militarily than mercenaries – a key argument of Machiavelli's. Despite these references, which are perhaps better explained by Barbon's perception of his readership's prejudices (he refers to 'the country gentleman' as troubled by new building in the Preface to the *Apology*), the entire thrust of the *Discourse* is counter to the use that was made of Machiavelli. This can be appreciated when his argument is contrasted with that of Andrew Fletcher. Fletcher linked his support for militias with the standard civic republican denunciation of the corruption of luxury and *inter alia* the associated 'perpetual change of the fashions in clothes, equipage, and furniture of houses' *Discourse of Government with relation to Militias* [1698] (ed. Daiches: p. 5). As we shall see it is precisely such changes that Barbon applauds.

Ease and Luxury, which made their Bodies unfit to endure the Labour and Hardships of War' (*Discourse*: p. 6).

While neither Livy nor Machiavelli discussed trade, Barbon also believes that those who did take up the subject frequently failed to appreciate its proper significance. The only writer he cites here is Mun. This citation provides further evidence of Barbon's self-conscious awareness of the polemical character of his *Discourse*. Mun's work on foreign trade, according to Barbon, better shows how to become an accomplished merchant than it demonstrates how trade 'may be most Profitable to the Nation' (p. 6).

Barbon's criticism of Mun is instructive for a further reason. The root of Mun's error is said to be his simile between an individual's expenditure and that of the nation (cf. Mun: p. 126). This simile was in fact so integral to the argument over trade as to constitute a cliché. In this light Barbon's position appears distinctly radical. Child (*New Discourse*: p. 124), for example, in the course of a debate, nonetheless agrees with his protagonist that certainly 'there is a great similitude between the affairs of a private person and a nation' (see Viner, 1937: p. 33n for further citations). Barbon's radicalism is further confirmed when it is noted that even Smith observes in the *Wealth of Nations* (p. 457) that what is prudent for a family can 'scarce be folly' for a great kingdom.

In view of his radicalism it is, therefore, worth noting in what way Barbon rejects this standard argument. Barbon's own style of argument is definitional *per species et differentiam*. He starts with a definition of the chief end of trade as 'to make a profitable Bargain' and then proceeds to identify five aspects of 'making a bargain'. The first of these concerns what is traded. This, too, is analysed and yields therefrom a basic dichotomy between natural and artificial wares. This distinction does not correspond to the difference between staple and non-staple commodities, since the former are simply what abound in a country. There can, however, be foreign staples which occur when a country either obtains a monopoly on trade, as the Dutch had with spices, or has sole possession of a particular art, as the Venetians had with glass. (*Discourse*: p. 10.)

From these distinctions Barbon draws three conclusions: that foreign staples are an uncertain source of wealth because the monopoly of either trade or artifice, as both the Dutch and Venetians found, is removed by competition; that the native staple is the foundation of foreign trade and that the native staple is infinite as is the artificial stock derived from it. It is this last point that renders erroneous the simile between a nation and an individual: the latter's stock/estate is always finite while the former's is infinite. By 'infinite' Barbon means intrinsically renewable – every spring brings new crops – or quantitatively inexhaustible as with 'the minerals of the earth'. It follows from this, according to Barbon, and here is where his argument connects again with our theme, that the moralising injunctions – be parsimonious, avoid prodigality – are beside the point (p. 11). More than that, he is able to declare, exploiting the disanalogy between individual and national expenditure, that prodigality is 'a Vice that is prejudicial to the Man but not to Trade' (p. 32). As we shall see, Mandeville will make this beneficial outcome of vices central to his argument. John Houghton [1681–3], writing before Barbon, had similarly commented that those 'guilty of Prodigality, Pride, Vanity and Luxury' create wealth for the kingdom while running down their own estates (quoted in Appleby, 1978: p. 171 – Appleby points out the adaptation of the 'deadly sins' that occurs here). Despite this precedent, Barbon's *Discourse* remains a fruitful text for our purposes. We can, that is to say, use his text to illuminate the issues involved in the 'de-moralisation' of luxury.

WANTS AND NECESSITIES

To Barbon the value of 'wares' derives from their use and the criterion of usefulness is 'to supply the Wants and Necessities of Man' (p. 13). In line with his style of argument he proceeds to identify two general wants, where 'generality' means those wants that 'mankind is born with'. The two sorts of wants are those of the body and those of the mind. Since Barbon immediately refers to these as 'necessities', 'want' here appears to have the force of 'need'. It is to supply these necessities that 'all things under the sun became useful and therefore have a Value' (p. 14).

Bodily wants correspond to the traditionally identified set of basic needs, namely, 'the three General Necessities of Man, Food, Clothes and Lodging'. Barbon does not remain content with a standard reference to this trio, which he himself had already given in an earlier pamphlet (*An Apology for the Builder*: p. 5). He adopts a more rigorous attitude and, in so doing, implicitly distinguishes animal from human needs. This rigour is manifest in his observation that, of this trio, only food is absolutely necessary since a 'great Part of Mankind go Naked and lye in Huts and Caves'. A consequence of this is that, even within the traditionally identified set of basic needs, it allows great scope for variation and fluidity. This means that the supposed fixity and 'natural' limits upon consumption set by these needs are attenuated. Having thus implicitly weakened the fixity of even bodily 'wants', Barbon is able to 'break free' of these limits through his notion of 'wants of the mind'.

It is in this notion, and its consequences, that we can discern Barbon's fundamental rupture with the moralistic tradition. Given the weight that I am attaching to this point, it is proper to supply a lengthy quotation,

Wares that have their Value from supplying the Wants of the Mind are all such things that can satisfie Desire; Desire implys Want: It is the Appetite of the Soul, and is as natural to the Soul, as Hunger to the Body. The Wants of the Mind are infinite, Man naturally Aspires and as his Mind is elevated, his Senses grow more refined, and more capable of Delight; his Desires are inlarged, and his Wants increase with his Wishes, which is for every thing that is rare, can gratifie his Senses, adorn his Body and promote the Ease, Pleasure and Pomp of Life. (*Discourse*: p. 14)

(This last phrase also occurs in both the *Apology* (p. 6) and the *Coining* (p. 3).)

Before proceeding to examine that passage we can append some others to complement it. Having narrowed down bodily necessities to food, Barbon later observes that necessity is not the cause of trade because 'Nature may be satisfied with little' (*Discourse*: p. 35). Rather, the usefulness of most things, and thence trade, stems from meeting the wants of the mind and most of them stem from 'imagination' (p. 15). There is, in consequence, an ineradicable fluidity. Barbon gives a striking illustration. 'Fashion', he writes, is 'an invention' which serves in effect to 'Dress a Man as if he lived in a perpetual Spring; he never sees the Autumn of his cloaths' (p. 33). Fashion, as we might now say, is 'consumer-led'; it is, for Barbon, a product of the 'Fancy and Approbation of the Buyer' (p. 13). Hence, rather than fashion being an occasion for moralistic indignation as in Mun, or Locke, for example, it is for Barbon thoroughly to be commended for providing a 'livelihood for a great part of Mankind' (p. 33). We will pursue the question of the benefits of trade and luxury consumption later but we must now scrutinise Barbon's current argument.

REVALUATION OF DESIRE

The first aspect to pick up is that we have here a picture of Man as naturally a desirous creature. This picture is recognisably 'modern'.

While Barbon, given the character of his *Discourse*, forbears from citing any 'authority' here, we can supplement his discussion by citing writings that have come to be seen as emblematic of this modern picture. Hence Hobbes, whom Child (*New Discourse*: p. 108) does cite in support of the proposition that all men are naturally equal, linked desire with appetite in that desire signified the absence of an object (*Leviathan*: 6 p. 38). It is 'want' in this sense of absence or lack that Barbon is utilising when he declares that 'desire implys want'. It is this utilisation that is characteristic of the 'new' way of thinking. An important, because influential, further testament of this thinking is John Locke's philosophical psychology. Locke defined desire as 'uneasiness of the mind for want of some absent good' (*Essay*: 2–21–31).

Because this 'modern' link between want, desire and lack is an important element in the de-moralisation of luxury, a brief comparison with the hitherto dominant Aristotelian account will be helpful. For Aristotle, too, it might seem that there is a link between desire and deficiency. For Aristotle, however, the deficit is always in terms of a normative standard – a proper mark or objective (*telos*). This mark is constituted unrestrictedly by the essential nature of whatever 'thing' is in question. In the case of humans, all aim at ('desire') *eudaimonia*, which is a 'perfect and self-sufficient end' (*Nic. Eth.*: 1097b). Those who attain *eudaimonia* are living life as it should be led and because this is a complete life, that is one without any lack or deficiency, then 'desire' for these individuals is at an end. In this very precise sense 'desire' is limited: the 'end' of food is to assuage hunger and thus, to desire food when not hungry is to miss the mark. (In this context, Aristotle typically uses *epithumia* for 'desire' and this can equally be translated as 'appetite' or, as by the Christian Fathers, as 'lust'.) As we have seen, it is a consequence of this perspective that to pursue desires beyond their appropriate end is to fail to live as a human should – is to lack virtue.

By contrast, the 'modern' view in rejecting this teleological perspective (Hobbes explicitly denies that there is a *summum bonum* or *finis ultimis* (*Leviathan*: 11 p. 70)) also rejects the possibility of a perfect desire-less state and, in consequence, rejects further the idea that desires can be accordingly limited to some fixed end. The only way to be 'free' of desire is to be dead. Motion or uneasiness is the correct description of the way the world (including mankind) is. But for Aristotle, mutability – as opposed to the purposiveness constitutive of the realisation of a *telos* – was characteristic of normative imperfection. This establishes the basic classical/Christian distinction between the tranquil and/or ascetic life, devoted to the contemplation of the immutable First Cause or eternal perfection of God, and the mundane life which is unceasingly at the beck and call of the demands of bodily desires. Hence the classical paradigm whereby luxury is understood as a corrupt preoccupation with bodily pursuits and hence, too, now, from this modern perspective, the potential for luxury to be de-moralised.

Central to this de-moralisation is the re-evaluation of mundane life. From being deprecated because of its concern with the recurrent necessities of everyday living – as soon as one meal is over, it is time to prepare the next – it is *within* this necessity that a new source of certainty could be located. Once the objective/teleological framework is dismissed, the consequence is not dis-order because the 'modern psychology' itself identifies a certainty and predictability in human affairs by virtue of Man's material nature. All humans enjoy pleasure and avoid pain – these are, as Bentham was to say, their 'sovereign masters' (*Principles of Morals*: p. 125). And Hobbes allowed that there was a *summum malum* in the form of violent death.

The most palpable evidence of such a constancy is the 'fact' of the salience of self-interest in human nature. As Slingsby Bethel put it in 1680, 'it being *natural* to all men to seek their own profit' (quoted in Ashcraft, 1980: p. 77; my emphasis). And Adam Smith's statement that the desire to better one's condition is 'natural' can be read as merely the culmination in politics and morals, as well as in economics, of this rejection of the Aristotelian teleological conception of nature. Without spelling out this philosophical backcloth, Joyce Appleby (1978: p. 184) regards this constancy, as expressed in market behaviour, as 'responsible for economics becoming the first social science', although Hobbes had declared that political science (or civil philosophy) was no older than his *De Cive* (*De Corpore, Ep. Ded.*, quoted in Watkins, 1965: p. 51).

We can usefully reinvoke at this point the hypothesis concerning the inter-relationship between desire, need and politics that we examined in Chapter 3. This rejection of the Aristotelian view of nature displaces 'needs' from their location within a rational or purposive order which desires, if unchecked, threaten. Instead, as we shall see further in Chapter 7, needs are either relegated to Man's animal nature, in the form of 'basic needs', or (as in Barbon) become, in the form of 'volitional needs', assimilated to desires, as they become viewed as the moving principle in humans. Corresponding to this re-location, the political order is based on facilitating, not proscribing, the satisfaction of desires. Hobbes's sovereign will enforce the conditions to enable its subjects to pursue their desires for 'commodious living' (*Leviathan*: 13 p. 90). It is the particular desires of individuals that determine what they judge subjectively to be commodious, not, as with Aristotle, that something is objectively commodious and therefore individuals desire it. The sovereign's interest lies not in the specific content as such of the desires only in the likelihood of these desires not peaceably co-existing.

Since in Chapter 3 we examined the hypothesis by means (in part) of an investigation of Roman sumptuary laws, then if the hypothesis carries any weight, we should expect these changes in the evaluations of needs and desires to accompany a shift in attitude toward such legislation. And, given Barbon's rejection of the traditional under-standing of luxury, we should expect him to reject sumptuary legislation. This expectation is borne out. In his critique of Mun, in the opening pages of the *Discourse*, he upbraids him for commending 'Parsimony, Frugality and Sumptuary Laws as the means to make a Nation rich' (p. 11).

Barbon is not alone. Generally speaking, and in line with the hypothesis, the attitude towards the efficacy and propriety of sumptuary laws is one reasonably reliable indicator of a writer's conception of luxury (and also of what comes to be seen as its concomitant, namely, commercial society). Hence Barbon's contemporary, Dudley North, in his *Discourses upon Trade* [1691], judged that 'countries which have sumptuary laws are generally poor' because these laws discourage industry and ingenuity, based as they are in 'the exorbitant Appetites of Men' (in McCulloch, 1952: pp. 528–9). And in the eighteenth century, we find, on the one hand, Berkeley, who thinks luxury does 'violence to our natures', declaring, in his aptly named *Essay toward Preventing the Ruin of GB* (pp. 76–7), that sumptuary laws are a necessary corrective and on the other hand Adam Smith, who thinks opulence a 'blessing' (see Chapter 6), remarking in the *Wealth of Nations* (p. 346) that sumptuary laws represent the 'highest impertinence and presumption on the part of kings and ministers in their effort to watch over the economy of private people'.

Of course we should not expect a simple black-and-white picture; the hypothesis does not pretend to formulate a social scientific 'law'. Charles Davenant is a good example of an author who does not neatly fit into the picture. As a stalwart advocate of Machiavelli and public virtue (cf. Hont, 1990: pp. 57–9), he supported the principle of sumptuary laws in order to cure 'excess and luxury' (*Foreign Trade Beneficial*: I, 390–2). In a closely related fashion, he also averred that 'ancient frugality' should be restored (ibid.: I, 348; cf. *Essays on Peace and War*: IV, 424). These sentiments suggest that his conception of political order is distinct from one that bases it upon the satisfaction of desire. However, when he advocated the restoration of frugality, he was careful to say that he did not mean hoarding but rather a 'general good oeconomy in the minister' (*Essays*: IV, 431). Moreover, he also thought 'laws to compel the consumption of some commodities and prohibit the use of others . . . needless, unnatural and can have no effect conducive to the public good' (*East India Trade*: I, 99; cf. p. 114). What Davenant does portend, and this does endorse the hypothesis, is a change in the conception of 'public good'; a change that is embodied in Smith as we shall see in Chapter 6.

INFINITE DESIRES

It is against the backcloth of the rejection of Aristotelian psychology that Barbon's assertion that the mental wants are infinite is to be understood. Since there is no supposed 'natural limit' that ought not to be passed, the inherent tendency for desires to feed upon themselves limitlessly is not a process of corruption but is itself rather the 'natural' way of things. The dynamism of human desires is self-generating. As he points out, they increase with wishes and are capable of creating, through the imagination (see later), objects of desire *ad infinitum*. What is noteworthy is that this dynamism expresses itself in what we have termed 'qualitative refinement'. In his *Apology for the Builder*, Barbon had commented generally that as riches increase so do wants and, specifically, that 'the rich have a variety of dishes, several suits of clothes and larger houses' (p. 6). Humans, he also believes, will come to desire what is rare and what will adorn both themselves and their dwellings. Indeed, it is expenditure upon 'cloaths and lodging' that most promotes trade (*Discourse*: p. 32).

Although Barbon does not provide an explanation of why this should be so, it can be explained along the lines indicated in Chapter 1. Clothes and lodging are basic needs which are constants in human experience but, as we have already observed, Barbon is aware that these are subject to 'mental wanting'. In our terms, they are susceptible to qualitative refinements. It is these refinements that generate employment and trade. Hence bodily adornment in the form of clothes requires 'the Glover, Hosier, Hatter, Semstriss, Taylor, and many more, with those that make the Materials to Deck it; as Clothier, Silk-Weaver, Lace-Maker, Ribbon-Weaver, with their Assistance of Drapers, Mercers, and Milliners, and a Thousand more' (pp. 21-2). The same stimulation to employment, indeed even more so, is provided by expenditure on building – it is 'the chiefest Promoter of Trade; it Imploys a greater number of Trades and People, than Feeding and Cloathing' (p. 34).

Barbon is well aware that such expenditure is the product of a concern with the 'ease, pleasure and pomp of life'. The latter especially requires the support of 'infinite' trades (p. 21). The reason for this is that such wants are socially generated. It is through expenditure on pomp that a 'proper and vible Distinction of Riches and Greatness' is maintained (p. 33; cf. *Coining* where expenditures on the 'Pomp of Life' serve as 'Badges of Riches' that 'make distinction of Preference amongst men' (p. 3)). The 'Hobbesian' element is again discernible though given an explicitly social context. To Barbon, Man is 'Naturally Ambitious' so that social life is an occasion for emulation, with individuals 'Out-Vying one another in Apparel, Equipage and Furniture of the House' (*Discourse*: p. 34; cf. *Apology*: p. 23). Barbon here adverts once again to the different circumstance of food because that would only be the 'chiefest Expence' if Man 'lived solitary alone' (*Discourse*: p. 34). Child distinguished food similarly, claiming that expenditure upon it, unlike that devoted to 'household stuffs', did not generate trade; indeed if 'our bellies' were the object of our greatest expense, then it would be 'the most destructive consumption that can happen to a nation and tending only to nourish idleness, luxury and beggary'. (*New Discourse*: p. 42). It is worth noting parenthetically that in this last phrase Child is illustrating his allegiance to the moralistic tradition of 'luxury'; again, Barbon's silence on this point is eloquent testimony to his subversion.

Barbon's sensitivity to social context also made him aware of the so-called 'Veblen effect'. While in general opposed to the balance of trade argument that exports should be curtailed, Barbon does admit that if foreign imports serve to hinder consumption of the domestic product ('which will very seldom happen') then duties (not prohibition) should be levied upon them. These duties will serve to make the imported goods dearer. The effect of that will be to hinder 'common consumption' and confine it to the 'Gentry'. They, however, may well esteem these now expensive imported goods 'because they are Dear' (*Discourse*: p. 37). Locke had argued to somewhat similar effect that 'things of fashion' will be had 'whatever rates they cost . . . because they are dear' (*Consequences of the Lowering of Interest and Raising the Value of Money*, in *Works*: p. 598).

FANCY, IMAGINATION AND SHAFTESBURY

While Locke and Barbon might thus both be aware of the Veblen effect, Locke retains much of the older censorious moralistic tone in his treatment of fashion as the cause of this perverse phenomenon. Barbon connects fashion with 'imagination' and 'fancy'. Here, again, the force of his argument stems from what he does not say. He does not inveigh against the fancy because of its fickle and insubstantial character nor, relatedly, does he set up a value-laden dichotomy between the 'real' and the 'fanciful'. The appreciation of Barbon's position will be aided by a brief comparison with the thought of a significant contemporary, Ashley Cooper, Third Earl of Shaftesbury.

Shaftesbury deliberately and self-consciously set himself against the 'new' psychology. Interestingly, in view of his own close relationship to Locke (he was his tutee), he not only realised that Locke was following Hobbes here but also that, because of his notoriety, Hobbes's impact was less damaging than Locke's for it was he who 'threw all Order and Virtue out of the World' (Letter to Ainsworth [1709], quoted in Voitle, 1984: p. 119).

To Shaftesbury, imagination or fancy is the source of appetites and desires (*Characteristics*: I, 207) but is so indiscriminately. The imagination 'runs free'. In line with his adoption of the 'ancients' over the 'moderns', he explicitly invokes the Stoic injunction – he cites Aurelius and Epictetus – that imagination must be controlled (ibid.: II, 278–9). When this control is present then I am genuinely in possession of 'my good', but in its absence, I am subject to 'the tutorage of fancy and pleasure, and the easy philosophy of taking that for good which pleases me, or which I fancy merely will in time give me uneasiness sufficient' (II, 280). It is due to 'fancy merely' that the (delusory) 'force of good' is attributed to 'things of chance and outward dependency'. As examples of such 'things', Shaftesbury, like the Stoics, identifies 'plate, jewels, apartments, coronets, patents of honour, titles or precedences' (II, 278). The desire for these emanates from the imagination. Significantly Shaftesbury goes on to argue that 'therefore' these 'things' are sought 'not as mere conveniencies, means or helps in life' but (perversely) as 'excellent in themselves' and as 'directly and immediately causing my happiness and giving me satisfaction'. The fancy is thus, *inter alia*, covetous and ambitious (II, 281).

The connexion between these censures and the traditional indictment of luxury is not missed by Shaftesbury. He supplies, in the current context, a cross-reference to an earlier discussion where the 'muse' Fancy is explicitly linked to the fostering of luxury (II, 203). While Shaftesbury does associate luxury with ease and indolence he also alludes to the 'modern' morally neutral argument. He remarks that Luxury herself has learnt that 'life and happiness consist in action and employment' (II, 206) but, nonetheless, Shaftesbury retains the older moralistic usage. He contrasts the purpose of toil for 'the provision against want' with luxury as that which is over and beyond such provision. In line with his Stoicism, he juxtaposes a 'just frugality', the parameters of which are naturally determined, with 'imperious luxury' which 'forces us to sacrifice honour to fortune and runs us out into all irregularity and extravagance of conduct' (I, 326, 323). Once the natural limits are transgressed then no regulation can be effectively applied to 'mere imagination or the exorbitancy of fancy in adding expense to expense or possession to possession' (I, 327).

We can usefully relate Shaftesbury's account of imagination or fancy to the earlier analysis of need. Need-statements refer to states of the world – either something is needed or it is not. The implicit objectivism here removes questions of need from the realm of subjective belief. Imagination, however, inhabits this realm since, seemingly by definition, it does not refer to, in Wiggins's phrase, the way the world *is*. The imagination is thus able to go beyond the fixed and determined parameters of needs. And once the fixity of needs is passed, then all manner of 'flights of fancy' are possible.

Shaftesbury wishes 'reason', by virtue of its ability to discern the objective standards, to curb such flights. Barbon says nothing about reason as such, but the materialist psychology he assumes debars reason from that role. Hobbes is again the clearest exponent of the 'new philosophy'. To him, reason is a calculative faculty that works out the most economic/efficient means to a predetermined end. Crucially, the end itself is not reason's province; we do not do something because it is rational but because we *want* to do it. (*Leviathan*: 5 and 6.)

What Barbon does discuss is the imagination as a source of these 'wants'. The imagination is able to cause 'uneasiness' and thus prompt 'desire'. That is to say, we can perceive as a lack that which we can imagine. Such a lack or want generates the desire (makes us want) the object of our imaginings and prompts our activity. Once again Hobbes can be cited appositely; for him 'the Imagination is the first internall beginning of all Voluntary Motion' (*Leviathan*: 6 p. 38). In contrast to this apparently neutral description of imagination's role it was commonly deprecated. In Mackenzie's telling phrase, luxury and avarice have made men poor as well as wicked as they attempt to 'satisfy their Imaginary fantastick Necessities' (*History of Frugality*: p. 291, cf. p. 349). A good illustration (from a perspective sympathetic to Stoicism) of this mechanism is provided by Rousseau in *Emile* (p. 44):

it is imagination which enlarges the bounds of possibility for us, whether for good or ill, and therefore stimulates and feeds desires by the hope of satisfying them. But the object which seemed within our grasp flies quicker than we can follow; when we think we have grasped it, it transforms itself and is again far ahead of us.

I will pick up these references to 'imagination' in the context of Smith in Chapter 6, but there are two more immediate important ramifications to consider.

THE MUTABILITY OF MONEY

The first concerns the role of money and credit in society. Davenant in his *True Picture of a Modern Whig* (IV, 250) provides a succinct illustration of how this role could be viewed pejoratively.

DOUBLE: We, you know, are masters of most of the ready money, having robbed the whole people of it; and when things go not to our minds, we give the word out, That everybody should sell; which immediately sinks the value of stocks, tallies and all publick funds . . .

WHIGLOVE: And when things go to your fancy you fall as fast a buying, which raises the market, so you stockjob the nation.

What fuels the opprobrium here is the implicit contrast with the solidity of landed property, owned by country gentlemen, who, because they are not given to the whim of 'making markets', have a firm stake in the nation; they will not 'stockjob' it. This stake gives them a permanent interest in the public good. They are, in Bolingbroke's metaphor, the 'true owners of our political vessel' while the 'moneyed men as such are no more than passengers in it' (*Some Reflections on the Present State of the Nation* [1749], quoted in Dickson, 1967: p. 28). Money, unlike land, is fluid (liquid) and mobile. The echoes of the classical denunciation of the effeminacy of luxury can be heard. Whereas landed property possesses appropriately masculine traits of resolution, firmness and commitment, money is feminine in its potential to flit from market to market in search of the highest return (*Varium et mutabile semper Femina (Aeneid*: 4. 569)). By concerning itself only with immediate gratification and being always on the 'look-out' for a more profitable deal, the 'monied interest' is especially susceptible to the play of fancy and the caprices of imagination. This set of ideas reaches its apogee in the idea of credit. Davenant states the essence of the complaint when he describes credit as having 'existence only in the minds of men, nothing is more fantastical and nice . . . it hangs upon opinion; it depends upon our passions of hope and fear' and, as such, 'it comes many times unsought for and often goes away without reason' (*Concerning Credit*: I, 151). Barbon (*Discourse*: p. 18) for his part, also connects credit with 'opinion', the former 'is a Value' raised by the latter, but does so in a typical matter-of-fact manner.

As John Pocock (1975; 1985) has demonstrated, the late seventeenth and early eighteenth century witnessed intense debate as to the relationship between the world of commerce and credit and the idea of virtue understood as a civic disposition to uphold the *res publica*. This disposition is a restatement of 'classical republicanism' and the incipient de-moralisation of luxury in Barbon is a fundamental challenge to the tenability of that restatement. This challenge will be mounted by Mandeville in the next generation and carried to fruition by Hume and Smith. We will discuss this in Chapter 6.

FASHION

What lies within Barbon's account is the realisation that goods are produced and consumed not because they meet some fixed 'needs' but because they are 'wants of the mind' and serve our vanity, which 'is always founded upon the belief of our being the object of attention and approbation' (*Discourse*: p. 50). The second ramification is closely related to this last point.

A prime object of vanity is clothing and the elusive, evanescent character of imagination gives it its natural affinity to 'fashion'. Hence Locke talks of the 'habits of fashion' producing a 'fantastical uneasiness' that gives 'the itch' after honour, power, riches (*Essay*: 2–21–45). And elsewhere in his 'economic' *Treatise on Interest* he repeats this terminology when he refers to the 'costly itch' for materials of 'pride and luxury' being brought into 'fashion' (*Works*: p. 607). These references to Locke confirm that he does not eschew the moralistic perspective on luxury (cf. Vaughn, 1980: p. 24).[5]

Viewed against this intellectual backcloth, as provided by both Locke and Shaftesbury, Barbon's own treatment of fashion represents a clear break. Of course, neither this backcloth nor Barbon's views exist in hermetic isolation from the concrete particularities of economic change in contemporary society. These particularities, such as the diffusion of consumer goods and development of a mass market in household goods (cf. Thirsk, 1978: ch. 5), should themselves not be regarded as existing as some 'thought-less' or 'concept-free' environment. Thinking about change is no less 'real' than the number of knitted garments for sale. And, as the notion of fashion illustrates, the identification of a state of affairs as 'change' is a qualitative as well as a quantitative matter.

Barbon views fashion positively. Rather than the evanescent and transient quality of fashion being a categorical demonstration of the fickle, and thence morally dubious, character of fancy, this mutability is a recommendation. It should be encouraged because it provides 'a Livelihood for a great Part of Mankind' as clothes and the like are replaced before they are worn through (*Discourse*: p. 33). Cary, writing in 1695, aped this when he argued that 'all would grow rich' from the variety of fashions which, by adding 'wings to Men's Inventions', increase circulation of money and trade (quoted in Heckscher, 1955: p. 170).

There is a further consequence implicit in this positive assessment. The very changeableness that characterises fashion serves to undermine the fixity of 'value'. For Barbon 'nothing has Price or Value in itself'. (*Coining*: p. 10, *et passim*). Since mental wants largely proceed from the imagination and 'Humor and Fancy' (ibid.: p. 4), then as the mind changes, so 'things grow out of use and lose their value' (*Discourse*: p. 15).[6] The only accurate determination of value – 'the best judge' – is

---

[5] Further evidence is to be found in his major political work, the Second *Treatise of Government* [1690]. There he couples, in the traditional way, luxury and ambition (p. 11) and talks of a Golden Age that existed before 'the desire of having more than Men needed had altered the intrinsick value of Things' (p. 37). Barbon's *Discourse concerning Coining* is an explicit rejoinder to Locke and in it he was particularly severe on this notion of 'intrinsic value' (see *Coining*, esp. pp. 6–8).

[6] Cf. Bowley (1973: p. 31) for Barbon's development of the 'pure theory of value'.

the market; goods are worth just what they can be sold for (ibid.: p. 16).

The assessment of desire as fickle here comes into its own. For since trade responds to desire, and desire to attain 'imagined' goods is both infinite and indeterminate, then to prohibit the import of a particular good (Barbon mentions Flanders lace, French gloves and Westphalian bacon) does not entail that the domestic equivalent will be consumed (ibid.: p. 35). The very fluidity of fashion means that, should one good be prohibited, another imported product is likely to be 'taken up' so that too would have to be banned. Barbon, indeed, turns the tables on the proponents of balance. It is when trade is prohibited that native products lose their value and rents, for example, fall (ibid.). And, of course, once one nation allows in only those goods it deems advantageous, then other nations will reciprocate to the resultant ruin of all foreign trade (ibid.: p. 37).

Two morals follow from this. First, the attempt to engineer a favourable balance through manipulation of particular trades is misconceived. Though implicit in his *Discourse on Trade*, this is developed at greater length by Barbon in his later critique of Locke (see *Coining*: §3). As Child had similarly argued, to attempt to arrive at a computation of 'balance' in this way is 'fallible and erroneous' (*Trade*: p. 116). Second, the alternative to Dalby Thomas's 'pruning and loping' and the attempt to act in such a way as to predetermine the balance of trade, is to give 'the market' its head. One consequence of this, as we have seen, is the overthrow of sumptuary legislation since there is, as Mun and Bacon ('Of Seditions and Troubles' [1625] p. 42) exemplify, a close affinity between such legislation and the determination of a favourable balance.

Another more direct consequence is free trade. The traditional picture put a premium on controlling the influx of luxury goods. If there was no control then luxuries would flood in and become, as Livy had said, *semina futurae luxuriae* (*History*: 39.6) to the ruin of social virtue. In direct contrast, as Barbon explicitly spelt out in his pamphlet on the *Coinage* (p. 59), 'the freer the trade is, the better the nation will thrive'. His position was echoed by others.[7] For example,

---

[7] It is in this context that Barbon, North, Davenant and Child are typically bracketed together as 'free-trade Tories'. The source for this label appears to be Ashley (1900) who is followed by Cunningham (1910: pp. 405–6) and Gooch (1915: ch. XI) whence it appears to have attained the status of received wisdom (see, e.g., Kramnick, 1968: p. 279; Goldsmith, 1987: p. 240; Gunn, 1969: p. 261; Novak, 1962: p. 18). Ashley's argument, which itself relies heavily on some judgments of Macaulay, and as crystallised by Gooch, is that it is Tory (Stuart) support for trade with France and Whig opposition thereto that lay at the root of this advocacy of 'free trade' (see also Packard, 1923; but cf. Priestley, 1951).

Notwithstanding the frequency with which this view is promulgated, it is of doubtful

the judgment that trade should 'flow freely' was explicitly made in the
Preface to North's *Discourse*; 'no laws can set Prices in Trade, the
Rates of which must and will make themselves'[8] and Davenant held
that trade should be allowed to find its own course (*Publick Accounts*: v,
387, cf. p. 452; *East India Trade*: 1, 86).[9]

SOCIAL BENEFIT AND INDIVIDUAL WELL-BEING

There is one final aspect of Barbon's account that we can note. What
we find in Barbon is the incipient shift in the context within which
luxury is viewed. In essence, luxury can be looked upon as socially
useful and not as a source of social and individual corruption. As we
have seen, for Barbon, it is expenditure upon clothing and lodging

validity and even less utility. It gives to this quartet an unwarranted homogeneity. We have
already noted that Davenant, unlike North and Barbon, has some residual sympathy at least
for sumptuary legislation. Another instance of divergence among this quartet is that between
Child as an ardent advocate of the legal reduction of the interest rate (p. 6) and North who
dismisses such a scheme on the grounds that money is a commodity like any other and will
(and should be allowed to) find its own price (Preface). Barbon, for his part on this issue, is to
be found on the side of Child rather than North (cf. *Discourse*: pp. 41–2). In addition the
prohibition of French goods had long been standard 'mercantile' practice (cf. Cherry, 1953:
p. 109) and although the Whigs were closely associated with the silk and woollen interests who
benefited from such a policy, 'protectionism' was scarcely a Whig prerogative, the East India
Company, for example, suffered most at the hands of a Tory government in 1689 (cf. Thomas,
1926: p. 96). But perhaps the chief reason why the label for these four as 'free-trade Tories' is
misleading is that the labels 'Tory' and 'Whig', especially in this period, are shifting. It is
well-established that the last decade of the seventeenth century witnessed, in Plumb's words,
'the Whig party's volte-face' (1967: p. 133) in its concern to strengthen not limit monarchy
and authority. Davenant neatly exemplifies this in his dialogue *The True Picture of a Modern
Whig* [1701–2], a central theme of which is the distance between 'modern' and 'old whigs',
with the former looking upon the latter (Davenant's own view) as their 'worst of enemies' (IV,
152) since, for example, they still oppose a standing army (see, e.g., IV, 152, 198, 256) (cf. Hill,
1976: p. 87).
8 Joyce Appleby, while citing Ashley's linking of North with Barbon, Child and Davenant as
Tories is unpersuaded, somewhat along the lines of Thomas (whom she cites), by his
argument that their politics explained their opinions. Her own apparent alternative is to
'read-off' their advocacy from their social/occupational position. She states that it is 'no
accident that' these advocates of free trade (she cites among others North and Barbon) were
'merchants, bank promoters, stock jobbers and projectors'. For her it is seemingly decisive
that none of these occupations was involved (unlike manufacturers) in the mobilisation of
labour (Appleby, 1978: p. 262). Child and Davenant are not mentioned here even though
neither of them was a manufacturer. Child, whom one authority has declared to be a Whig
(Spiegel, 1983: p. 707), indeed was a prominent member of the East India Company, while
Davenant in his *True Picture* dialogues identifies himself as 'Old Whig' (see n. 7 *supra*).
9 Hont puts Davenant's advocacy of free trade down to his realisation that trade was now the
way to glory and dominion, and to his Machiavellian opposition to 'universal empire' which
France most notably represented (1990: p. 69). In a digression in his *Discourse* (p. 24), Barbon
alluded to the French attempt to 'Raise Empire' but considered there to be overwhelming
difficulties against their success.

that most promotes trade. The general underlying principle is that it is the 'wants of the mind, fashion and desire of Novelties and Things scarce that causeth Trade' (*Discourse*: p. 35). Trade in its turn brings manifold advantages – it provides employment, improves the natural stock of the country, raises rent and improves yield, occasions peace, increases revenue, enlarges defensive capabilities and can help in the 'Inlarging of Empire' (ibid.: pp. 22–4).[10] Trade thus benefits government but it also, Barbon claims, helps mankind or the general population. All the inhabitants are well-fed, clothed and lodged, that is, their basic needs are met. More pointedly, these needs are better met than if a country were to follow the injunctions of the moralists and practise parsimony and abjure luxury.

While he himself refers only to 'the Richer sort' being furnished with all things to promote 'ease, pleasure and pomp' *all* desire what these 'things' promote. Indeed it is the universality of that desire that underpins the universal practice of status-differentials – 'there never was any part of Mankind . . . but they had Difference and Degree of Men amongst them' (as manifest in differences in apparel) (ibid.: pp. 14–15).

In sum, we can detect in Barbon's argument that fashion and luxury goods can be justified by their instrumental promotion of trade. The benefits of trade in turn are justified by their positive effect upon social well-being. Yet what is valuable in such well-being is the possession of goods, for they are the occasion for 'the refinement of the senses' and the 'increase in delight'. That Barbon does indeed deem these valuable has, it is true, to be inferred from the text. This is an argument that will be developed, notably, by Hume and Smith in the next century. What underlies it is the definitive 'modern' perspective that the satisfaction of material needs and the promotion of material well-being are important, together with what Charles Taylor (1989) has called 'the affirmation of ordinary life'. Concomitantly, this perspective and affirmation involves the downgrading of the Classical concern with virtue as well as of the Christian concern with salvation, since both of these exhibit a disdain for, or distrust of, such materialistic considerations.

[10] The obverse of Barbon's argument that France would have difficulty achieving a land empire (see n. 9, *supra*) is that England, as an island, and enjoying the 'largest Freedoms and Best Government in the World' and thus equipped for world trade, could raise a sea-based empire of greater extent than either Alexander's or Caesar's (*Discourse*: p. 31).

CHAPTER 6

The eighteenth-century debate

The eighteenth century was the period when the debate as to the meaning and value-laden status of luxury came into prominence. The 'de-moralisation' undertaken by Barbon as part of his limited and polemical aims was pursued more directly by others and the increasing publicity for this view (especially following Mandeville's contribution) produced, in reaction, a re-vindication of the traditional, moralist – whether humanist or Christian – view. It is important testimony to the salience and implicit seriousness of this debate that it was taken up and pursued throughout the world of letters from St Petersburg to Boston, from Naples to Aberdeen.

The sheer size of the literature makes a comprehensive survey impossible but since any such survey would reveal enormous duplication, it would of itself serve little purpose. Accordingly my strategy in this chapter is to concentrate on Hume and, especially, Smith. It would, however, be untrue to the debate to ignore its breadth of expression and reiterative quality. Additionally, of course, the comprehension of Hume (section III) and Smith's (section IV) own contribution is bound up with an appreciation of the general debate. To that end, therefore, the first section of the chapter will examine briefly Mandeville's historically key presentation. This will be followed (section II) by noting, again cursorily, the diffusion of 'his' ideas, especially in France, and a concluding section (v) will acknowledge the 'popular' dimension of the debate.

I

MANDEVILLE

Owing in no small measure to its initial mode of presentation in what he himself called 'this little Whim' (*Fable*: I, 9), Mandeville's thought has been open to diverse interpretations. There has been extensive debate as to whether he is a mercantilist or instead an advocate of laissez faire or, again, simply neither of these (see Landreth (1975) for a convenient summary). There are those who would stress the political context of his writing and his relationship to civic humanism and Whiggism (see, e.g., Horne, 1978; Gunn, 1983; Goldsmith, 1985). Others again have fastened on to his ethical or moral thought (e.g., Monro, 1975; Colman, 1972) and yet others seek to do justice to the literary and satirical character of his writing (see, e.g., Castiglione, 1986; Hopkins, 1975). Unsurprisingly, amidst this volume of comment Mandeville's view of luxury has not escaped notice (see especially Gunn (1983) and Goldsmith (1985)) and I have no wish merely to add to this volume. My remarks will therefore be brief and directed at the issue of de-moralisation begun in Chapter 5.

If what Mandeville says about luxury is examined in isolation it contains little that is not implicit in Barbon. But a large factor in Mandeville's historical significance is that he is explicit (recall how Barbon mentions 'luxury' only once in his *Discourse on Trade*). In addition, and not coincidentally, Mandeville's comments occur within a deliberately provocative context. The very fact that Mandeville enjoyed such a *succès de scandale* ensured that it was his work that became the reference point for subsequent investigation.

The increasingly elaborate and extensive Remarks that Mandeville attached to subsequent editions of the *Fable of the Bees*, together with a greatly expanded Second Part (1727) and the separately published *Enquiry into the Origin of Honour*, leave no doubt that he is aware of the intellectually iconoclastic character of his argument. He realised that his comments on luxury required him to deal with such standard issues as the example of the Dutch, as portrayed by Temple (*Fable*: 1, 189–91) and the paradigmatic status of Sparta as a virtuous republic (ibid.: 1, 245–6) as well as more directly answering objections. He devoted the whole of Remark L to that latter task, and supplemented it with further discussions in Remarks M, O and P.

Mandeville identified as the 'main Design' of the *Fable* the demonstration that it is impossible to enjoy 'all the most elegant Comforts of Life', as they are experienced by an 'industrious, wealthy and powerful Nation', while simultaneously enjoying 'all the Virtue and Innocence that can be wish'd for in a Golden Age'. More pointedly, he wished 'to expose the Unreasonableness and Folly' of those moralists who decry the 'Vices and Inconveniences' of 'an opulent and flourishing People' yet who are 'wonderfully greedy' for the benefits of material prosperity (i, 6–7). Thus stated, Mandeville's target might be thought to be narrow and incapable of creating a furore. But that would be to underestimate the solidity of the conventions he was assailing. What Mandeville's argument was thought, by his contemporaries, to mean was that all upholders of virtue, that is, all right-thinking individuals, were hypocrites. Certainly an attack on hypocrisy was never far from Mandeville's mind – 'the Contempt of Riches is seldom sincere' (ii, 113) – and one of his major strategies was to identify from the practice of mankind what *in fact* were their 'real pleasures', namely, that which is 'worldly and sensual', rather than what they *say* (frequently in Stoic language (cf. i, 151)) is truly pleasurable (i, 166). It is not surprising, therefore, that Shaftesbury's *Characteristicks* comes in for rough treatment.

Significant though this element was, the chief factor determining Mandeville's notoriety was his claim that the benefits of industry, wealth and power are associated with various inextirpable vices of mankind, not with their virtues. To use this claim as the basis of his exposé required Mandeville to adopt ostensibly conventional usage. Hence in a manner perfectly consonant with the moralistic tradition, Mandeville not only regards luxury, characterised by effeminacy and enervation, as one of these vices but also openly admits its close relationship to pride, avarice, fraud, envy and vanity. However – and here is the source of his notoriety – he nevertheless openly points out its connexion with public benefits.

This was disconcerting or paradoxical because it broke the links in the accepted causal chain. The accepted line of reasoning was that beneficial effects must have appropriately worthy causes, while bad causes produce injurious outcomes. Thus if a people indulge themselves intemperately in a life of luxury then 'these sort of sins are natural causes of weakening the power and interest of a nation' (Edward Stillingfleet, Bishop of Worcester, quoted in Speck, 1975: p. 69). The converse of this is that the 'good/Christian society' must therefore consist of good actions performed by virtuous individuals.

Mandeville has no quarrel with that so long as the 'good society' means one where comfort and ease are not enjoyed and where power and plenty are absent. But once comfort, plenty and the rest are admitted into the definition of a 'good society' (as the *practice* of men now reveals to be the case) then luxury, and the rest, must also be admitted. What Mandeville leaves equivocal is the goodness of material satisfactions, though to maintain that truly he is an ascetic runs against the grain and tone of his argument (cf. Goldsmith, 1987: p. 247); certainly none of his contemporaries read him that way.

At one level Mandeville's argument is definitional. Strictly understood, luxury is 'everything not immediately necessary to make Man subsist as he is a living Creature' (*Fable*: 1, 107). He immediately follows up this definition by agreeing with the putative criticism that it is 'too rigorous' since it implies that nothing other than luxury is to be found in the world because 'even among the naked Savages' some 'Improvement upon their former manner of Living' has been made.

This manoeuvre on Mandeville's part serves two purposes. It enables him to claim (strictly) that everything is a 'luxury' but, of course, this is also to say equally that nothing is a luxury. This undermines the possibility of any secure benchmark from which to judge whether any particular state of affairs is luxurious; there is no room for the traditional standard of fixed, natural limits. The second purpose reinforces this. Mandeville is able to say that although the definition is defective it is so *faute de mieux* because any alternative is even worse, precisely because 'if we abate one Inch of this severity I am afraid we shan't know where to stop'. He presses home this point by drawing attention to the experientially warranted fact that what is thought superfluous by one rank in society is looked upon as a necessity by another, superior, rank. Typically he supplies a clerical example,

People may go to Church together, and be all of one Mind as much as they please, I am apt to believe that when they pray for their daily Bread, the Bishop includes several things in that Petition which the Sexton does not think on. (Ibid.: 1, 108)

Mandeville does reveal why this rank-relativity, in effect, denies the existence of luxury. His governing principle is akin to Barbon's. He states bluntly (that is, without any attendant argument) that 'if the wants of Men are innumerable then what ought to supply them has no bounds'. Although phrased conditionally, it is clear that for Mandeville this is, again, underwritten by experience. Wherever we look, whether it be Hottentots or bishops, we find improvements in living as well as social differentiation and emulation. There are two points here. First there is a universalism which is traced back to (post-lapsarian) human nature and, second, there is an acknowledgement of the presence of 'improvements' which, though a loaded term, is the meaning conveyed by Mandeville's term 'public *benefits*'; the counterpart to 'private *vice*' is not 'public *virtue*' (cf. Castiglione, 1986: p. 466). At the heart of Mandeville's argument is an account of the relationship between these two points.

Human nature is constant but Man is a 'taught animal' (*Fable*: I, 286) so that in society he is 'quite another Creature from his savage state' (I, 205). This raises the question, what changes and what remains the same? What are constant are passions and appetites – 'The Seeds of every Passion are innate to us and no body comes into the World without them' (I, 281). What changes is the degree to which these seeds germinate, and this depends on historical experience (Mandeville's alertness to the historical dimension has earned him the praise of commentators, especially Hayek (1967)). Men learn from experience (*Fable*: I, 171) and what they learn is what 'pleases'. And human nature being what it is, what pleases is what gratifies the passions and makes life more comfortable. The learning curve starts from 'primitive simplicity' (I, 169) and, given earlier definitions, develops through the acquisition of 'luxuries' and a concurrent 'germination' of pride, ambition, avarice and the rest. The upshot is that what is now thought to be a necessity, even for those who are miserably poor, was once looked upon as the 'Invention of Luxury'. Strictly, of course, the 'necessity' is not a necessity at all. Mandeville is thus being consistent with his own definition when he remarks that the consumption of meat by the poor is a luxury 'that is not look'd upon as such' (I, 172). At times his consistency slips, as when he contrasts in contemporary society the 'Variety of Services that are required to supply the Luxurious and Wanton Desires as well as real Necessities of Man' (I, 299).

If we look beyond Mandeville's definition, we find an affirmation of the benefits of luxury and a rejection of standard objections. It would defeat Mandeville's 'main design' if he simply stated the utilitarian (as we would term it) position that since luxury produces good effects, it is therefore good. On the contrary, he has to insist, for the reasons noted earlier, that luxury is 'bad . . .' and then add the rider '. . . but if you wish power and plenty then you must also have luxury'. It is in line with this strategy that he draws attention to how such unambiguous vices as thieving provide employment for locksmiths (I, 86). Once that connexion is admitted, he is able (he seemingly believes) to establish a more general argument. Hence he argues that it is the activities of the 'sensual Courtier', the 'fickle Strumpet', the 'profuse Rake' and the 'haughty Courtesan' (1, 355) – in short, all those who live a life of 'Pride and Luxury' (1, 85) – which 'sets the Poor to Work, adds Spurs to Industry and encourages the skilful Artificer to search after further Improvements' (1, 130; cf. 1, 85).

Why does Mandeville deem work, industry and improvements to be benefits? The answer is the standard mercantilist one (cf. Heckscher, 1955: 1, 157–72). Politically, wealthy societies are more powerful than poor ones. The basis of the power is partly a simple question of numbers. In Mandeville's terms a frugal and honest society, that is, one bereft of vices, would be unable to support a large population (*Fable*: 1, 184–5). One significant use of large numbers is the maintenance of substantial armed forces and the consequent aggrandisement of political clout (1, 287). The source of wealth itself is trade, and a 'Multitude of laborious Poor' (ibid.). The 'Greatness and Felicity of Nations' rests on 'the fruits of the Earth and the Labour of the People' (1, 197).

The inclusion of 'felicity' here indicates more general benefits. A poor society will be 'almost wholly destitute of what we call the Comforts of Life' (1, 183). These comforts form the standard array of luxury goods – sustenance, habitation, clothing (and potentially we would want to add, leisure) (1, 169–73) – that in a more opulent society are enjoyed by the poorest,

> . . . Ingenuity,
> Which join'd with Time and Industry,
> Had carry'd Life's Conveniences,
> It's real Pleasures, Comforts, Ease,
> To such a Height, the very Poor
> Liv'd better than the Rich before,   (*Fable*: 1, 26)

These goods are increasingly served by the development of technology and its attendant social division of labour. Technological inventions (tools, instruments and engines) are the product of the 'Excellency of Human Thought and Contrivance' (1, 367, cf. 1, 184). In contrast, an economically underdeveloped society is characterised not only by 'Slothful Ease' but also 'Stupid Innocence' (1, 184).

The general premise that underpins this connexion between lack of economic development, sloth and stupidity (as well as the obverse connexion between industry, excellence of thought and wealth) is the materialist psychology discussed in Chapter 5. In Mandeville's version, 'grafted' into every individual (1, 200) is the desire to enjoy

pleasure and avoid pain – to be happy (1, 139; *Enquiry*: p. 21).
Mankind, however, is also naturally lazy (*Fable*: 1, 192, 242, 289) and
never exerts itself unless roused by desire (1, 184). In brute form, these
desires comprise hunger, lust and fear (1, 200–8) but in society these
desires are activated by pride, envy, avarice and the rest. Once these
vices begin inevitably to operate, they initiate the chain of events that
results in greatness and felicity. In this process, as technology develops
and individuals become less ignorant, so desires are enlarged and
'consequently . . . Wants and Appetites are multiply'd' (1, 206).[1]

We can usefully gloss this. With economic development I can now
want a silk waistcoat. Such objects have to be a possibility in order for
my desire to be aroused. But, of course, for Mandeville it is more than
simply the increased number (above those supposedly present in an
honest, frugal society) of objects available to choose from that
generates desire. In addition I can want a silk waistcoat because my
neighbour has one, while my neighbour, for his part, wishes to
emulate the squire with his exquisitely embroidered version (cf. 1,
130). In this way Mandeville, like Barbon before him, sees shifts in
fashion as an economically productive flux. And, given the desirous
nature of mankind, together with their openness to the private vices of
pride, envy and so on, there can be no end to their wants and luxury.

Mandeville realises that to portray luxury in an approbative
context runs foul of the 'receiv'd Notion that Luxury is as destructive
to the Wealth of the whole Body Politic, as it is to that of every
individual Person who is guilty of it' (1, 108). His subsequent
discussion focuses on two aspects of the received view. First he tackles
the issue that 'foreign' luxury impoverishes and, second, he meets

---

[1] Mandeville supplies his own particular twist to this. Given natural laziness and the
multiplicity of desires consequent upon increased knowledge he advocates (especially in his
essay on charity schools) that for the sake of 'Welfare and Felicity' the knowledge of the
working poor should be confined (*Fable*: 1, 288). In comparison to working, schooling is a state
of idleness and, except for those who need to be numerate and literate, such skills are 'very
pernicious to the Poor'. Similarly over-extensive charity is good for little other than the
breeding of drones and is thus destructive of industry (1, 267). The governing principle of
policy should, therefore, be to relieve the wants of the poor (including treatment when sick
and support when disabled) but not to cure them (1, 248). The incentive should be sufficient
money to stop them starving but not so much that they can save (1, 193).

   That this critique of charity schools and advocacy of low wages was Mandeville's own twist
is demonstrated not only by its later repudiation by Hume and Smith, but also by the fact that
it was no necessary accompaniment of mercantilism. Child, for example, increasingly paid
attention to the problem of poverty and advocated high wages – 'wherever wages are high . . .
it is an infallible evidence of the riches of that country' (quoted in Wilson, 1965: p. 233; cf.
Wilson, 1959).

head on the complaint that luxury encourages avarice and effeminacy.

On the first count Mandeville remains within the balance-of-trade orthodoxy. He charges the government to 'keep a watchful Eye' over the general balance and, provided that their 'dextrous Management' ensures that imports never exceed exports, then (by the conventions of the doctrine of balance) 'no Nation can ever be impoverish'd by Foreign Luxury' (1, 116). This position enables Mandeville to hold simultaneously that, provided there is no net outflow, there can be no objection based on how much luxury is imported, and that these luxuries themselves can still be thought to 'taint' societies (1, 286).

The second objection appears, however, to deal with the moral dangers of luxury. In essence, Mandeville deflects this accusation. As we have already seen he has no wish to deny that effeminacy and corruption are 'terrible Things' but he does deny that luxury is to blame. Once again politicians are called into play. It is the fault of 'Male-Administration' and 'bad Politicks' if this terrible behaviour makes a country easy prey to invaders (1, 115). He then proceeds to deal directly with the particular connexion between luxury and military weakness that had always lain at the heart of the charge of effeminacy.

One ploy is to produce counter-assertions in order to undermine any supposed necessary connexion between luxury and cowardice. Hence in Spain and Flanders the 'embroider'd Beaux with fine lac'd Shirts and powder'd Wigs' have stood up as well under fire as any 'stinking Slovens'. Similarly, 'wild Rakes' whose health has indeed been impaired by 'Excesses of Wine and Women' have still fought bravely (1, 122–3). Another ploy is to concede the principle but deny its applicability. Hence even if soft living renders men unfit for battle those affected will be the rich, but these men do not fight – their military contribution is financial by means of taxation (1, 119). Mandeville's tacit acceptance here of a professional/standing army is in line with what Davenant would have called his 'new' Whiggism; his anti-Country, anti-civic republican sentiments. As we will explore more fully later such sentiments are an integral part of the 'defence' of luxury within the eighteenth-century debate. Mandeville goes on to remark that those who actually do the fighting are 'the meanest Indigent Part of the Nation' and, in an economically developed society, there will always be enough spare man-power or enough of those whose daily labour is of an arduous, physical sort that they will not suffer any enervation – the supposed ailment of the luxurious.

Mandeville even proceeds to plug the one apparent loop-hole in his ploy, the officers. His argument here is that this class is preoccupied with questions of honour, and such a preoccupation has two effects. First, when strictly analysed, 'honour' is fear of shame and a vain concern with posthumous reputation (I, 313)[2] and these are sufficient to render such men valorous (I, 214). Second, the maintenance of the dignity commensurate with the honour of being an officer involves such expense on finery and equipage that there is little left over for physically debilitating debauchery (I, 121). And, to meet a final contingency, even if none of that applied it matters not because 'Robustness is the least Thing requir'd in an Officer' (I, 123).

There is one last objection that Mandeville feels it incumbent upon him to rebut. This objection saw in the desire to live a luxurious life – the lifestyle of a superior rank – a source of ruin. Here Mandeville simply retorts that any such ruin is the fault of folly not luxury, since whoever lives above his income is a fool (I, 249). The corollary of this is that one can be as extravagant as one likes within one's income (I, 304) just as a nation can import any amount of goods as long as exports overbalance it. As with nations, so with individuals; the significant implication of Mandeville's rebuttal is that there is nothing inherently injurious about so-called 'luxuries'. This, of course, follows from the fact that judgments as to *what* is a luxury, and what, by the same token, is a necessity, have changed over time. However, contrary to some 'strong' primitivists this has not meant a diminution of physical strength since 'clean Linen weakens a Man no more than Flannel . . . and a rich Couch, or a gilt Chariot are no more enervating than the Cold Floor or a Country Cart (I, 119).

II

AFTER MANDEVILLE

Historically important though Mandeville's defence of luxury was, it would be misleading to think that that defence was the sole source of his notoriety. If any one aspect was responsible for his reputation, it would be his view of virtue. What was upsetting was not so much his definition in terms of self-denial (*Fable*: I, 156; cf. *Enquiry*: p. vi) (though that did mean that in the supposed pristine state of slothful

---

[2] In the *Enquiry* (p. 15), Mandeville says this is the 'Gothick' meaning which was invented to influence men over whom religion had no power.

ease and stupidity there was little occasion for virtue) as his claim that virtue was taught by 'skilful Politicians'.[3] In a phrase calculated to enrage moralists, both Christian and humanist, he declared that 'the Moral Virtues are the Political Offspring which Flattery begot upon Pride' (*Fable*: 1, 51). Even Hume, who himself argued for the artificiality of crucial social virtues and, indeed, thought sufficiently highly of Mandeville to mention him with approval, nevertheless baulked at reducing *all* virtues to the 'artifice of politicians' (*Treatise*: p. 500). Hutcheson's response is more typical. Within an acute dissection of the inconsistencies and ambiguities in the *Fable*, Hutcheson incorporates an analysis of the account of luxury (*Observations*: pp. 80–100). This is typical in so far as Mandeville's view on virtue was used as a stick to beat his apologia for luxury, and his defence of luxury was used contrariwise to berate his pernicious notion of virtue (see, also, for another example, Dennis's aptly named *Vice and Luxury; Public Mischiefs* (cf. *Fable*; ed. Kaye: II, 407–9)).

Outside Britain, Mandeville's greatest impact was felt in France. This does not mean that the ground was unprepared. In fact Mandeville's own ideas were shaped to no small extent by French sceptics and epicureans like La Rochefoucauld and St Evremond as well as Bayle. What Mandeville was perceived by contemporaries to have done was to transform *luxe* from a theological to a political/philosophical notion.[4]

Although the *Fable* was only translated in 1740, it was known earlier. There is in fact a passage in Montesquieu's *Lettres Persanes* [1721] (hereafter *LP*) that, in the words of one commentator, contains Mandeville's whole message within one page (Morizé, 1909: p. 61). The page in question is in Letter 106, where the view that luxury engenders effeminacy is rejected and the argument put forward that a state without *la volupté ou la fantaisie* would be the most miserable in the world. Moreover, as Parisian society testifies, it is refined pleasures that provide work and industry and a powerful prince must procure superfluities for his subjects as earnestly as he

[3] Indeed, Mandeville's own resolution of how it was possible to link private vice with public benefits was that it was by the interposition of 'the dextrous Management of a skilful Politician' (*Fable*: 1, 371; cf. Goldsmith, 1985: p. 62, for such a politician being a 'fictive literary device', an 'elliptical way' of referring to general social development).

[4] According to Pluquet's *Traité philosophique et politique sur le luxe* [1786], Mandeville's ideas transformed the question of luxury from 'the object of zeal of theologians and religious moralists' into a 'philosophical and political dispute in which one took sides either with Mandeville or with the English theologians who had sprung up to attack him' (quoted in Ross, 1976: p. 1906).

pays heed to their necessities (*LP*: pp. 222–3). Montesquieu certainly knew his Mandeville, citing him explicitly in *De l'Esprit des Lois* [1748], but it is unclear whether he knew of the 1714 edition of the *Fable*. Similarly, while there is also no categorical, but much circumstantial, evidence that Mandeville was known to Voltaire and Melon it is their work (the latter's in particular) that gave the greatest initial impetus to the French debate.

Voltaire's witty poem *Le Mondain* [1736] cocked a snook at ascetic morality and moralising and he followed it a year later with a sequel revealingly entitled *Défense du Mondain ou L'Apologie du Luxe*. Although Voltaire impishly caught the flavour of Mandeville's own paradoxicality with his oft-quoted line '*Le superflu chose très nécessaire*', it was Melon's *Essai politique sur le commerce* [1734] that 'gallicised Mandeville' (Strugnell, 1983: p. 83). Melon devoted a whole chapter to the issue of luxury. Therein he defended the relativity of the notion and rejected the standard critique that it induced military weakness. More positively, he asserted its value in destroying idleness by creating employment and thus strengthening the state. This last aspect is particularly significant. At the beginning of the chapter he defines luxury as '*une somptuosité extraordinaire*' (*Essai*: p. 742) that supplies wealth and security to a government; it is indeed a necessary effect of all societies '*bien policées*'. Melon stakes his claim on the facts – the everyday consumption by the present generation of what was 'extraordinary' for their fathers. His explanation for this change rests on the materialist conception of Man (human nature) as a creature of the passions – especially the Mandevillean ones of ambition and greed. It is against the backcloth of this professed realism that Melon also remarks that the word *luxe* lacks any clear meaning; it is a composite of vague, confused and false ideas (p. 744) and, accordingly, he wishes it to be banned from discourse on *police* and commerce. This is not simply for clarity's sake but also because he is afraid that the effect of this sloppy usage would be to stifle the source of industry itself. What he has in mind here are the moralistic injunctions (he mentions Cato) to impose sumptuary laws.

Rather than chart the various arguments as different individuals came to make them – frequently re-stating well-rehearsed positions – it will suffice to take as an example one piece that explicitly sets out the various positive and negative arguments. The piece in question is St Lambert's article *Luxe* in *L'Encyclopédie* (vol. IX). The author lists six arguments that have been made in favour of luxury – it encourages population and the well-being of states; it facilitates the circulation of money; it reforms manners; it favours the progress of knowledge and the fine arts and it increases the happiness of individuals and the power of nations ('Luxury': pp. 204–5). After each argument, St Lambert supplies objections. These objections take the form of counter-examples rather than statements of principle. The same ploy is then executed with respect to arguments critical of luxury. Five such arguments are cited – luxury co-exists with extreme inequality of wealth; it ruins the countryside by attracting men to cities; it contributes to de-population; it weakens courage and it stifles love of country – to each of which a counter is supplied.

Although at the end of what is a lengthy article, St Lambert concludes that his readers should reject the extremes of both Sparta and Sybaris (p. 232), the balance of the discussion is that since luxury does contribute to the greatness of states it should be encouraged (and directed) (p. 230). This does not mean imposing sumptuary laws (save possibly and only as a tax on certain foreign imports) but keeping luxury within bounds by *l'esprit de communauté* (p. 226) – it is unregulated luxury that destroys itself (p. 232). This, on balance favourable, assessment (not echoed elsewhere in *L'Encyclopédie* – see, most famously, Rousseau's article on 'Political Economy') is to be expected, given St Lambert's opening paragraph where he attributes to 'all men' a desire to increase their well-being (p. 204) and his conclusion, where he remarks that the desire to become rich (and to enjoy one's riches) is part of human nature (p. 230). It follows from this universality that luxury exists in all states and societies – 'the savage has his hammock which he buys with pelts' (p. 204).

What is apparent from St Lambert's article is his awareness that the various pro and contra arguments took a predictable or standard form. Throughout the literature, certain characteristics recur. Those in favour of luxury emphasise employment or industry as a source of national strength, while those opposed emphasise military valour and associated traits as the chief prop of states. Again, both sides could agree that population size was an important factor in the well-being of a society, but disagree on whether luxury aided or hindered that well-being (cf. Spengler, 1942; Eversley, 1959). What connects these two concerns is the 'classical' link between luxury and effeminacy. While the ancients were, on balance, more concerned with the lack of military virtue exhibited by the effeminate, in the modern period the lack of procreative potency associated with the effeminate came more to the fore.

What emerges from this predictability is that both sides are engaged in the same task, namely, the identification of the appropriate criteria by which to assess the 'good society'. For the traditional moralist, luxury was inimical to the maintenance of such a society because of its effects both on individual citizens and the conduct of the 'public thing'. The de-moralisation of luxury from this traditional context, begun by Barbon and carried dramatically forward by Mandeville, raised the issue of the morality of a good society once that de-moralisation has taken place. The proponents of luxury become increasingly aware, especially after the furore stirred up by Mandeville, that it is the charge of abetting immorality which must be met. One way of doing this was to deflect the charge. This deflection could be achieved by making an overt distinction between questions of government or commerce and those of morality.

A good example of the openness of this distinction is found in Sir James Steuart's *Principles of Political Oeconomy* (1767). In Chapter 6 of Book I, Steuart defines luxury in 'a political sense', by which he means 'as a principle which produces employment and gives bread to those who supply the demands of the rich' (I, 44n). As such, he says, it necessarily produces 'good effects'. But in this same note he is at pains to dissociate his discussion from the 'doctrine of morals' and he feels obliged to declare defensively that he is 'no patron either of vice, profusion or the dissipation of private fortunes'.[5] Much later (Bk II, ch. 20), Steuart devotes a chapter to luxury. In a manner reminiscent of Melon's comments on the term's vagueness, he produces a series of stipulative distinctions. He distinguishes luxury from sensuality from excess (although he admits that generally they are treated as synonyms). Once distinguished, however, Steuart is able to defend luxury without committing himself to upholding excess (of which, he says, nobody has ever seriously been an apologist); hence, 'luxury consists in providing the objects of sensuality, so far as they are superfluous. Sensuality consists in the actual enjoyment of them and excess implies an abuse of enjoyment.' And in the provision of these

---

[5] Cf. J. Harris who encapsulates Steuart's argument in the following sentence, 'The word luxury hath usually annexed to it a kind of opprobrious idea; but so far as it encourages the arts, whets the inventions of men and finds employments for more of our own people, its influence is benign and beneficial to the whole society' (*Essay on Money and Coins* [1757] quoted in Viner, 1937: p. 91n; also quoted by Johnson, 1937: p. 297; and Sekora, 1977: p. 123).

'objects' luxury gives bread to the industrious and encourages 'emulation, industry and agriculture' (1, 266). These are presumably the 'good effects' referred to earlier. The good society is one that possesses these 'effects' and, although Steuart himself does not make the point, this means that the traditional 'doctrine of morals' that condemns luxury no longer has a monopoly of virtue.

Two developments are now made possible. First the way is opened for a critique of luxury on *economic* rather than moral grounds. This now explains (or at least helps to explain) a significant thrust in the argument of the Physiocrats (cf. Labriolle-Rutherford, 1963: pp. 1034–6). Baudeau in his *Principes de la Science Morale et Politique* (p. 14) defines luxury as '*l'interversion de l'ordre naturel*'. He does not mean by this the surpassing of 'natural limits' but the proportion of national expenditure given over to unproductive expense to the prejudice of that directed in support of production. Luxury is not the same as prodigality. In Physiocratic terms luxury is 'sterile' and refers, in general, to *luxe de décoration* (cf. Mirabeau in Meek, 1973: p. 139). What makes ornamentation 'unproductive' is the Physiocrats' identification of agriculture as the criterion of productivity. Hence the actual amount *spent* on 'luxury' is not vital, it is the direction and the proportion of total expenditure that is crucial (cf. Meek, 1962: p. 317). This development presages the role (sometimes positive, sometimes negative) that 'luxury' comes to play in nineteenth-century political economy as it tackles the increasingly technical issues of consumption and saving, to culminate in the theories of demand elasticity that we noted in Chapter 1.

The second development is the articulation of a doctrine of commerce, incorporating luxury positively, that will underwrite a new understanding of a good society. I shall examine this more direct response, as made by Hume and Smith, shortly.

LUXURY AND IDEOLOGY

But first I want to change tack briefly in order to consider how this 'new' understanding might be interpreted. Although it is easy to exaggerate and fall into undue hyperbole, this understanding can be seen to indicate the presence of a fundamental fault-line in European thinking. The interpretation of that fault-line that I wish to consider regards it as marking the transition from feudal to capitalist relations of production. The debate over the status of luxury can be situated at what this interpretation would call the 'superstructural' or ideological level. Given its close relationship to questions of trade and commerce then 'luxury' would indeed appear to be a prime candidate for retrospective re-analysis along class/ideology lines. These lines run somewhat as follows.

The defenders of luxury were, *inter alia*, defenders of mobility, both financial and social. If, in accordance with a familiar model of ideological analysis, we ask, 'who benefits?' the answer is the middle-class or bourgeoisie. This benefit, according to the model, gives them an 'interest' that expresses itself in two characteristic ways. First in an opposition to the (feudal) landed aristocracy, which wants (has an interest in) to keep mobility to a minimum in order to retain its own advantages as the uppermost rung in a stable hierarchy. Primogeniture, entailment and sumptuary laws are all practices that this aristocratic interest would support and the bourgeois interest oppose. However, secondly, the bourgeoisie are also opposed to granting any economic or political power/privileges to the poor ('the working class'). Accordingly, the bourgeois interest invests private property with exclusatory rights and underwrites such practices as enclosures and clearances, the punishment of vagrancy and the enforcement of labour.

The model is not without its merits. There is no denying that these various practices do characterise the eighteenth century. But to admit their presence is not to admit that the appropriate explanation is provided by the model. The difficulty is partly one of levels of abstraction. Meszaros (1990: p. 25), for example, writes, 'the practical rehabilitation of luxury represents an objective structural imperative of the capitalist system as the new regulator of the social metabolism'. Even apart from its hypostatisation this declaration affirms the consequence. The effects are only 'read' as those effects because they presuppose a pre-identification of effective causality. If we examine the debate itself, the identification of the requisite 'interest' is not clear-cut and this lack of precision makes it difficult (to put the point neutrally) to assess independently the adequacy of this explanation. Indeed it is hard to know what could, independently of the model, count as an objection.

For example, it is impossible to identify the arguments of the protagonists in the debate with their own 'class positions'. By definition, none of the participants belongs in the illiterate peasantry but, beyond that, they range in origin from sons of landed aristocracy

(Holbach) to sons of minor gentry (Hume) to sons of low-grade functionaries (Diderot); in professional occupation from church (Lessing) to university (Kant) to law (Montesquieu), and in contemporary status from 'outsider' (Rousseau) to the pinnacle of 'establishment' respectability (Robertson). The only safe generalisation is the expected one, namely, that they come from the educated/ professional stratum of their societies. This very similarity, when juxtaposed against the fact that we are here dealing with a *debate*, means we cannot collapse the different sides into different class positions. This is dramatically illustrated by the case of David Hume and his cousin Henry Home (Lord Kames – a legal title) since the former was a defender of luxury while the latter was a steadfast opponent (see section v).

Of course, when viewed from the perspective of the 'imperatives' of 'capitalism', it is possible to relegate these considerations as relatively unimportant (Marx himself was an educated professional from the bourgeoisie). Or, again, they can be thought to be too narrowly focused on individual intention. Galliani (1989: pp. 366–7), for example, purports to explain the opponents of luxury in France (including Rousseau) as being under *l'influence de l'idéologie nobiliaire* even if they (but not including Rousseau) were unaware of the fact. But the cost of such relegation is the purchase of an interpretative package that regards, for example, the Christian moralists' objections to luxury as, in effect and independently of any motivation, a reactionary defence of a weakening material interest.

If instead of invoking an interpretation that relegates contemporary perceptions, we fasten on to those perceptions themselves, then we can do justice to those social changes that were occurring.[6] More than that, we can do justice to the conceptual resources that were brought to bear in an attempt to comprehend those changes. In this way a

---

[6] There is a large literature, especially regarding Britain, on 'economic' change in the late seventeenth and eighteenth century. Much of this is retrospective in that it is motivated by a concern with the preconditions or triggers of the 'Industrial Revolution'. The role of consumption patterns and the diffusion of domestic consumer goods (the 'spread of luxuries') has come to be seen as an important element. Sombart (1913: p. 140) is an unacknowledged pioneer with his argument that the demand for luxury goods created markets and, as such, played a decisive role in the emergence of capitalism. For an influential, more recent statement see Perkin (1985: pp. 91, 93), who declares at one point that consumer demand was 'the most important economic factor in the genesis of industrialism' and that it was contemporaneously perceived 'luxuries' that formed the basis for the industrial revolution. For a useful overview of the literature and its controversies that focuses on consumption see Weatherill (1988).

more plausible account of why *luxury* should be the focus of debate is made possible. The crux is that luxury has the particular history that it does. That is to say it is because 'luxury' had for so long provided an account of how wealth and private interest damaged both self and society that it achieved a salience in a society where these factors were coming increasingly to the fore. In effect, 'luxury' became an omnicompetent explanation-cum-scapegoat for various social ills.[7] But even this is too mechanical. We must not lose sight of the literary dimension. Not all societies were experiencing these changes to an equal (even any) degree, but that did not stop the literati throughout the world of letters from engaging with equal vigour in the debate. And it is bad metaphysics or presumptive prejudice to think that somehow 'ideas' are less 'real' than the number of shopkeepers in London.

The eighteenth-century debate over luxury was thus both a debate about the character of contemporary society, and itself a characteristic of that society. The contemporary description of this society was that it was 'commercial'. We have already observed that the shifts in the evaluation of luxury first appeared in discourses on trade, and it was in writings on commerce or political economy that the 'new understanding' burgeoned.

III

HUME

Hume's essay 'Of Luxury', first published in 1752 but re-titled 'Of Refinement in the Arts' in 1760 (hereafter RA), is his most obvious contribution to the eighteenth-century debate; indeed, this essay is designedly organised as a response to Mandeville. Hume's contribution is not confined to that essay and I shall, in this brief examination of his position, make reference to other essays, especially the contemporaneous 'Of Commerce' (hereafter Com.).

Rather than provide a résumé of Hume's argument, I will concentrate upon one very particular aspect of his discussion and use

---

[7] A good example of this phenomenon is Fielding's *An Enquiry into the Late Increase of Robbers* [1751]. As part of his recourse to 'history' he cites in his Preface Middleton's recent [1741] account of the fall of Rome, and in the text refers to Cato's Orchian sumptuary law. These pieties are supplemented by identifying the 'vast Torrent of Luxury' (ed. Zirker: p. 77) as the cause of unwanted diversions among the vulgar, of drunkenness and of gaming; all of which contribute to the predicament indicated in the title of his pamphlet.

that to illuminate his general position. The aspect in question is his treatment of Sparta. This treatment is apt because of Sparta's long-standing (indeed proverbial (cf. Rawson, 1969)) association with the virtues of military prowess and concomitant abjuration of all 'softness'. It is further testament to the aptness of Sparta for our purposes that, as we noted in passing, Mandeville also had felt the need to treat, though in an atypically anodyne way, this exemplar explicitly. Against this traditional understanding and its rhetorically potent image, given a recent boost by Rousseau's prize-winning *Discours* on Arts and Science [1750], Hume declares the Spartan regime to be contrary to human nature. How is that possible?

The argument is intricate since it combines sociological, historical and philosophical ingredients. Philosophically Hume's 'science of man' (*Treatise*: p. xxi) leads him to attach explanatory weight to the 'natural bent of the mind'. And since this 'science' must be gleaned from 'cautious observation of human life' (p. xxiii), the data of sociology and history must be taken on board. Historically this means that the circumstances of city-states like Sparta are no longer applicable. Sociologically the character of modern commercial society reveals the ways in which that lack of applicability is evident.

Like Melon before him and Steuart after him, Hume worries about terminology. He opens 'Refinement in the Arts' by stating that 'luxury' is a word of 'uncertain signification'. Accordingly he immediately provides a general definition of luxury (which perhaps explains his later change of title): luxury is 'great refinement in the gratification of the senses' (RA: p. 268). 'Refinement' is used in a social as well as an individual sense. He refers to 'ages of refinement' which correspond, in their fullest and proper sense, to the modern world of commerce. He remarks significantly of these ages that they are 'both the happiest and most virtuous' (RA: p. 269). The significance of this remark stems from the radical break from the moralistic tradition that the Spartan case represents.

The 'arts of luxury' are, for Hume, conterminous with the 'finer arts' (Com.: p. 256) and he places them in a chronological sequence. Hume's initial phase, corresponding, as we shall see, to Smith's first state of society, is a subsistence economy devoted to hunting and fishing and called by him a 'savage state'. Thereafter societies support a population who devote themselves to agriculture and manufacture, with the former initially predominant (Hume cites Melon in an accompanying note, though only to criticise him for assuming that agriculture continues to predominate). Once, however, agriculture is improved, it can support more than those needed to labour upon it. These 'superfluous hands' now apply themselves to the arts of luxury. These arts add to the 'happiness' of states since *many* (my emphasis) now have the 'opportunity of receiving enjoyments with which they would otherwise have been unacquainted' (ibid.).

It is important that happiness is enhanced and diffused by this progress of events, and we shall come back to Hume's account of happiness. However, Sparta stands as a case where this series of events did not transpire and, because Sparta embodies 'classical' virtue, its example constitutes a moral reproach to those countries – commercial nations – where such enjoyment is to be had. In the Spartan case the superfluous hands were explicitly devoted to public service (military duty) and not to the private pursuit of commerce, luxury and refinement. Sparta is cited by Hume (Com.: p. 257) as proof of the general proposition that 'the ambition of the sovereign must entrench on the luxury of individuals; so the luxury of individuals must diminish the force, and check the ambition of the sovereign'. There is a seeming opposition, Hume remarks, between the 'greatness of the state' (its military power) and the 'happiness of the subject'. That this is in fact, for Hume, only 'seeming' will become apparent.

If ages of luxury are happier ages, in what does happiness consist? Hume identifies three ingredients (RA: pp. 269–70). Of these, indolence or repose is derivative and only relished as a contrast to the second ingredient 'action'. Action, 'being occupied', or industry is of itself enjoyable, even apart from the pleasures derived from the fruits of that activity. Pleasure is the third ingredient, and is clearly linked with action both intrinsically and extrinsically. Action invigorates the mind – it enlarges its powers and faculties – and, in so doing, it not only satisfies 'natural appetites' but prevents the growth of 'unnatural' ones. The latter are commonly engendered by ease and idleness and it might now seem that Hume is paying his dues to the moralist tradition. As we know, traditionally *luxuria* was judged to be an unnatural appetite; a perversion of the essentially instrumental and finite business of meeting needs by allowing the inherent limitlessness of desire to hold sway. It was also, typically, associated with 'soft' living and not the 'hard life' of frugality. But the whole tenor of Hume's argument runs counter to the tradition.

The crux of Hume's argument lies in his notion of 'action'. When he praises action he is celebrating the private endeavour of industry, not the Ciceronic preoccupation with public or political affairs – the *res publica*. We shall return to this last point when we discuss Smith but, for the present, we can profitably enlarge upon Hume's understanding of the role of action *qua* industry. This enlargement concerns both the motives and consequences of 'action' in Hume's account. Humans are motivated, are roused to activity or industry by a 'desire of a more splendid way of life than what their ancestors enjoyed' and by the hope of attaining the 'pleasures of luxury' (Com.: p. 264). In the moralistic tradition these desires and pleasures were treated with opprobrium because they gratified bodily desires. As we saw, Hume, too, has defined luxury in terms of sensory (sensual) gratification but, once again, his project is effectively to dissociate it from the tradition. This he achieves partly by his notion of 'innocent' luxury, whereby only those 'disordered by the frenzies of enthusiasm' (that is, monks – those in the Christian ascetic tradition) can regard delicacy in apparel or food as a vice/sin. But he also achieves it by developing an important association between refinement, luxury and civilisation. Hence, the more pleasure is refined the less excessive indulgence is practised – it is the Tartars feasting on horsemeat who are gluttonous, not the courts of Europe with their 'refinements of cookery' (RA: pp. 271–2). Since it is the luxurious ages that are refined, it follows that the moralistic indictment of 'excess' is misdirected at modern commercial societies.

The consequences of action/industry are the advantages it bestows. By drawing attention to these advantages Hume is at the forefront of the utilitarian strategy, broadly-conceived to dissociate luxury from a negative assessment of the 'good society' and view it positively, *because* of its effects, as an ingredient in a civilised society. Somewhat akin to the Physiocrats, this does enable him to hold that 'luxury' is only pernicious ('vicious') when it ceases to be socially beneficial.

Without the presence in society of these energising desires, 'habits of indolence' will prevail. If indolence prevails, then it cannot be a true ingredient of happiness because, as we saw, its value was as a relief from labour and, if bereft of that connexion, it constitutes lethargy which 'destroys all enjoyment' (RA: p. 270). It is precisely this languor that is the 'unnatural appetite' mentioned above. With the advent of industry, far-reaching *progressive* changes occur. 'Every art and science' is improved so that 'profound ignorance is totally banished'. Echoing the earlier remark about refined pleasures, a consequence of this banishment is that 'pleasures of the mind as well as those of body' are cultivated (RA: p. 271).

Ignorant and, thus, barbarous or savage nations are non-urban which means, for Hume, that they lack sociability and humanity. This implicit defence of urban life ran counter to the conviction that the dangers of luxury were inextricably bound up with the corruptions of cities. Cities were not only 'nurseries of debauchery and voluptuousness' (Price [1769], in Glass, 1973: p. 54) but acted as a magnet drawing simple peasant folk away from the land (see, e.g., Goldsmith's Dedication to the *Deserted Village* [1770] (*Works*: II, 32)). What lies behind this antipathy to the urban is the model of the virtuous citizen as the proprietor of a landed estate; in a very strict sense, luxury is a 'bourgeois' phenomenon.[8] We shall consider this ultimately Aristotelian position in the next section. For Hume, civilisation, civility and the civic life are all linked. Accordingly we find him elsewhere referring to the Koran as a 'wild and absurd performance' and declaring its 'treachery, inhumanity, cruelty, revenge, bigotry' as 'utterly incompatible with civilized society' (*Essay*, 'Standard of Taste' [1757]: p. 229). On the positive side, along with these traits of sociability and humanity are developed 'laws, order, police, discipline' (RA: p. 273). In short, Hume affirms that it is 'peculiar' to 'polished or . . . luxurious ages' that 'industry, knowledge and humanity are linked together by an indissoluble chain' (RA: p. 271).

If we now return to Sparta, Hume is explicit that Sparta's power 'was owing entirely to the want of commerce and luxury' (Com.: p. 257). It is an implication of Hume's argument that they are an uncivilised people (Rousseau had cited their '*heureuse ignorance*' (*Discours*: p. 9)). Because they eschewed commerce and luxury and devoted themselves to military prowess, they abjured all 'ease and delicacy' (RA: p. 257). But it is a mark of the growth in 'humanity' that it has, in part, expressed itself in the 'tempers' of men being 'softened' (RA: p. 274). Hume is here providing his version of what Hirschman (1977: p. 60) has called 'the doctrine of the *doux commerce*'. As Hirschman points out, the most influential exponent of this doctrine was Montesquieu in his *De l'Esprit des Lois*. For Montesquieu it is '*presque une règle générale*' that commerce and '*des moeurs douces*' are associated. He is, however, less than forthcoming about the content of this 'softness', except from the general statement that a natural effect

---

[8] Cf. Galliani (1989) who, while criticising anachronistic accounts of Rousseau, nevertheless moves from the precise sense of *bourgeois* (as manifest in the wording of various sumptuary laws; compare here the reference to 'burgesses' in the English Act of 1363 (see ch. 2, *supra*)) to talking of '*la société bourgeoise* (e.g., pp. 11, 228, 247) and '*l'individualisme bourgeois*' (e.g., pp. 12, 372).

of commerce is that it leads to peace (*Esprit*: xx, 1.2). Hume, too, picks up this aspect. One manifestation of the softening of manners is that wars are less cruel and the aftermath less 'brutal', that is, more 'humane' (RA: p. 274).[9] Corresponding to this is a relative, and beneficial, downplaying of the virtue of courage – this pre-eminently military virtue predominates in 'uncultivated nations' (*Inquiry (Morals)*: p. 79).[10]

Nonetheless Hume denies that this softening has enervated the 'martial spirit'. One strand in this denial is to undermine the supposed causal link – contemporary France and England demonstrate that there is no constant conjunction between luxury and military weakness (RA: p. 275). Another strand is to claim that the corruption of Rome was not the product of luxury (as Sallust and other 'severe moralists' liked to maintain) so much as (here echoing Mandeville's references to 'male-administration') an 'ill modelled government' as well as 'the unlimited extent of conquests' (RA: p. 276). A final strand is to develop a positive alternative account, the nub of which is the articulation of a 'modern' notion of liberty. This alternative was more fully worked up by Smith, and we shall examine this strategy as he prosecutes it. Before turning to Smith, there are still aspects of Hume's account of Sparta that require examination.

Hume draws attention to the sociological fact that Spartan society

[9] Adam Ferguson (*Essay* [1767]) interestingly comments that the dissociation of 'glory' from 'destroying the vanquished', and use of force only for justice, is 'perhaps the principal characteristic' that makes us call 'modern nations' 'civilized or polished'. But Ferguson goes on promptly to deny that this develops *pari passu* with the 'progress of arts' (p. 200). This is symptomatic of his willingness, without adopting Rousseau's extremism, to treat Sparta's commitment to public virtue with more respect than Hume (see esp. pp. 158–61). In a letter to Hume, Ferguson remarked that if he 'were to plead the cause of Sparta' then he realised that he 'must appeal elsewhere' (quoted in Rawson, 1969: p. 350).

[10] While Ferguson (*Essay*: p. 258) was disturbed by the consequences that follow from lack of courage and other active virtues, where 'contempt of glory' passes as wisdom, Smith, like Hume, downplays courage. Not only have modern conditions of battle reduced the 'skill factor' but more significantly the very individualism, the heroism, of the virtuous/courageous man is rendered suspect. He points out that 'the most intrepid valour may be employed in the cause of the greatest injustice'. Courage, while sometimes useful, is 'equally liable to be excessively pernicious' and will be called upon when law and justice are 'in a great measure impotent', that is, 'in times of great public disorder' (*TMS*: p. 241, cf. p. 264). The contrast is with 'the gentler' exertions of temperance and modesty, of chastity and industry, that 'can seldom be directed to any bad end'. It is indicative of the generality of these sentiments that we find them echoed, for example, in Hegel. In the *Philosophy of Right* (p. 212(328 Remark)) he remarks that 'the principle of the modern world ... has given courage a higher form' as the invention of the gun has made bravery less personal and more abstract. Relatedly, Hegel thinks that virtue proper is commoner in uncivilised communities (*ungebildeten Gemeinwesens*) where ethical conditions are more a matter of private choice; in the modern state, virtue is to be found in adherence to a rational system of laws (ibid.: p. 108 (150 R), cf. p. 260).

was rigidly stratified between the helots, whom he here calls the labourers, and the Spartans themselves who were 'the soldiers or gentlemen' (Com.: p. 257). Their military power was underpinned by what was effectively slave labour. One important consequence of the growth of luxury is to erode those underpinnings. The way that erosion occurred is discussed briefly by Hume (cf. RA: p. 277; *History of England*: e.g., III, 99) and more fully by Smith, whose account we will discuss.

In another of his Essays of this time ('Of the Populousness of Ancient Nations'), Hume remarks that slavery is 'disadvantageous' to 'happiness' (*Essays*: p. 396). Of the three ingredients of 'happiness' noted above, that which here seems most applicable is 'pleasure', understood straightforwardly in terms of material well-being. (The intrinsic enjoyability of 'labour' is unlikely to be widespread under conditions of slavery, where the requisite repose will not be forthcoming.) Unlike Sparta, a society that indulges in foreign trade, and which abounds accordingly in industry and luxury, will be not only rich but happy as its members 'reap the benefit of these commodities, so far as they gratify the senses and appetites' (Com.: p. 263). A more explicit statement of Hume's allegiance to the 'modern' materialistic psychology and rejection of the classical concern with due and proper limits is hard to imagine (cf. MacIntyre, 1988: p. 305). If we now recall Hume's reference to 'unnatural' appetites, we can appreciate that his usage refers not to some teleological discourse of proper ends but to a description of what in fact, that is as a material cause, motivates human behaviour. It is this fundamental difference that enables Hume to couple rather than sever virtue and luxury.

Hume's naturalism has a further role to play. Though he draws attention to some similarities between the conduct of Sparta and the early years of Rome, he remarks that Spartan society was exceptional. He goes so far as to say it would have been thought impossible, were it not so well-attested (Com.: p. 259). What gives the impression of impossibility is Hume's general philosophical judgment that 'ancient policy was violent and contrary to the more natural and usual course of things' (ibid.). In a somewhat backhanded confirmation of this point, Rousseau's rhetoric had led him to proclaim Sparta a republic of demi-gods (*Discours*: p. 9). Hume's judgment underwrites the significant historical conclusion that, *because* of this contrariness, contemporary sovereigns cannot return to that policy. The conclusion and the judgment combine to signal Hume's awareness of the decisive sociological difference between the contemporary world of commerce (and luxury) and earlier ages.

He supposes that if a 'city' today became a 'fortified camp' such that its inhabitants had both a 'martial genius' and 'passion for the public good' then industry sufficient to maintain the community might be undertaken – in which case the modern community could emulate Sparta and banish all arts and luxury (Com.: pp. 262–3). But this supposition is unrealistic. The touchstone of realism is human nature – 'the natural bent of the mind'. The requisite devotion to the public good is 'too disinterested' to have an effective purchase upon human behaviour. While Hume had argued that on the basis of 'common experience' an individual's 'kind affections' overbalance the selfish, yet 'in the original frame of our mind, our strongest attention is confin'd to ourselves' (*Treatise*: pp. 487–8). Two noteworthy consequences follow. First, civic virtue, or a 'passion for the public good' is too fragile a base on which to erect a system of government (cf. Moore, 1977: p. 820). Second, and relatedly, this means that in the normal run of things governments must govern men by those passions that most effectively animate them. In practice this means they must 'animate them with a spirit of avarice and industry, art and luxury' (Com.: p. 263).

Once again Hume's couplings are significant. Avarice the *bête noire* of 'severe moralists' is associated with – or even the 'spur of' ('Civil Liberty' [1741] (hereafter CL): p. 93) – industry, 'exercise and employment' for which 'there is no craving or demand of the human mind more constant and insatiable' ('Of Interest' [1752]: p. 300). And avarice itself, Hume had attested in an earlier essay, was universal, operating 'at all times, in all places and upon all persons' ('Rise and Progress of Arts and Sciences' [1742] (hereafter RPAS): p. 113). This universality is significant. The aim of his 'science of man', as originally proclaimed, was to provide a 'solid foundation' to all sciences, and to attain that goal 'we must endeavour to render all our principles as universal as possible', consistent with 'experience' constituting the guarantor of the foundation's solidity (*Treatise*: pp. xx–xxi). Though Hume was to exhibit less confidence in the speed with which this foundation might be laid, he never repudiated the aspiration. It is one of the themes of his Essays to sift out 'certain and stable' ('natural') causal associations from those 'owing to chance'

(RPAS: p. 111). It is, accordingly, sensible and, in practice, greatly preferable to conduct public affairs upon the solid foundation of man's natural inclinations and motivations rather than upon what transpired in Sparta – justly esteemed 'a prodigy' by everyone 'who has considered human nature' (Com.: p. 259).

We can discern this general line of argument in 'Refinement in the Arts', where Hume declares it would require 'a miraculous transformation of mankind' to treat it as endowed with every virtue and free from all vices (RA: p. 280). The magistrate, however, is not in the business of miracles, he must deal with men as they are. Accordingly, the magistrate can 'very often' only cure one vice by encouraging another, where the latter's effects are less prejudicial to society. What underpins this strategy is Hume's 'modern' epistemology. In contrast to the classical framework, where the proper response to unruly passions was the cultivation and application of reason, Hume regards reason itself as inert. (*Treatise*: p. 458). What has been traditionally thought to be the *work* of reason has been confounded with the operations of 'calm passions' (ibid.: pp. 417, 437).[11] Accordingly, the task of government cannot be to impose the 'rational' solution, and it makes no sense to censure the magistrate for not implementing an objective doctrine of the 'good life'. Rather, given that human nature cannot be changed, the task of government is to change the situation (ibid.: p. 537) so that the passions are channelled constructively. It follows for Hume that the appropriate judgment is the constructiveness or otherwise of the channelling. And one of the crucial criteria of constructiveness is whether public policy promotes the material well-being of the individuals under its jurisdiction. In these terms, luxury can be justly cultivated because it is superior to sloth when it comes to such promotion.[12]

This defence of luxury also enables Hume to admit that luxury can be vicious as well as innocent, that is, when it is injurious to that well-being. But it also enables him to criticise Mandeville for calling

[11] Hirschman (1977: pp. 65–6) remarks how the pursuit of wealth was linked by Hutcheson with 'calm desire' and quotes Smith on the 'calm and dispassionate' desire to better our condition (see later). He also quotes Hume on the difference between calm and weak passion but this is too elliptical to make his point which is that 'money-making' came to be regarded as a calm passion. However, in our current context this is too general because the vital issue is the more specific, and more normatively charged, issue of luxury.

[12] In a possible allusion to Hume's argument, Ferguson (*Essay*: p. 160) remarks that Sparta's government's aim was 'to inspire the virtues of the soul' and was 'not calculated to prevent the practice of crimes by balancing against each other the selfish and partial dispositions of men'.

'vicious' even that luxury which nonetheless produces benefits.[13] Yet even with that admission it is clear that for Hume 'vicious luxury' will be rare and even then the fault lies most properly at the door of the government for its lack of what Mandeville called 'dextrous Management' (*Fable*: 1, 364). *Because* of its beneficial effects it will, in general, be preferable to accept luxury 'warts and all' than attempt fruitlessly – in the sense both of ineffectively and deleteriously – to extirpate it.

Hume's defence of luxury because of the positive advantages it conveys, and because it is sometimes the least damaging policy, commits him to a particular reading of a 'good society'. He is well aware that this reading is contrary to the tradition that regards a luxurious/commercial society as lacking in greatness. Hume's argument is, however, far from defensive – he holds, on the contrary, that 'industry and arts and trade encrease the power of the sovereign'. Moreover this increase is not – unlike in Sparta – bought at the cost of 'the happiness of the subjects'. Nor is this combination of sovereign power and subject happiness fortuitous, it rather accords with 'the most natural course of things' so that to attempt to separate the combination does 'violence' (Com.: p. 260).

Since a state's 'greatness' is a synonym for its military power it means that Hume – in an argument that Smith was to echo – contends that a trading nation is potent and is not emasculated. His contention has both negative and positive aspects. Negatively he holds that the population of a non-trading society will be indolent. The soldiers, like the farmers, in such a society will be inept since they will lack knowledge, skill and industry. This ineptitude will make them fit only for sudden confrontations, while regular attack or defence cannot be executed (Com.: p. 261). Positively a civilised nation, *because* of its other attributes, will be an effective military power. The root cause is that a state's power increases in proportion as it increases labour employed 'beyond mere necessaries'. The effect of this cause is that the society possesses a storehouse of labour (RA: p. 272; Com.: p. 262). This store can be drawn upon to meet military need. In a civilised nation, an army is raised by imposing a tax, the

---

[13] It is perhaps on these grounds that Hume judges Mandeville to be a man of 'libertine principles'. However Hume's major objection is to Mandeville's doctrine that all moral distinctions are the invention of politicians. This doctrine runs foul of Hume's naturalism – the most politicians can do is extend the natural sentiments, they cannot 'furnish the materials' of morality which must come from 'nature' and which 'give us some notion of moral distinctions' (*Treatise*: p. 500, cf. p. 578).

effect of which is to reduce expenditure on luxury goods and thus release the manufacturers of such goods for military service (Com.: p. 261).

Though Hume lays great stress on the energising effects of the provision of, and desire for, luxury goods and how this increases both power and happiness, an equally significant dimension to his analysis is the attention he draws to the increase in liberty that is associated with the growth in commerce. Sparta, it will be recalled, was a slave society. Sparta was also, and not coincidentally, uncivilised, and it is the element of civilisation that is crucial in the link between commerce and liberty. To lay stress upon *civilisation* is to attach less weight to formal constitutions. Hence Hume declares (echoing here a theme present in both Temple and Barbon)[14] that 'civilized monarchies', no less than republics, are a government of laws not men (CL: p. 94; cf. RPAS: p. 125). It is 'absolute government' that, of its 'very nature', is 'hurtful to commerce' (CL: p. 92) and hence also that 'the poverty of the common people is a natural, if not an infallible effect of absolute monarchy' (Com.: p. 265). This link between commerce, luxury and liberty, and the dislodging of liberty from republics are both important points that I will now develop in the context of Smith.

IV

SMITH AND MODERNITY

Adam Smith, in his lectures at the University of Glasgow, is reported to have professed that 'opulence and freedom' were 'the two greatest blessings men can possess' (*Lectures on Jurisprudence* (hereafter *LJ*): p. 185). My object here is to bring out how that pairing embodies the peculiarly modern understanding of liberty and how, as such, the whole tradition that pitches luxury against 'good and politic order' is, in principle, overturned. It is as well to be candid at the outset and admit that I shall seek to realise this objective through an interpretative

---

[14] Temple, having noted that trade seemed to flourish in commonwealths (he mentions, among others, Tyre and Venice as well as Holland), cites the cases of Bruges and Antwerp where trade reached heights under the rule of princes. This shows positively – he argued – that trade can thrive under 'good Princes and legal monarchies as well as under free States' and, negatively, that 'under arbitrary or tyrannical power it must of necessity decay and dissolve' (*Observations* [1754]: 1. 120). Barbon thinks the English monarchy, where legislative power is 'in both the Prince and People' is 'Best for Trade' since 'men are most industrious where they are most free' (*Discourse of Trade*: pp. 27–8).

(and hence deliberately selective) exposition of his thought. Smith is a subtle thinker and it is a sad fact that much Smith scholarship, until quite recently, has paid scant heed to that subtlety. Nowhere has this been more apparent than in his treatment of liberty. Partly in an attempt to do justice to Smith's own thought, but mainly because it fits the overall design of this work, I shall conduct my interpretation in the light of pre-modern views of liberty.

There are two such 'classical' views of relevance. There is the pre-eminently Stoic view, found in Seneca or Epictetus for example, where liberty is a state of tranquillity, where bodily desires are firmly controlled by force of decision or the rational will. There is also the 'civic' view, found in Cicero or Livy for example, where liberty consists of activity in the political world, where individuals act purposively and directly to realise both their own and the common good. The two views are, of course, related and, as we explored in Chapter 3, nowhere is this more evident than in their common stand against corruption as embodied in a life given over to luxury. In essence, Smith rejects the passivity enjoined by the former view, but also the purposive political character of the activity advocated by the latter (it is this latter view upon which we shall concentrate).

Looking through Smith's eyes we can see that the key to the modern world is that it is a world of commerce. It is a world where everyman 'becomes in some measure a merchant' (*Wealth of Nations* (hereafter *WN*): p. 37). A society wherein this was true would, for classical thinkers from Plato onward, be corrupt. For Smith, on the contrary, this universality harmonises with a basic trait of human nature; it is a natural 'propensity to truck, barter and exchange one thing for another' (*WN*: p. 25). As befits a natural trait, this is co-eval with human society but it is only in a commercial society that it attains full expression. A commercial society is thus a 'natural' society (whence Marx's charge that Smith was hypostatising bourgeois relationships).

That this is at odds with the classical conception of 'nature' is readily apparent. Smith assesses 'desire' positively. He remarks that the 'desire of bettering our condition [is] a desire . . . which comes with us from the womb and never leaves us till we go into the grave.' Nor is this a mere background condition for, in accord with modern psychology, he also declares 'there is scarce perhaps a single instant in which any man is so perfectly and completely satisfied with his situation as to be without any wish of alteration or improvement of any kind.' The positive consequence is that this restless desire creates opulence because 'an augmentation of fortune is the means by which the greater part of men propose and wish to better their condition' (*WN*: p. 341). Moreover, the very grounding of this restlessness in the facts of human nature means that it is the Stoic ideal of 'tranquillity' that is 'unnatural'; it teaches a perfection 'beyond the reach of human nature' (*Theory of Moral Sentiments* (hereafter *TMS*): p. 60, cf. p. 292).

The Stoic perspective, and the teleological view more generally, understood 'nature' normatively. It was not that men could not adopt a commercial life but that such a life was unworthy. Hence, from this perspective, to associate positively opulence, or luxury, with freedom was to yoke together two mutually incompatible 'forces' – selfishness and the public good. But in Smith's eyes, this 'selfishness', properly understood, is everyone's natural desire to better his or her condition. Relatedly, and here is the nub of his rejection of the civic view of virtue, the arena for this activity is not the public or civic life, with its goals of honour and glory, but the private, self-interested 'economic' life. Meeting household (*oikos*) needs or procuring the basic wherewithal for life that, as Cicero had observed, was the inferior, sub-human/masculine, concern of animals and slaves, has become, in Smith, the natural business of humanity.

Where everyman lives by exchanging, there is a network of interdependence: in a 'civilized and thriving country' (a description that is a significant synonym for a commercial society) even the 'very meanest person' could not be provided with even his woollen coat without the 'joint labour of a great multitude of workmen' (*WN*: pp. 22–3). This identification of interdependence as the heart of a commercial society is significant for two general reasons. To appreciate the first of these it is necessary to heed the heavy conceptual load that the notion of 'dependency' carried.

CIVIC HUMANISM

Smith states that the dependence of one individual on another is corrupting (*LJ*: p. 333). That statement is impeccably classical in its associations. Indeed it is central to that tradition of thought we have learnt to call civic humanism (or 'classical republicanism'). The civic humanists linked together the ideas of freedom and independence. This linkage was sustained by an ultimately Aristotelian conception of virtue whereby the human (male) personality was only fulfilled in political participation, in the practice of citizenship. The hallmark of this practice and virtue was free activity; as Aristotle said, the polis was a community of free men (*koinónia tôn eleutherôn*) (*Pol.*: 1279a). This virtue rested upon a civic or political equality that stemmed from proprietorship of a household. Ownership of real property gave independence, and its function was to permit the taking on of public tasks such as defence (warfare). To use one's property to accumulate private profit or to indulge in personal luxury was to be corrupt.

This 'model' of political liberty proved enduring. As outlined by J.G.A. Pocock (1975) – the writer who has done most to bring out the presence of this tradition – the model was re-formulated by Machiavelli and other Florentines whence it was transported into seventeenth-century English republican thought by James Harrington and his associates. By the eighteenth century, the chief source of corruption and threat to virtue was thought to lie in the growth of credit and commerce (recall Davenant and the quotation from Bolingbroke in Chapter 5, pp. 120–1). The crucial assumption was that, without the presence of a stable foundation for virtuous activity, society, shorn of the bearings needed to direct it to the public good, would be cast adrift on the sea of contingency that an economy based on commerce and credit represents.

If we now return to Smith's statement, we discover that far from echoing this line of argument he is repudiating it. Immediately after having proclaimed the link between dependence and corruption, Smith remarks that 'commerce is one great preventive' of its occurrence. Commerce is not a disease but a core functional ingredient in the maintenance of a healthy constitution. What underpins Smith's very different understanding is his account of the history of social development. For the civic humanists, including their contemporary exponents like Rousseau or John Brown, history represented the growth of corruption; it was a story of degeneration. For Smith, on the contrary, history is a story of progress.

THE FOUR STAGES

Smith's progressive account is expressed in the so-called 'four-stages' theory. I shall not expound this theory in any detail (I shall address it again in the next chapter) but shall highlight certain crucial episodes.

According to this theory, the 'lowest and rudest state of society' – Hume's 'savage' age – is the age of hunters (*WN*: p. 689). The rudeness of that age is marked by its poverty and that, in turn, means 'there is scarce any property' and little or no inequality, subordination or dependency (*WN*: p. 709). By contrast, in the second age (*LJ*: p. 14) – that of shepherds – there is great inequality associated with a vast disparity in property and great subordination and dependency. The Tartar chief maintains a thousand men to whom he is 'necessarily both their general and their judge, and his chieftainship is the necessary effect of the superiority of his fortune' (*WN*: p. 712). A similar picture is painted of the third age – the age of husbandmen or farmers. Just as the Tartar chief was such by virtue of his being the greatest shepherd, so the leaders in the third age are the greatest landlords (*WN*: p. 717).

We can interpose at this point to indicate the depth of Smith's subversion of the assumptions of civic humanism. Most obviously, Smith differs by correlating the presence of property (especially in its landed form) with dependency, and its absence with independence. But this is not a radical difference because the civic humanists, such as Machiavelli and his heirs, were opposed to property being concentrated in the hands of a prince or of the *grandi*. However, Smith's disagreement is more profound since his argument cuts deeper. What he severs, by means of his account of the 'natural progress of opulence' (society's development from barbarism to civilisation), is the distinctive humanist linkage between politics, property and dependency. The (political) equality presumed by the civic humanists was based on property held by citizens, but this, in practice, presupposed widespread (social) inequality between citizens and non-citizens. What Smith's historical argument, associating social equality with the absence of property and political inequality with its presence, has served to do is to isolate the particular political emphasis in civic humanism. As we will see later, this argument enables him to displace the connexion these humanists made between liberty and the *vivere civile* or active political life.

To return to the four stages: the fourth, or commercial, age marks a decisive change but one which, unlike the earlier transitions, stems not from population pressure but directly from the natural human propensity to truck, barter and exchange being allowed to establish a network of interdependency. This brings us to the second general point of significance that lies in the centrality with which Smith endows interdependence. Whereas Rousseau sees in the commercial age only a deepening corruption, Smith sees a superior form of freedom – that of liberty under law, the hallmark of civilisation.[15] The explanation of this superiority lies precisely in the social conditions and model of human relationships that Rousseau abhors, namely, luxury and loss of independence. This is because the conditions that make luxury possible also, in a mutually complementary fashion, make possible this superior form of freedom.

How, according to Smith, does this conjunction of opulence and freedom, luxury and civilisation, occur? Again he provides a historical account. It is this account which, he explicitly observes, is also to be found in Hume's *Essays* (and which Hume himself had reiterated in his *History*: iii, 99; cf. ii, 602). The focus of this account is the collapse of the age of farmers, in the guise of feudal lords.

A great proprietor uses his surplus in the same way as the Tartar chief had done, namely, to maintain a multitude of retainers and dependants whose only means of reciprocation is obedience (*WN*: p. 413). However, this employment of the surplus is explained by the absence of any other outlet, in particular any outlet that would permit the proprietor to expend the surplus on personal consumption. Once the opportunity for such consumption arose it was seized upon. This opportunity was provided by 'the silent and insensible operation of foreign commerce'. In a celebrated passage Smith outlines the effect of this commerce:

For a pair of diamond buckles perhaps, or for something as frivolous and useless, they [the great proprietors] exchanged the maintenance, or what is the same thing, the price of the maintenance of a thousand men for a year, and with it the whole weight and authority which it could give them. The buckles, however, were to be all their own and no other human creature was to have any share of them; whereas in the more antient method of expence they must have shared with at least a thousand people . . . and thus for the gratification of the most childish, the meanest and the most sordid of all vanities, they gradually bartered their whole power and authority. (*WN*: pp. 418–19)

The presence of these buckles ('trinkets and baubles' (*WN*: p. 712) or 'domestic luxury' (*LJ*: pp. 227, 416, 420)) in the feudal era results ultimately in the members of a commercial society being free of the thrall of personal dependency (*WN*: pp. 419–20). Once the tenants

---

[15] Smith reviewed the 'Second Discourse' for the short-lived Edinburgh Review of 1755–6 (see *Essays on Philosophical Subjects*: pp. 250–4) where he interpreted Rousseau as replying to Mandeville.

had attained their independence, then the proprietors 'were no longer capable of interrupting the regular execution of justice'. As we shall see, it is such regularity that characterises a society wherein every man is a merchant, and hence also characterises modern liberty.

It is noteworthy that in this process of social change, which Smith calls a 'revolution of the greatest importance to the publick happiness', luxury plays a positive role. (Hume too had given such a role to luxury (*History*: II, 53–4).) While this is in marked contrast to the classical accounts, where luxury is always a sign of degeneration, the way it plays its role is also significant. This process of social change cannot be put down to any deliberative individualistic explanation. Neither proprietors nor merchants had 'the least intention to serve the publick' and neither had 'knowledge or foresight of that great revolution' (*WN*: p. 422). The public happiness, the general good, was not brought about by a deliberate intention to achieve that end. This, for Smith, is a general truth about social life. Moreover, it is a truth that belies the civic humanists' conjoined emphasis on the primacy of the political and the necessity of individual virtue. I will return to this point.

As a consequence of this series of events, individuals in a commercial society enjoy a liberty from dependence on particular masters. They enjoy independence but, and this is what distinguishes commercial society, this independence is achieved through an interlocking social system (the market) so that these individuals (merchants) are truly interdependent. We now need to examine more closely the liberty that, on Smith's understanding, comports with a commercial society. There are two related dimensions to this liberty, which conventionally we can term the private and the public or political.

PRIVATE LIBERTY

We can approach the first dimension by means of the link Smith makes between opulence and freedom. The degree to which the propensity to exchange expresses itself depends on the size of the market: the bigger the market for goods the greater the specialisation, and the greater the specialisation the higher the productivity. Hence, in the famous example of pin manufacture, through the division of labour ten individuals could make 48,000 pins a day – equivalent to 4,800 each – whereas each working on his own could not have produced twenty a day.

What this means in a developed market society is the presence of a 'universal opulence which extends itself to the lowest ranks of the people' (*WN*: p. 22). By contrast, those who best embody Rousseauan independence are 'miserably poor'. Nor should we look for any redemptive or ennobling qualities in this poverty. These same people, Smith observes, frequently resort to the policy of 'directly destroying, and sometimes of abandoning their infants, their old people, and those afflicted with lingering diseases, to perish with hunger, be devoured by wild beasts' (*WN*: p. 10). It is, in this context, worth recalling that Smith calls 'opulence' a *'blessing'*. Only in a developed market society is material happiness enjoyed, for example, the 'common day labourer in Britain has more luxury in his way of living than an Indian sovereign' (*LJ*: p. 429) and his accommodation 'exceeds that of many an African king, the absolute master of the lives and liberties of 10,000 naked savages' (*WN*: p. 24).

Here Smith is unequivocally contrasting poverty and luxury. The Stoics, however, as we saw in Chapter 3, distinguished between poverty and frugality and associated the former with luxury, in as much as both embodied unruly desires. The 'classic' virtue of frugality (and its Christian equivalent) manifested the 'natural life'. For Smith, 'frugality' is the virtue of 'saving' and the source of 'stock' (capital investment). Indeed in this same paragraph Smith links frugality with industry in the person of a 'peasant' who, nonetheless, as part of a 'civilized and thriving' nation enjoys a better material standard of living than any savage. It is true that the abodes of the lowest rank in commercial society are far inferior to those of the rich but, though there is this inequality, there is also there present the second great human blessing of liberty.

Since in a commercial society individuals are not tied into relationships of dependence, they are, for example, able to change trades as often as they please (*WN*: p. 23). As an illustration Smith cites the practice (the 'police') of Indostan and ancient Egypt in forcing a son to follow his father's occupation; a practice he judges 'violent' (*WN*: p. 80)). Smith is, moreover, explicit that it is the presence of a choice of occupation, together with the ability to have one's children inherit and dispose of one's effects by testament, that makes individuals 'free in our present sense of the word Freedom' and its absence is the principal attribute of 'villanage and slavery' (*WN*: p. 400).

The roots of this modern liberty of choice lie, as we have seen, deep in human nature. However, to enable that natural desire to better their condition, to generate opulence efficiently, individuals should enjoy the private liberty to decide for themselves how to deploy their resources (*WN*: p. 454). This is the 'obvious and simple, system of natural liberty' where every man 'is left perfectly free to pursue his own interest his own way' (*WN*: p. 687).

This emphasis upon private liberty and the corresponding attention paid to economic activity does not leave the political world unaffected. We now turn, therefore, to the second – the public or political – dimension of the liberty enjoyed in commercial society. It is worth adding the point that Smith's stress on the universality and ubiquity of this desire 'to augment fortune' means that the pursuit of 'luxury goods' is not something confined, as was implied in the accounts of Barbon and Mandeville, to the behaviour of the rich. The motivation of the feudal lord to have a diamond buckle is perfectly generalisable and comes to fruition (or potentially so) in a commercial society.

POLITICAL LIBERTY

For Smith, as we observed in Chapter 5, it is the 'highest impertinence and presumption' of kings and ministers 'to watch over the economy of private people' by such measures as sumptuary laws (*WN*: p. 346, cf. p. 630). Hence, the opulence that comes from the interdependence of individuals pursuing their private economic liberty rests upon the confidence provided by the impersonal rule-governed system of public liberty, and not on a system that enjoins and relies upon virtue – direct, personal political will.

We need to enquire further as to why Smith thinks this modern rule-governed political liberty is superior to that activist political liberty advocated by Aristotle and his heirs. In shorthand terms, Smith is able to uphold the superiority of the modern understanding of liberty by restricting its requirements while extending its application. Smith's political liberty under law is a liberty to be enjoyed by all, but, as he points out, like Hume had done in the case of Sparta, the Aristotelian political liberty was only enjoyed by a few and was only sustainable by the enslavement of a sizable proportion of the population (*LJ*: p. 226). Slavery is not only morally objectionable (as Rousseau – though not all civic humanists – would agree)[16] but also

---

[16] Even a comparatively late exponent like Andrew Fletcher of Saltoun advocated as part of his package of economic reforms that estates should directly employ vagabonds, who, if in local excess, should be sold to other estates where there was a lack (see his *Second Discourse on the affairs of Scotland* [1698] ed. Daiches). While Fletcher denies that he was thereby advocating slavery, he makes clear that this was the policy of the 'ancients'. Pocock (1975: pp. 427–32) included Fletcher in his civic humanist camp and Fletcher's importance to the Scottish Enlightenment has been maintained by G. E. Davie (1981) and N. Phillipson (1981: pp. 19–40).

economically unproductive (*WN*: pp. 387, 684). Contrary to Mandeville, for Smith wealth is increased by the 'liberal reward of labour', since where wages are high there 'we shall always find the workmen more active, diligent and expeditious' (*WN*: p. 99). Given further that 'servants, labourers and workmen' (*WN*: p. 96) constitute the bulk of a society's population, then what improves their lot makes for a happy and flourishing society.

Smith's rejection of slavery constitutes his extension of liberty, and his theory of justice constitutes his restriction of its scope. While Smith is critical of Hume for reducing justice entirely to utility, the role and prominence of justice in his theory closely followed Hume. For Smith, what is necessary for social existence is not the positive virtue of beneficence, since a company of merchants can subsist without it (*TMS*: p. 86), but the negative virtue of justice. This is because society cannot subsist at all amongst individuals who are ready to injure each other, that is, where injustice is prevalent. Justice, therefore, is 'the main pillar that upholds the whole edifice. If it is removed, the great, the immense fabric of human society . . . must in a moment crumble into atoms' (*TMS*: p. 86; cf. Hume, *Treatise*: p. 497). Justice is negative because it requires abstention from injuring others so that indeed 'we may often fulfil all the rules of justice by sitting still and doing nothing' (*TMS*: p. 82).

It does not follow from the practical priority that he assigns to justice that Smith denies the virtuousness of benevolence. While society can subsist without benevolence, such a society would indeed be as a consequence 'less happy and agreeable' (*TMS*: p. 86). Moreover, it is clear, in the *Moral Sentiments*, that he thinks 'bare observance' of rules without more positive acts of virtue is to lack certain feelings of humanity (*TMS*: p. 82). But justice and benevolence are not inversely related; one who acts justly will also exhibit great humanity and benevolence (*TMS*: p. 218), as well as being the recipient of esteem.

Nevertheless, in the context of his theory of political liberty, Smith's negative account of justice is contrary to both Rousseau and Aristotle, who stressed active participation, since, for Smith, it is possible to fulfil our public/political duties passively. In our conduct with others it is sufficient to follow rules in order to practise the virtue of justice and enjoy thereby freedom under the law. And, provided that society is peaceable (itself a characteristic of the humanising or softening attributes of commerce), support of the established government is the 'best expedient' to promote the interests of our fellows and to be, thereby, a 'good citizen' (*TMS*: p. 231). Furthermore, by making few demands in this way, freedom and the just life can be in the reach of all and need not be reserved to those with the resources necessary to underpin an active political life. This is Smith's above-mentioned severance of the civic humanists' linkage between property, politics and independence. In summary terms, Smith believes that a society based on a system of rules is superior to one that embodies the 'republican' practice of political virtue.[17]

Since for Smith civilised societies enjoy liberty under law, he does not share the qualms of even a moderate civic humanist like Adam Ferguson that rule-following will be detrimental to the civic spirit. In his *Essay on the History of Civil Society* [1767] Ferguson argued that liberty was never in greater danger than when national felicity is measured by 'mere tranquillity which may attend an equitable administration' (p. 270). A government that bestows tranquillity and interrupts commerce minimally is 'more akin to despotism than we are apt to imagine' (p. 269). The reason for this is that when the emphasis is placed upon the provision of security, no effort is required from the individual citizen (pp. 191, 223). The result is that improvements of civil society (whose reality Ferguson is not concerned to deny) 'lay the political spirit to rest' and 'chain up the active virtues' (p. 221). Hence while the 'modern' constitution embodies important freedoms 'its members become unworthy of the freedom they possess' (ibid.). For Ferguson, civil liberty can rest on no other foundation than the 'right of the individual to act in his station for himself and the public' (p. 167). Although Ferguson does here, and elsewhere, talk of rights (to property, for example (p. 186)) and is clear that the Spartan model is inappropriate (cf. p. 161), the 'rights' in question are 'rights of the mind' which can only be sustained by individual political action.

INVISIBLE HAND

Smith is sceptical of this reliance upon civic spirit, resting as it does on an unjustified and overblown conception of the human will. As the collapse of feudalism testified, the public good (Rousseau's 'general will') does not depend upon being willed as such. Rather, the public

---

[17] MacIntyre (1985: p. 236) says Smith was a life-long republican. His unacknowledged source for this would appear to be J. Rae's *Life of Smith* (1965: p. 174). Rae himself quotes Smith's pupil, the Earl of Buchan, as evidence. For wise words on the limited weight that such 'republicanism' can bear see D. Forbes (1975b).

good will be promoted through (in Rousseau's terms) particular wills. This, of course, is the force of Smith's evocation of the 'invisible hand' – the individual 'intends only his own gain' but society does not suffer because, through pursuit of his own interest, he 'frequently promotes that of the society more effectually than when he really intends to promote it'. Indeed Smith goes on the offensive – 'I have never known much good done by those who affected to trade for the publick good' (*WN*: p. 456). Politicians, who exercise their will in directing others, are, in fact, a threat to the liberty enshrined in the rule of law. They will pursue policies that will affect their citizens differentially – as in the prohibition of wool exportation to promote manufactures – and which will, as such, be 'evidently contrary to the justice and equality of treatment which the sovereign owes to the different orders of his subjects' (*WN*: p. 654). In Smith's view, political will should confine itself to external defence, the maintenance of justice internally through 'regular administration', and the provision of 'certain publick works' (*WN*: pp. 687–8). The complexity and systematic interdependence of commercial society makes redundant (even delusory) the approach of the civic humanists, who generally believe that the common good can only be achieved through the direct, purposively willed actions of politically motivated individuals.

There is a broader more general point here. Though Smith's 'invisible hand' is generally read as an *economic* dictum, that is to construe it too narrowly. We have seen that it was in the late seventeenth century, in writings concerned with trade, and as illustrated by Barbon, that the traditional vocabulary and context of luxury became de-moralised. What we can now discern in Smith (and Hume) is a de-politicisation of the idea of the 'public good' that luxury had been presumed to corrupt. The public good loses its supra-individual character, as manifested in Pericles' Oration, where private citizens (*idiotas*) are declared to benefit more when the polis as a whole is successful than when they prosper as individuals, though the community itself is ruined (Thucydides, *History*: ii, 60). Once individual happiness, or material well-being, is placed centre-stage, then the identification of the 'good' as something other than that 'happiness' loses its previous salience. Since material well-being is the product of commerce, then the only defensible idea of a public good must be one that underpins rather than undermines that activity.

We can reinforce this point by recalling the earlier discussion of sumptuary laws. Whether part of the aristocratic (marking social hierarchy) or republican (upholding the public over private good) tradition, these laws expressed the belief that it was necessary to control 'desire'. Erasmus, for example, in his *Institutio Principis Christiani* [1516], advocated sumptuary laws because he believed it preferable to restrict the free disposition of property by individuals than to allow luxury to undermine *mores civium* (p. 266, tr. p. 194). From Smith's perspective, on the contrary, because the effectiveness of commerce in producing widespread opulence (the consumption of 'luxury' goods) reposes on private liberty, it is plainly inefficacious to replace that with some political *qua* supra-individual conception of liberty or civic norms. Not only is a politically motivated personality (one possessed of Ferguson's 'rights of the mind') inappropriate, it is injurious to this 'new' idea of public good.

The source of the injury lies in the general phenomenon of 'unintended consequences', of which the 'invisible hand' is merely one manifestation. Once the essential interdependence of social relationships is grasped, it renders inadequate any conception of society that relies on individual acts of will having a predictably decisive effect. And since a commercial society is one precisely characterised by that interdependence then in those circumstances the actions of an individual ramify out of control. Given that individual actions have unintended consequences, then the area of individual moral responsibility is also correspondingly curtailed. This now opens up further the 'space' within which luxury can be de-moralised.

Because of this dissonance between individual responsibility and social effects, Smith is able to maintain simultaneously that the consequences of luxury are beneficial while treating the cause itself contemptuously – the diamond buckles were 'sordid and childish vanities'. (As John Burrow (1988: p. 50) observes, this dissonance is obviously reminiscent of Mandeville's 'paradox'.) Though many commentators detect Stoic sympathies here, the dissonance that lies at the heart of this position effectively counts against giving this idiom great weight. This conclusion can even be sustained in the face of a passage in the *Moral Sentiments* that possesses seemingly impeccable Stoic credentials. In this passage Smith contrasts the 'real happiness of human life' that is to be found in 'ease of body and peace of mind' (as enjoyed by the beggar) with the deceptive 'pleasures of wealth and greatness' (as enjoyed by lordly masters and kings) aroused by the imagination (*TMS*: pp. 183–5).

If, however, we pursue the reference here to 'imagination' we can not only appreciate that Smith's argument exploits rather than endorses the Stoic perspective, but also connect it with Barbon's de-moralisation of luxury. The first and most obvious remark is that Smith here is placing the role of imagination within an economic context.[18] The role played is that of deception or delusion (cf. *TMS*: p. 51). From its 'modern' origins in Hobbes, imagination had been closely associated with fictiveness. Since for Hobbes imagination is 'nothing but decaying sense', then the mental conception of (say) a centaur is a compound of the sight of a man and of a horse, and such a 'compound imagination' is 'properly but a Fiction of the mind'. (*Leviathan*: 2 p. 16). The imagination is, however, a powerful motivator and Smith follows, in broad terms, Hobbes's account of human motivation. It is because 'the *pleasures* [my emphasis] of wealth and greatness . . . strike the imagination as something grand and beautiful and noble' that men embark upon 'toil' and the 'continual motion of the industry'. It is this industry which is responsible for all 'the sciences and arts which ennoble and embellish human life' (*TMS*: p. 183).

But as his references to ennoblement and embellishment indicate, this is not a matter for regret.[19] If mankind had attended to what makes for 'real happiness' then they would be bereft of 'all the sciences and arts'. In a similar vein he later remarked that manufactures and commerce are 'real improvements' that have 'ennobled' human nature (*TMS*: p. 229). Hence Smith, while not denying that there is indeed a distinction between the real and the imagined, points to the latter to account for the transformation of 'rude forests' into 'agreeable and fertile plains'. This now enables him to argue that those, like the Stoics, who wish to confine human endeavours to real satisfactions are, in practice (in 'reality'), advocating a miserable impoverishment

---

[18] It is also worth noting that this same passage contains Smith's reference in *TMS* to 'an invisible hand'. In outline, the argument is the same as in the later *WN*. The rich, in gratification of their 'own vain and insatiable desires' (Smith even refers to 'baubles and trinkets' as the object of these desires), are 'without intending it, without knowing it' led by the invisible hand to 'advance the interest of the society' by giving employment to thousands. It is 'luxury and caprice' not the moral motivations of 'humanity or justice' that have produced this advance.

[19] A good case can be made that Smith has Rousseau explicitly in mind in this whole passage (cf. Ignatieff (1984) and the editors of *TMS* (Macfie & Raphael)). In his review of the *Second Discourse*, Smith quoted the passage where Rousseau declares that once co-operative labour and property are introduced then (in Smith's translation *Essays*: p. 252) 'the vast forests of nature were changed into agreeable plains'. For a more developed account see Berry (1989b).

of mankind. We have already linked this last point with a critique of
Rousseau and it is germane to add that Rousseau himself remarked in
the *Discours de l'Inégalité* (p. 62) that, unlike among 'us', in *sauvages* the
imagination was inoperative and, moreover, that once their needs are
satisfied they lose desire. Finally we can also add (interpretatively)
that the 'beggar' in modern society is qualitatively better off because,
in principle, he now enjoys freedom under the law (cf. *TMS*: p. 223).

What lies within Smith's account is the realisation that goods are
produced and consumed not because they meet some fixed 'needs' but
because they are what Barbon had called 'wants of the mind' and
serve our vanity, which 'is always founded upon the belief of our being
the object of attention and approbation' (*TMS*: p. 50). He had made
the point unambiguously in his lectures,

The whole industry of human life is employed not in procuring the supply of
our three humble necessities, food, cloaths, and lodging, but in procuring the
conveniences of it according to the nicety and delicacy of our taste. (*LJ*: p. 488)

I shall seek to bring out the full import of that passage in the next
chapter.

MODERN MORALITY

In the original Aristotelian formulation 'politics' was a matter of
'ethics', and 'economics' was put firmly in its proper subordinate
place. To shift that 'place' means also shifting the primacy of political
ethics (cf. Teichgraeber, 1986: p. 10). Moreover, since man naturally
is a *zôon politikon* (or possessed what was called above a 'politically
motivated personality'), this same shift will also dislodge that
understanding of 'human nature'. Once the primacy of the virtue of
political actors – their purposive deliberations on the 'public thing'
and 'heroic' actions on the public stage – is displaced, it opens the
way, as part and parcel of the re-assessment of human nature, for
another conceptualisation of morality. As politics enters into what we
now call its liberal mode, namely, the formulation of general rules to
provide the (neutral) framework for private (economic) activity, so
morality, too, becomes a private question of choice, and the nature of
humans is revealed in the material motivations underlying these
choices. In Alasdair MacIntyre's (1985: ch. 3) terms, what comes
'after virtue' is the morality of the role-less individual, culminating
(absurdly so for MacIntyre) in emotivism.

It would take this discussion too far afield if MacIntyre's argument was subjected to a thorough analysis, but for two reasons something needs to be said. Firstly, because in Part IV we shall be considering the morality of private choice or desire and, secondly, because MacIntyre's account is misleading if it is taken to imply that Smith's 'new morality' is radically individualistic.

We have seen that central to the superiority of the modern world is the belief that the just life is in the reach of all. What sustains this view is Smith's sociological account of morality. Quite simply, for Smith, morality is a matter of social interaction. A significant instance of this is when, at the conclusion of his explicit discussion of virtue in the *Moral Sentiments*, he remarks that 'respect for . . . the *sentiments of other people* is the *sole* principle which, upon most occasions, overawes all those mutinous and turbulent passions' (*TMS*: p. 263: my emphasis). The sage, in his independence from all worldly and personal attachments, would be incapable of a life of Smithian virtue; he would lack the 'mirror' of society in which to see the 'beauty or deformity of his own mind' (*TMS*: p. 110).

Smith's social morality is intrinsic to his conception of commercial society, and its superiority. For him to be so confident about the rectitude of commercial society means that he must also be confident that general rules will be adhered to in a society where everyman is a merchant. Smith's confidence rests on a new assessment of individual relationships. In a civilised (market) society the individual 'stands at all times in need of the cooperation and assistance of great multitudes, while his whole life is scarce sufficient to gain the friendship of a few persons' (*WN*: p. 26). This means that the individual in a market society deals preponderantly with other individuals who are strangers to him. In that circumstance they must, as Rousseau had lamented, appeal to advantage. Hence it is that,

It is not from the benevolence of the butcher, the brewer, or the baker, that we expect our dinner, but from their regard to their own interest. We address ourselves, not to their humanity but to their self-love, and never talk to them of our own necessities but of their advantages. Nobody but a beggar chuses to depend chiefly upon the benevolence of his fellow-citizens. (*WN*: pp. 26–7)

But Smith's account of morality is devoted to showing how social interaction humbles the arrogance of self-love (*TMS*: p. 83). The lynchpin of this account is Smith's analysis of the principle of sympathy. Sympathy, in Smith's technical sense, is the human faculty of compassion or fellow-feeling. By use of imagination one individual sympathises with another and feels what the other feels (or should feel) (*TMS*: p. 10). Because there always remains an inevitable shortfall between the two, since no compassion can ever match up exactly with the original, then one consequence is that the bereaved (to use one of Smith's examples) learns to lower the pitch of his grief so that spectators can the more easily sympathise.

It is important that this is a learning exercise. Individuals (unlike sages) learn from experience of life what is proper. Morality thus becomes a matter of socialisation, of 'insensible habit and experience' (*TMS*: p. 135). The effects of social intercourse teach the individual what behaviour is acceptable and, in due course, the individual internalises these social judgments as conscience by viewing his or her actions and motives as an 'impartial well-informed spectator' would (*TMS*: p. 130). Through the dynamics of this social interaction there will be a degree of concord sufficient for 'the harmony of society' (*TMS*: p. 22).

On Smith's account (though this is implicit rather than explicit), the circumstances of commercial society are well suited to maintain social concord. It is this fit, so to speak, that explains Smith's confidence that the general, and thus impersonal, rules of justice will be adhered to in a society where everyman is a merchant – that is, as we have seen, where the bulk of relationships take place on a non-personal footing between strangers. On Smith's account of the dynamics of sympathy, an agent can expect less sympathy from a stranger than from a friend. The effect of this is to make the agent moderate his emotions to a greater extent, so that more tranquillity is called forth in the presence of strangers than in that of friends (*TMS*: p. 23). In the light of the Stoical view, it is possible to interpret Smith as associating the ideal of tranquillity with the modern world of commercial interdependence and not with the miserably impoverished world of self-sufficiency.

Furthermore, this socially-induced ability on the part of the agent to tone down his emotions is the source for Smith of that central Stoic virtue of self-command, the virtue from which, Smith allows, 'all the other virtues seem to derive their principal lustre' (*TMS*: p. 241). Because of this, MacIntyre (1985: p. 234) claims that Smith is to be accounted a Stoic. But this doesn't amount to much. The thrust of Smith's analysis – as MacIntyre himself perhaps concedes when he notes Smith's link between virtuousness and rule-following – is to undermine, in ways we have already addressed, both the philosophical and civic assumptions of the Stoics. A commercial society of strangers has the effect of strengthening the character by making habitual the need to moderate one's emotions (cf. *TMS*: p. 147). In this way it is a stranger rather than a friend who is more like the impartial spectator (cf. *TMS*: pp. 153–4). It is this spectator who corrects 'the natural misrepresentations of self-love' and who 'shows us the propriety of generosity and the deformity of injustice' (*TMS*: p. 137). Moreover, commercial society need not go to the extremes of 'savages and barbarians' where self-denial is cultivated at the cost of humanity (*TMS*: p. 205). Indeed, when self-denial expresses itself in suffering torture without any complaint whatsoever, then the whole merit of self-command is taken away (*TMS*: p. 245).

There is thus a wide difference between the degrees of self-command required in a 'civilized' and in 'barbarous nations'. The latter – as the case of the passive victim of torture exemplifies – 'necessarily acquire the habits of falsehood and dissimulation', and when they give way to anger their vengeance is 'always sanguinary and dreadful' (*TMS*: p. 208). The former, by contrast, become 'frank, open and sincere'. It is in the world of commerce that honesty is the norm. This point is made explicitly in the *Lectures*, 'when the greater part of the people are merchants they always bring probity and punctuality into fashion, and these therefore are the principal virtues of a commercial nation' (*LJ*: p. 539). The very interdependence of that world contributes to the maintenance of these virtues, because there is a preponderance of men 'in the middling and inferior stations of life,' none of whom can ever be great enough to be above the law but are, rather, overawed into respect for 'the more important rules of justice' (*TMS*: p. 63). (Hume had made exactly the same point in his essay 'Refinement in the Arts' (p. 277).)

VIRTUE AND COMMERCE

Despite Smith's commitment to the superiority of commercial society he is not blind to its drawbacks. There are two aspects of these drawbacks that deserve a brief discussion. The first concerns the effects of the division of labour. Although specialisation enhances dexterity this is achieved at the expense of the 'intellectual, social and martial virtues' of the great body of the people (*WN*: p. 782). In the light of the classical view of virtue it is noteworthy that Smith lays some stress here on the enervation of 'martial virtue' and the deleterious consequences of cowardice. These consequences affect both the individual and his society. Regarding the former, cowardice necessarily involves 'mental mutilation, deformity and wretchedness', while regarding the latter the 'security of every society depends, more or less' upon the martial virtues (*WN*: p. 787). These sentiments are also to be found in the earlier *Lectures* where Smith even links commerce's enervation of the 'martial spirit' with the effeminacy of men who are 'constantly employed on the arts of luxury' (*LJ*: p. 540). Albert Hirschman (1977: p. 106) quotes this last remark and declares that Smith is 'totally espousing the classical "republican" view'. Though these remarks do indeed indicate Smith's appreciation of the classical conception of virtue he is not to be placed in the camp of the civic humanists.

In the *Lectures* Smith is cataloguing objections to commerce rather than necessarily endorsing them. At best it is a recognition of the drawbacks; in no way is it tantamount to an argument urging a retrenchment and return to some pre-commercial era. The context is similarly crucial in the *Wealth of Nations*. His concern is that modern militias are an ineffective means of sustaining the 'martial spirit'. Smith has already demonstrated that the division of labour in modern societies, together with advances in military technology, have made professional standing armies, and *not* the citizen militias favoured by the civic humanists, the superior force (*WN*: p. 700). He even argues that so long as the civil and military authorities are complementary then, contrary to 'men of republican principles,' a standing army is favourable, not dangerous, to liberty (*WN*: pp. 706–7). The admitted advantage of martial virtue is that it would enhance that process and also help to reduce the size (and hence implicitly the cost) of a professional army (*WN*: p. 787). Smith does allow that commercial society threatens this advantage and that, in consequence, some governmental action should seek to offset it as part of its general educational responsibilities (one of its public works). And it is to that end that he cites the example of the Greeks and Romans, with their compulsory military exercises and provision of prizes for those who excel.

When all allowances have been made, what remains decisive is the superiority of 'opulent and civilized' over 'poor and barbarous' nations (*WN*: p. 708). The *historical* fact of artillery is crucial. This bears directly on the general shift in the catalogue of virtues that we remarked upon earlier in the discussion of Hume, whereby courage and those associated with martial pursuits are demoted relative to industry and other 'gentler' ones. And, of course, such a shift is symptomatic of a profound re-orientation of human values, which itself is indicative of a change in self-understanding or conception of human character and personality. To regard oneself as 'civilised' meant not that one's emotional life should be sternly controlled in the manner of Brutus judging his sons, but that it was capable of peaceable expression. To be a 'man of feeling' and undertake a 'sentimental journey' was not to lose one's *manhood* but to bear witness to one's *humanity* (cf. Taylor, 1989: pp. 283–4). Similarly, since self-understanding is attained in a mutually reciprocal fashion through an understanding of one's own society, then one could be, without self-contradiction, a 'man' and a merchant. It is 'natural', that is it is consonant with human nature, to seek enjoyment in private pursuits – to aspire to a life of luxury.

The second aspect worthy of attention is that one consequence of specialisation is to confine some individuals to 'performing a few simple operations', the very simplicity of which makes them incapable of 'conceiving any generous, noble or tender sentiments and consequently of forming any just judgment concerning many even of the ordinary duties of private life' (*WN*: p. 782). This is serious, given the importance that Smith attaches to private concerns. It is likely that the obligations of justice will suffer and that the pervasive 'torpor of the mind', and attendant ignorance, will enervate the self-command of these individuals and will fuel 'enthusiasm and superstition', a frequent source of 'dreadful disorders' (*WN*: p. 788).

Confronted with these consequences, while firmly accepting the desirability of their causes, Smith seeks to palliate their impact. He sees it, accordingly, as a further legitimate task of government in commercial society to finance the instruction of those 'in the lowest occupations' that they might acquire the 'most essential parts of education' ('read, write and account' together with some 'elementary parts of geometry and mechanicks') (*WN*: p. 785). The effect of such instruction, he believes, would be to instil self-respect and to promote thereby decency and order. This, in its turn, would further the stability of the entire society because that rests ultimately on confidence in general rules. What lies behind this advocacy of education is Smith's subscription to that most characteristic of all Enlightenment tenets – Voltaire's battle-cry *écrasez l'infâme*. Science, he declares in this definitive Enlightenment idiom, is 'the great antidote to the poison of enthusiasm and superstition'. Accordingly, Smith advocates the state making almost universal 'the study of science and philosophy' among the middling (and above) ranks. Since this would make these ranks immune then, thanks to their example, 'the inferior ranks' too would be little exposed to the poison (*WN*: p. 796).

Of course, in a thinker as subtle as Smith, his writings can be made to tell different stories. As the venerable 'Adam Smith Problem' on the relationship between the *Moral Sentiments* and the *Wealth of Nations* (abetted more recently by debate on the significance of the changes between the sixth and earlier editions of the *Moral Sentiments* (cf., e.g., Dickey, 1986)) indicates, this has been long recognised. More particularly, as we have seen, Smith does on occasion use the moralised language of 'luxury',[20] and there are elements in Smith that suggest a residual sympathy for some aspects of both civic humanism[21] and Stoicism.[22] Nevertheless his fundamental argument is that both these classical views, in effect, prevent mankind enjoying both of their greatest blessings – opulence and freedom. The modern world of commerce, even with its drawbacks, alone offers the prospect of those twin delights.

It is worth stressing the element of modernity here. The circumstances where human will might seem to have some moment – when there was room for heroes or Machiavellian princes suffused with *virtu* – no longer obtains. Yet it is just such times that the civic humanists presuppose in their critique of credit or commerce. To this critique Smith is able to rejoin that it is not only anachronistic, but also unsoundly (unscientifically) based on a view of a free society as the direct and deliberate outcome of human (perhaps even 'superhuman') will. To similar effect, Smith is able to rebut the Stoic view because it too suffers from an over-individualistic and an overdemanding (superhuman) understanding of liberty as an exercise of will. It too is profoundly anachronistic. Modern liberty, as found in Smith, thus

[20] Cf. 'Luxury in the fair sex, while it enflames perhaps the passion for enjoyment, seems always to weaken, and frequently to destroy altogether, the powers of generation' (*WN*: p. 97).
[21] In addition to Hirschman, J. Robertson (1983) argues that Smith adopts the conceptual framework of civic humanism even as he 'transforms' it. A similarly qualified version is put forward by McNally (1988). See also D. Winch (1978), but his essay (Winch, 1983) makes clear the limitations of viewing Smith in these terms.
[22] In addition to MacIntyre, others who argue that Smith subscribes to a good measure of Stoicism include most notably the editors of *TMS*. (See also N. Waszek, 1984; Dwyer, 1987.)

accords with a realistic account of human nature and, in that sense, it is less exclusive than the classical versions, which are, in comparison, elitist (and sexist).

V

LUXURY REDIVIVUS

We should not, however, fall into the trap of confusing Smith's subsequent dominance, which is itself not a straightforward story (but see Fontana, 1985; Collini et al., 1983), with contemporary triumph. The eighteenth-century debate does not end with Smith. The traditionalist, moralistic understanding of luxury still played an important role in both 'academic' and 'popular' literature. As testament to that fact I will cite very briefly some examples which, for added emphasis, I shall draw from Scotland.

The language of luxury and corruption was certainly used in the popular periodicals of later eighteenth-century Scotland. John Dwyer and Alexander Murdoch (1983) cite numerous passages from the *Mirror*, the *Lounger* and the *Caledonian Mercury* in support of that statement and I shall draw upon their article. Since the authors themselves are concerned to fit these passages into what they call 'the linguistic paradigm of civic humanism' (Dwyer & Murdoch, 1983: p. 242) it is not surprising that they select such passages for illustrative quotation. It matters not for our purposes whether this is an overly rigid interpretation, it is the presence of the vocabulary that serves my limited ends. Dwyer and Murdoch, influenced by Pocock (1975) and Phillipson (e.g. 1973; cf. Berry, 1986b), detect in these periodicals a defence of the landed interest and a corresponding distrust of monied men and the *nouveaux riches*. Such an editorial line accords with the inferential evidence that it was the gentry who constituted the bulk of the readership, whose numbers the authors declare to be 'not unimpressive', given the size of Scotland and the sale of between 400 and 600 weekly copies of the *Mirror* and the *Lounger* (Dwyer & Murdoch, 1983: p. 229).

From the evidence supplied by Dwyer and Murdoch, the evocation of 'luxury' followed closely the received conventions but that, of course, is the source of its power. Hence one writer cited 'luxury, effeminacy and debility' as the destroyers of Sparta and Rome and detected similar tendencies in his own society (ibid.: p. 231, quoting

Cal. Merc. 5 Oct. 1764). Luxury not only corrupted the 'manners' of the natural (that is, landed) elite by making them forsake their estates for the extravagance and degeneracy of city-dwelling, but also gave power to the stock-jobbers and those who deal in 'imaginary' and 'fictitious' paper money (ibid.: p. 232, citing *Cal. Merc.* 13 July and 21 Nov. 1772). This 'unsolid and burdensome property', as one correspondent called it, was directly linked to 'the great prevalence of pernicious luxury' (ibid.: p. 231, citing *Cal. Merc.* 17 Oct. 1764).

A second source of popular evidence for the contemporary recourse to the traditional vocabulary of luxury is provided by Hugh Blair's sermons.[23] Blair, as Professor of Belles-Lettres at Edinburgh, one-time Moderator of the General Assembly of the Church of Scotland and minister of the prestigious St Giles' Church in Edinburgh, was both a popular and influential preacher. According to one historian, his sermons were typical of 'Moderatism' in seeking to amalgamate 'elements of Stoicism, orthodox Presbyterianism, civic humanism and conservative Whiggism' in order to promulgate humane and enlightened principles within existing political and religious institutions (Sher, 1985: p. 211).

In line with this pedigree, Blair's sermon preached after Culloden in 1745 used the Jacobite rebellion as a signal that society had become wicked and corrupted with luxury (in Sher, 1985: p. 42). More expansively, in a sermon entitled 'On Luxury and Licentiousness' to a text from Isaiah (a favourite for these purposes), Blair adapted the 'classical' convention of primitive innocence. He observed how a 'sober and religious nation', experiencing a 'simple and pastoral life', had succumbed to the wealth obtained from conquest and commerce and 'contracted habits of luxury' with all their 'attending evils'. (*Sermons*: IV, 114). Blair immediately went on to proclaim that 'in the history of all nations, the same circulation of manners has been found' and Isaiah's reproof to the Jews was 'equally applicable to the manners of many in modern times'. When the 'refinements of criminal luxury' become habitual, 'all proper views of human life are forgotten' (p. 117). As befits a Christian minister – even one as worldly as Blair – the antidote to this corruption was religion; but a religion that preached not asceticism (St Giles' was the most fashionable kirk in Edinburgh) but enjoined '*manly* and becoming sentiments' (p. 125, my emphasis).

---

[23] The editor of the *Caledonian Mercury* praised Blair's sermons for uniting 'mild religion' with 'discriminating observations on the order of human conduct and the fortunes of human life' (quoted in Dwyer, 1987: p. 15).

There is no need to reproduce more examples because, to repeat, my point in citing Blair and the *Caledonian Mercury* was confined to illustrating that the issue of 'luxury' was very much 'alive' within eighteenth-century (Scottish) society. From our late twentieth-century perspective, we have the advantage of knowing that the issue will lose its sting and we know, therefore, that it is the views of Mandeville, Hume and Smith that will 'win' the debate. Their success was not obvious at the time, and we should be careful not to invest Smith and the others with some precognisance of this outcome. These trite observations are also intended to apply to the categories in terms of which the debate is seen to have been conducted. This goes beyond Macpherson's (1962) 'possessive individualism' or Meszaros's 'imperatives of Capital' to include also the two currently favoured 'paradigms' – civic humanism and natural jurisprudence (cf. Winch, 1988). As Pocock (1972) had originally argued, Kuhn's notion of a 'paradigm' was of use because of its inherent multivalency and, in the spirit of that argument, we should not treat civic humanism and natural jurisprudence as discrete categories. My final example in this chapter is intended to illustrate that point as well as provide evidence of the more 'academic' – as opposed to 'popular' – persistence of the traditional vocabulary of luxury. The example is the writings of Henry Home, Lord Kames.

I have, in my interpretation of Hume and Smith, emphasised their divergence from the civic humanist preoccupations of Rousseau and Ferguson and in so doing placed some weight on their conception of history. Kames is a worthwhile example because at one and the same time, seemingly, he was one of the earliest proponents of using differing modes of subsistence as a means of categorising social change and a resolute detector and denunciator of the evils of luxury.

Though the origin, development and articulation of the 'four-stages' theory is a matter of some dispute (cf., e.g., Meek, 1976; and Emerson, 1985) and its most definitive expression is to be found in Smith's *Lectures* of 1762 (*LJ*: pp. 14–16), Kames's writings, especially his *Historical Law Tracts* [1758] make use of it as an interpretative framework. However it is his most synoptical work, the *Sketches on the History of Man* [1774] that best serves my purposes. This book Kames himself considered to be his *magnum opus*, although it was less contemporaneously influential than either the *Tracts* or his *Elements of Criticism* [1762].

Kames devotes a whole Sketch to the 'Progress and Effects of Luxury', but a morally censorious attitude to the topic pervades the whole tome. Hence, for example, luxury is blamed for depopulation because not only does it enervate the capacity of both sexes for successful procreation but also reduces them to slavery and destroys industry (3rd edition, pp. 63–4). His most sustained attack is found in the Sketch on 'Patriotism'. He follows the Livian convention that Rome was corrupted by the importation of 'Asiatic luxury' (p. 473) and laments that 'the epidemic distempers of luxury and selfishness are spreading wide in Britain' (p. 477). Given the character of his own society, this implies a judgment about commerce. While he allows that commerce is 'immediately' advantageous in bestowing wealth and power, he judges that it is 'hurtful ultimately by introducing luxury and voluptuousness which eradicate patriotism' (p. 474). Indeed he had earlier declared in his typically forthright manner that 'luxury is above all pernicious in a commercial state' (p. 373).

But Kames's commitment to historical explanation gives an added dimension to these sentiments. He compares Livy and a fourteenth-century Lombard to illustrate the proposition that notions of luxury differ widely from age to age – new sources of sensual gratification are termed 'luxury' but then lose that label as they become habitual (p. 359). But what makes Kames apt for our purposes (though, of course, not uniquely – cf. Pescarelli (1978)) is that his 'Sketch on Patriotism' opens with a clear statement of the differences between the 'original state of hunting and fishing', where any notion of *patria* is absent, the shepherd state where common flocks produce an idea of common interest but not that of a *patria*, and the settled agricultural state where 'the sense of a *patria* begins to unfold itself' (p. 465). When 'manufactures and commerce' begin to flourish, as in Tudor England, patriotism is still present (p. 468) but when, as the Dutch bear witness (but also the Romans, of course), 'power and riches become the sole object of pursuit' then patriotism vanishes (p. 476). The only solution Kames sees is in 'pinching poverty' (p. 486) with the aim of encouraging a new beginning. Indeed Kames closes this Sketch with an avowal of the cyclicalism (hinted at above in Blair) that was a commonplace of classical and Renaissance thought (Clark, 1949; Pocock, 1975).

This last point serves succinctly to exemplify the limited purpose of my discussion of Kames. For all Kames's utilisation and advocacy of the historical method (see especially his Preface to the *Tracts*) his assessment of luxury remains steadfastly in the moralistic mode. The next chapter takes up the consequences of the 'historicist revolution' of the nineteenth century upon the concept of luxury.

CHAPTER 7

The historicity of needs

In Chapters 5 and 6, in discussions of Barbon, Mandeville, Melon, Kames and Smith, I referred in passing to the notion that 'luxury' can change over time. This chapter explores a crucial implication of this notion. If past 'luxuries' have now become 'necessities/needs' it also means that the latter too are subject to temporal mutability. The significance of this implication can be appreciated when the role played by needs, as constituents of a 'natural life', is recalled. This role was to act as a normative benchmark upon desires. In contrast to the insatiability and fickleness of the latter, needs were held, by writers from Plato onwards, to possess the virtue of fixity and permanence. Once, however, needs themselves are seen to be capable of change then their traditional role appears to be jeopardised. Indeed the very idea that there are inherent 'limits' to the meeting of certain finite needs is displaced by an emphasis on change manifest as 'progress'. The expansion of needs is a positive marker. In general terms, as an element of the so-called 'historicist revolution' of the late eighteenth and early nineteenth century, there is a shift from grounding norms in Space (the fixed natural life in terms of which change is corruption) to grounding them in Time (life is getting progressively better).

Chapter 8 will consider directly the normative relationship between needs and desires, as well as the practical and political aspects of the luxury-into-necessity dynamic as they apply in the contemporary world. The task in this chapter is to deal with the prior question of the temporality or historicity of needs. The task can be encapsulated in the question – in what sense, if any, can needs be said to have a history?

The focus of the answer to this question is Karl Marx; more precisely the focus is his notion, which he articulated on a number of occasions, that over time 'new needs' are developed. The focus is justified because Marx is very commonly associated with an affirmation of the historicity of needs. Moreover he is generally commended for that positive answer. Kate Soper (1981: p. 14), for example, states that it was 'Marx's crucial insight' to have recognised the 'historically developed nature of needs'. However, quite what that positive answer amounts to, what the proper interpretation of 'new needs' is, and the extent to which Marx's view is novel are all problematic. Partly to justify that claim but also to assist the integration of the discussion into our wider concerns, I propose to look at Marx's argument in the light of two of his predecessors – Smith and Hegel. My reasons for choosing these two thinkers will become apparent.

BASIC AND INSTRUMENTAL NEEDS

The first step, however, is to acknowledge that a negative answer to our guiding question is possible. One such answer is given by Collingwood. He argues that needs do not have a history because,

so far as man's conduct is determined by what may be called his animal nature, his impulses and appetites it is non-historical; the process of those activities is a natural process. Thus the historian is not interested in the fact that men eat and sleep and make love and thus satisfy their natural appetites. (Collingwood, 1961: p. 216)

To similar effect he says later that in so far as economic life means satisfying demands or needs which spring from our animal nature, then that life cannot be the subject of history (ibid.: p. 332). What this negative answer trades on is a set of associations between needs, animality and economic life. I will return to these associations. But first we need to ask how it is possible that there can be two such opposed answers to the question as those given by Collingwood and (putatively) Marx.

The most obvious place to look for the explanation is in the respective notions of need. We can here usefully reinvoke from Chapter 1 the distinction between basic needs and instrumental needs. At first sight it might seem that there is no contradiction between the two answers to our initial question because the negative answer refers to basic needs and the positive answer to instrumental needs. Although this is an attractively neat and simple solution, we should not be too quick to accept it without further consideration.

Braybrooke (1987: p. 31), for example, gives as the criterion of a basic need that it be 'essential to living or to functioning normally'. However, if we take the need for refined petroleum as an example of an apparently obvious instrumental need, it is quite easy to construct a case that, for those who live in remote rural districts, the practical necessity and indispensability of refined petroleum, as fuel for personal transport, put it on a par with food and drink. Taking 'practical necessity' and 'indispensability' as definitional markers (cf. Thomson, 1987: p. 4) then sustenance and petrol both appear to be basic needs. The effect of this is to recognise that the necessity built as a matter of definition into the concept of need can be seen to be social as well as physical. But once social necessity is admitted then it seems but the shortest of steps to incorporate history. Clearly in an earlier more self-sufficient age an available, efficient, long-range mode of transport was not needed in the Scottish Highlands.

If the various stages in this argument are accepted, then it might seem that what constitute 'basic needs' are, *pace* Collingwood, historical. We must now tread carefully. The reason for caution is that although petroleum in this example is indispensable it remains an instrumental need, it subserves the basic need for sustenance. That basic physical need has, as an end, remained unaltered; it is the socially-conditioned needs, as means, that have changed. In order therefore truly to demonstrate that basic needs have a history, a more fundamental claim has to be made. It has to be shown that the social and the physical interlock in a non-contingent manner. That is to say, it has to be shown that socially necessary instrumental needs actually affect the constitution of those who need them. We can express this abstractly as follows: at T_1 A needs X while at T_2 A needs Y such that the difference between X and Y effects a difference in A so that at T_2 we now have A'.

The argument that the social and the physical are necessarily interlocked is fundamental to the doctrine that I have elsewhere called contextualism (Berry, 1982; 1986). The heart of contextualism, on this understanding, is an attack on dualistic abstraction; an attack on the view that human nature is comprehensible independently of its particular socio-cultural context. The feminist distinction between sex and gender is a good example. The former is the appropriate sphere for physiological and other related data but such facts say nothing about the latter, that is, about the social position of women. Hence the definitive possession by males of a particular chromosome cannot serve as a causal explanation of their social dominance. It is an illicit dichotomy to separate 'nature', as cause, from 'society', as effect, for the simple reason that it is natural for humans to live in

The transition to modernity

society; thus, 'if we are concerned with humans as social beings then their natures, that is, the underlying structures that explain behaviour must be understood as socially constituted and historically evolving' (Holmstrom, 1982: p. 34). We can, therefore, hypothesise that the core of any argument to the effect that there can be a history of basic needs is an acceptance of contextualism. It is in the light of that hypothesis that we shall (in due course) examine Marx's positive account.

HISTORY, ECONOMICS AND HUMAN NATURE

The denial of that hypothesis is the implication of Collingwood's position. We concluded that his negative answer traded on a set of associations – needs, animality and economic life. These associations recall the original meaning of 'economics' as the ordering or rule (*nomos*) of the *oikos* or household. Aristotle's account was paradigmatic. Whereas the function or *telos* of the polis proper was the 'good life', the end of the household was life, the provision of the wherewithal to meet needs. As we noted in Chapter 2, household activity was instrumental, a means to the end of making the good life possible, and luxury was understood, in the classical tradition, as the corruption or perversion of this proper teleological ordering. The good life, the life of virtue, was devoted to intrinsically worthwhile, 'free' activity. The polis proper was a community of free men among whose virtues was courage, for they were expected to fight and hence risk death, since life (mere preservation) did not constitute their *telos*. Those who, like animals, have 'life' as their 'end' are natural slaves (Aristotle (*Pol.*: 1252a) said that oxen were the slaves of the poor).

A clear conceptual connexion between animality, economic activity and needs-satisfaction can thus be discerned in Aristotle. However, the obverse of this, namely, humanity (masculinity), the practice of virtue and the good life of intrinsically worthwhile activity, does not encompass any notion of history. Aristotle looked upon history as dealing merely with particulars (cf. *Poetics*: 1451b). This view was broadly typical of the Greeks. Even Thucydides, the greatest of the Greek historians, explicitly hinged his 'history' on its utility; it would act as a guide to the future because, thanks to the constancy of human nature, there is a repetitiveness in the affairs of men so that his study can become in his famous phrase, a 'possession forever' (1, 22).

If we now leap forward to the 'modern' world and its self-consciously 'new' philosophy based on the material facts of human nature, in the guise of the primacy of the passions, then history will simply be a record of the interplay of passions. This is exemplified by Hume. In his 'First Enquiry' he wrote,

> it is universally acknowledged that there is a great uniformity among the actions of men in all nations and ages, and that human nature remains still the same in its principles and operations . . .
> . . . so that it now follows mankind are so much the same in all times and places, that history informs us of nothing new or strange in this particular. Its chief use is only to discover the constant and universal principles of human nature by showing men in all varieties of circumstances and situations, and furnishing us with materials from which we may form our observations and become acquainted with the regular springs of human action and behaviour. (*Inquiry* (*Understanding*): pp. 92–3)

For Hume, the veracity of historians is assessable by the experience we today have of mankind. Crucially 'we' possess this experience because the principles of human nature are, as such, common to all and operate in a constant manner, so that the 'pastness' of what these historians relate is no obstacle to its comprehension. Human nature is not historically defined. In line with my earlier definition, this means that Hume is a non-contextualist (cf. Berry, 1982).

Hume, of course, practised what he preached and wrote an immensely popular *History of England*. But despite addenda that discuss the 'manners' of the age, the *History* focuses on political events. It is indeed in many ways itself a political document (cf. Forbes, 1975a) and, in that regard, it is interesting that in a letter, written as the first volume was being completed, Hume alluded to Thucydides in hoping that his book too might be a possession for all time. (*Letters*: I, p. 171). As we saw in Chapter 6, he did also write some influential 'economic' essays and chief amongst those influenced was Smith. It is Smith's account I now want to examine.

SMITH AND THE HISTORY OF NEEDED OBJECTS

In Chapter 6 we drew attention to Smith's history of economic life in the form of the 'four stages' – hunting, herding, farming and commerce.[1] As we emphasised in that chapter, those stages constitute

[1] There is considerable debate on the meaning and extent of 'materialism' in Smith's 'four-stages' theory – that is, that the stages are 'basic' modes of subsistence in some proto-Marxian sense. This view has been upheld in varying degrees by, for example, Pascal (1938), Meek (1967) and Skinner (1975); it is contested by, for example, Höpfl (1978), Haakonssen (1981) and Emerson (1985).

a normative progression marked by the transition from rudeness to civilisation. The difference between the first and the fourth state can be characterised as the difference between 'universal poverty' and opulence or, on another characterisation, between a society that is 'frequently reduced' to infanticide and one where the poorest enjoys liberty under the law (cf. *WN*: pp. 10–11).

Adapting Smith's argument, we can say that he has not provided a history of needs but a history of the mode of satisfaction of needs. This mode has become more complex and is charted by Smith in terms of the growth of markets and the division of labour. Hence whereas in the first age 'everyman provides everything for himself' (*WN*: p. 276), in the commercial age it requires the 'joint labour of a great multitude of workmen' in order to meet, for example, the need for a warm coat. To underline this point Smith promptly proceeds to list nine occupations involved in this 'homely product' and even that enumeration omits all merchants and carriers with their component trades (*WN*: p. 23). Thanks to this interdependence, each of those occupations needs the other; to meet his subsistence needs the spinner needs a weaver and vice versa, each is an instrument of the other. And since such specialisation results in the diffusion throughout society of a 'general plenty', then the needs of those in a commercial society are better met than would be the case in an earlier age. History is thus the history of the more effective meeting of needs.

We can detect here a crucial dualism. There is an implicit distinction between the subject of needs, or who it is that has needs (the 'need-bearer'), and the object of needs, or that which is needed (the 'needed object'). For Smith there is a conceptual separation between the two. Needed objects are instruments to serve the ends of the need-bearer. From the Smithian perspective the history of the growth of opulence is (though not coextensively) the history of the expansion of needed objects. For example, the need to be mobile in order to get from A to B can be satisfied now by a wide variety of means – cars, trains, planes and so on. These are functional equivalents but clearly represent a history of technology. This technology presupposes the need that it was designed instrumentally to meet. It is also possible to turn this around and maintain that developments in medical technology, for example, can generate a need for their utilisation.

It remains consistent with this general argument to hold that objects that were once needed can be made redundant; sharp flints would come into that category. Conversely, particular objects can now be needed which were unavailable earlier; as in the case of refined petroleum, which is needed to fuel a car for those who live in what have become, not unconnectedly, remote rural areas. Despite these changes, however, the need for transportation and for cutting-tools has not changed. The redundancy or novelty of needed objects is a separate matter from the persisting demands of need-bearers.

Such persistence implies a constancy in needs. Food, for example, is 'always' in demand. This example of Smith's is a good illustration of his non-contextualism. The demand applies to humans 'like to all *other* animals' (*WN*: p. 181, my emphasis) and applies, as a result, independently of any 'social' considerations – 'The rich man consumes no more food than his poor neighbour' and this for the simple reason that such consumption 'is limited by the narrow capacity of the human stomach'. What is without limit is the desire for the 'conveniencies and ornaments of building, dress, equipage and household furniture' (ibid.). These are the stuff of 'luxury' and their association with desire comes as no surprise. The rich man has more of these goods, enjoys more luxury, than the poor man (*WN*: p. 23). But the poor man in commercial society has more of them, and more luxury, than even the ruler of hunters (*LJ*: p. 562).

History is the history of opulence, not of (basic) need. But this does not mean that the daily requirements, the instrumental needs, of the hunter and merchant are identical. While a rod (or its functional equivalent) is needed by them both in order to catch fish, for the former that instrument possesses an exigency and primacy within the overall schedule of needs that is absent in the latter's schedule. This is because, thanks to the growth of opulence, fishing, once an activity pursued out of necessity, is later pursued as an amusement (cf. *WN*: p. 117). Nor is this to say that the perceptions of what is necessary to live have no history. Rather the natural progress of opulence/luxury is also a progress in such social perceptions. In Chapter 6 we quoted Smith's remark in the *Lectures* that human industry was employed to procure conveniences (determined according to delicacy of taste) rather than basic necessities. And to similar effect in the *Wealth of Nations*, in the context of a discussion of taxation (which we will consider in its own right in Chapter 8), Smith, contrary to Mandeville's rigorist definition, defines the necessaries of life as 'whatever the customs of the country renders it indecent for creditable people, even of the lowest order, to be without'. Thus a linen shirt is now in the eighteenth century, on that definition, a necessity although such a garment was unknown to the Greeks and Romans who lived, Smith supposes, 'very comfortably' without it (*WN*: p. 870).

It is important to appreciate correctly the significance of this example. The example does not make him a contextualist. The focus of Smith's notion of social necessity is customary conventions of decency and shame. This focus is what we should expect given, as we discussed in Chapter 6, Smith's 'sociological' account of moral judgments. The grounding of those judgments remains the pleasure that humans accrue from enjoying the sympathy of their fellows, whether friends or strangers. Chapter 8 will pursue further the place of luxury on this understanding of necessity but the remainder of this chapter will pursue the contextualist path to the establishment of the historicity of needs. This pursuit will also throw into relief and explain why Smith's account of necessity based on shame is non-contextualist.

In the interim the significance of Smith's account should be underscored. He does give us a history of needs – understanding these as instrumental needs. Consistent with that history, an account of the temporal mutation of luxury (what Smith generally calls 'opulence') into necessity can be given. But as his account of the linen-shirt demonstrates the location of 'necessity' lies in social norms. It is by virtue of these norms that a linen-shirt is a needed object. Accordingly the 'need' for it now, compared one can suppose to some earlier status as a 'luxury', does not represent a history of needs in the form of a history of need-bearers. Finally, one consequence of Smith's view should be noted. His history of needs is a natural history of opulence but this history, as we saw in Chapters 5 and 6, effectively de-moralises luxury. As we shall see, one element in Hegel's account of historicity enables 'luxury' to retain a place within a moral vocabulary, and an aspect of Marx's account of historicity does serve to retain the force of 'needs' as a critical perspective.

HEGEL AND THE HISTORY OF NEED-BEARERS

Smith's account is representative of that put forward by the political economists. It presents Man as a naturally self-regarding creature who participates in external exchange relationships to establish, in time, a society that best effects this nature, namely, a commercial or market society. In so far as history is relevant, it is an 'economic' history of the growth of markets and the division of labour.

This picture bears all the characteristics of Hegel's conception of the Understanding (*Verstand*). This is no accident since the work of Smith is, for Hegel, a prime example of the Understanding in operation. The Understanding is concerned to establish the fixed, separate and mutually exclusive character of phenomena. It deals with finite or external, mechanical relationships which separate form from content. It is a dualistic mode of thought *par excellence*. While this enables the political economists to come up with some valid inductive generalisations they are, according to Hegel, prevented from apprehending the true significance of human interaction because they remain fixed 'at the given'.

What they take as given is the nature of Man as a needy being who is prompted to act in order (in Smith's phrase) to 'better his condition' – a motivation that Smith goes on to characterise significantly as a 'uniform, constant and uninterrupted' effort which, though 'generally calm and dispassionate comes with us from the womb and never leaves us til we go into the grave' (*WN*: 341). How then, by contrast, does Hegel deal with needs?

Hegel, in that section of the *Philosophy of Right* (§190R)[2] concerned with Civil Society (*die bürgerliche Gesellschaft*), declares that Man simpliciter, as opposed to the legal person or the moral subject or the family member or the political citizen, is a needy being and, considered specifically as such, Man leads an economic life to satisfy his needs. But that life, and thence those needs, must not be seen as fixed. In particular they must not be seen as fixed at the level of satisfying requirements that are both physical and selfish. Rather there is within them an inner dynamic because these needs are *human* needs. Fundamental to Hegel's account is the conceptual distinction between animal needs and human needs. The former are fixed and determined; the latter are not. Humans *qua* humans transcend animal needs. But this transcendence is the work of history. The transcendence is witnessed by the increasing multiplication and differentiation of human needs. Hegel is here clearly echoing a Smithian analysis. However, given Hegel's project of transcending while preserving (*Aufhebung*) this is no mere echo.

In Hegel's terms, needs move from being concrete to being abstract and in so doing they become both social and mental (ibid.: §191).

[2] All references to *Philosophy of Right* will be to paragraphs, with the suffix R denoting 'Remarks' attached to the main text and A denoting 'Additions' collated separately at the end of the text. I have used the German text edited by J. Hoffmeister.

They become social because the satisfaction of needs can only be achieved in conjunction with others. More is involved here than the interdependence that a complex economy necessitates (recall Smith on the woollen coat). The additional factor can be grasped by exploiting the distinction between humans and animals. The panda satisfies its need for food by the direct and unmediated consumption of bamboo. But in humans food itself becomes a social fact; for example, the Jew *qua* Jew needs a specific diet. This need is no longer a mere natural unmediated fact but, and here is Hegel's contextualism linking together physical and social necessity, a culturally determined requirement. The need in this cultural sense has also become mental, because as a constituent of culture it is, for Hegel, *geistig* or thought-imbued. Hegel himself puts it that Man is now concerned with a 'necessity of his own making alone' (§194).

Hegel contrasts this self-made necessity with 'an external necessity, an inner contingency and mere caprice (*Willkür*)' (§194). To reinvoke our earlier terminology, the development of human needs affects not merely needed objects but also need-bearers; it is a development from external to internal necessity. This development is a *liberation*. It liberates Man from the 'strict natural necessity of need' (ibid.). Such natural or external necessity is experienced by the panda, which is restricted to its diet of bamboo. But it is the human prerogative to raise itself out of nature, so that Jews are able to discriminate between the meats they consume; for to be confined to 'mere physical needs (*Naturbedürfnis*) as such and their direct satisfaction would simply be the condition in which the mental (*Geistigkeit*) is plunged in the natural and so would be one of savagery and unfreedom' (§194R).

This association between 'the natural', 'savagery' and 'unfreedom' gives us, I think, the best insight into Hegel's position. Savages (*Barbaren*), he says, are governed, as befits their 'brooding stupidity', by 'impulses (*Triebe*), customs and feelings' but when, through the educative process (*Bildung*), there is developed a self-consciously articulated system of justice (*das Recht*) then 'every accident of feeling' vanishes, together with 'revenge, sympathy and selfishness' (§§192A, 211A). There is thus a move from the savage's schedule of needs, characterised by impulsiveness and selfishness, to a schedule where Man's rationality and spirituality come increasingly to the fore. In this process Hegel allots an important role to work. It too is liberating because it too puts a check on animalistic impulse. Hence a fixed agricultural life (Smith's third stage), unlike the nomadic life of savages (Smith's second stage), exhibits needs to care for the future and for a family (§§203, 203A). This process is even more apparent in Civil Society (Smith's fourth stage) where mental needs (*geistigen Bedürfnisse*) are preponderant (§194).

This in itself is indicative of the fact that Hegel, like Smith, is here telling a 'progressive' story. However, whereas Civil Society is the culmination of the story for Smith this is not so for Hegel, who sees this economic tale as deficient. One aspect of that deficiency is that the merely implicit Reason (*Vernunft*) of this Moment manifests itself in a sharp disparity between luxury and necessity (*Luxus/Not*). This disparity is the product of the inner dynamic of the division of labour and fissiparity of social conditions (§195).[3] Hence, despite a shared commitment to historical progress, Hegel's premises are far removed from those of Smith. On Hegel's account, contrary to the premises of Smith's conjectural history of economic life, the needs experienced by modern Man cannot be retrospectively attributed to an earlier age. The difference between the Roman noble and an eighteenth-century labourer is more profound than the presence or absence of the 'necessity' of a linen-shirt or the relative place of fishing-rods in their respective schedule of needs. In the terms of our earlier formula, the modern bearer of needs is a different 'subject' (A' at T_2) than the savage (A at T_1). In this sense therefore needs might be said to have a history.

This 'history' differs from Smith's in two important ways. Firstly it is a history of humans as bearers of needs, not a history of the things they need. This account of Hegel's is clearly premised on his Idealism – on his conception of Man as the embodiment of *Geist*. Hegel historicises human nature as a whole and, as a good contextualist, this historicisation is inseparable from its progressively adequate concrete embodiment in the world of objective *Geist*. This constitutes the second difference. There is no way that Hegel's history can accommodate a de-moralisation of needs. If anything, the obverse is true. Hegel's history is a history of their moralisation. This explains why he talks of liberation in the context of needs. One way of telling the story of the growth of freedom, the story of the meaning of history, is to relate how needs shed their cloak of naturalness *qua* instinctive

---

[3] Hegel's familiarity with the 'luxury debate' and the claim that this had an impact upon the formulation of his early thought is maintained by Dickey (1987: esp. p. 248).

drives to stand revealed as embodiments of the universal, rational human will (cf. §190A).[4] Here lies, we can add, the source of those arguments mentioned in Chapter 1 that seek to extend the scope of 'needs'. This extension aimed to move beyond viewing needs as the physical preconditions of existence to regarding 'autonomy' and the like also as needs. This issue we shall meet again in Chapter 8 when we discuss the debate over the 'relativity' of poverty.

In principle Hegel's version of the history of needs continues to allow 'luxury' to be criticised while admitting that as human society has developed so the standards in terms of which that criticism is made have also developed. Just as the virtue of 'courage' has lost its salience in the modern world (see Chapter 6) so, we may infer, to criticise luxury for engendering effeminacy will lose its force. Similarly as the modern world brings with it the 'problem of poverty' (§§241ff.) so, as his passing references in the *Philosophy of Right* suggest, luxury is criticisable now, in the world of commerce, for its capriciousness and its exemplification of the excesses of an unregulated Civil Society. This explains why, for example, Hegel believes, it is proper that the *Polizei* control the pricing of daily necessities (*Lebensbedürfnisse*) (§236).[5] As we shall see in Chapter 8, it is within this same context of lack of regulation and excess that certain contemporary criticisms of luxury occur.

MARX'S NOTION OF 'NEW' NEEDS

Part of the point of my illustrative use of Smith and Hegel can, I hope, now be glimpsed. Prima facie, Marx's doctrine of the 'history of material life' (historical materialism) would appear to combine Hegel's historicism with Smith's emphasis on economic life. The expectation is that his work will keep the latter's link between needs and economics with the former's deeper (in the sense that it applies to need-bearers as well as to needed objects) appreciation of historical change.

The *locus classicus* of historical materialism is the account in the

---

[4] For Hegel the *natürliche Wille* is composed of instinctive drives (*Triebe*), passions (*Begierden*) and inclinations (*Neigungen*) (see §11) and he invariably places needs in that context (see §§37, 123).

[5] A number of commentators have emphasised the influence of Steuart on Hegel (Hegel wrote a now-lost commentary on Steuart's *Principles* (see Ch. 6, *infra*)). See especially Chamley (e.g. 1965) (who is followed by Plant (1983)) and Dickey (1987: p. 200)) who stresses the affinity of Steuart's doctrine to the German tradition of *Polizeistaat*. For some doubts on Steuart's impact as opposed to Smith's, at least by the time of *Philosophy of Right*, see Berry (1982: p. 168n).

German Ideology. In that work Marx (with Engels) links the first historical act with the satisfaction of needs to maintain life. This – the production of material life – he explicitly states is 'the fundamental condition of all history' and, as such, it *must* be met (tr. Dutt et al.: p. 39). Indeed, as a necessity, it applies just as much today as it did thousands of years ago. This seems a clear reiteration of the position of the political economists. Marx even remarks that certain, though unspecified, French and English writers have made attempts at writing history with a materialistic base, that is, 'histories of civil society'. Nevertheless, Marx goes on immediately to say that the satisfaction of the first needs leads to 'new needs' and the production of new needs is also said to be the first historical act (*diese Erzeugung neuer Bedürfnisse ist die erste geschichtliche Tat*) (*Deutsche Id (Frühschriften)*: p. 355). History now becomes the history of 'new forms' of the materialistic connexion between humans, a connexion which is determined by their needs and their mode of production.

The nub issue is the status of these 'new needs'. It is possible to stitch together a quilt of quotations from the range of Marx's work that do seem to say that these 'new needs' represent merely a Smithian expansion of needed objects.

Certainly some of Marx's most prominent statements can be interpreted in that way. In the *Grundrisse* (p. 527) he even combines talk of luxury with historic needs. These needs are also 'social needs' because they are created by social production (cf. p. 409). As production develops and becomes more complicated so interdependence grows. Marx gives the example of the export of silk goods being necessary to procure guano. Of this example Marx comments that 'the manufacture of silk no longer appears as a luxury industry but a necessary industry for agriculture'. Capital has transformed the previously superfluous and 'so-called luxury needs (*sogenannte Luxus-bedürfnisse*)' into a 'historically created necessity' (p. 528). This is Marx's version of the luxury-into-necessity dynamic. What makes it Smithian is that the 'historically created necessity' is not what can be imputed to a 'natural subject' but what embodies certain developed social standards. Marx continues by observing that 'luxuries' too have developed so that in bourgeois society they still stand in opposition to these standards.

The Smithian echoes throughout this passage are also found in *Capital* (1, 171) in the discussion of the meaning of subsistence. Here Marx refers to natural needs, in the form of food, clothing, fuel and housing, which vary according to climatic and other physical conditions, that is, non-temporally. In addition, he refers to 'so-called necessary needs' which are the product of historical development.[6] This again appears very close to Smith's notion of necessity, especially since Marx's necessary needs incorporate the 'habits and degree of comfort' that form the socially accepted living conditions of the free labourers.

In the light of passages such as these, it would seem that the historically developed 'new needs' are needed objects. Thus interpreted, Marx's argument is a reprise of Smith's and those commentators, such as Soper, who have commended Marx precisely because he is, in their lights, not reiterating Smith are mistaken (cf., e.g., Heller, 1976; Gould, 1980). In the final analysis this may indeed be the correct conclusion to draw, but Marx himself is critical of Smith and so perhaps there is more. I thus push on to patch together another quilt in order to investigate what these 'new needs' might alternatively signify. Aside from the intrinsic merit of this investigation we will also uncover an implication that bears upon the wider design of this study.

Needs as qualitative change

Even in the part of the *German Ideology* already cited, Marx is explicit that the production of material life is both a natural and social relationship, thus suggesting a contextualist rejection of Smith's dualism. He is also explicit that the satisfaction of new needs and the production of material life are not chronological stages but 'moments' that exist simultaneously (ibid.). And, if we look elsewhere, we come across the fact that for Marx a Smithian expansion and multiplication of needs, and of the means of their fulfilment under capitalism, produce perversely the 'bestial degeneration' of the worker (*Early Writings* (hereafter *EW*): p. 359).

I believe the term 'bestial' (*viehische*) (*Frühschriften*: p. 256) here provides an important clue to another understanding of 'new needs' within Marx's work. This point is at least partly confirmed by the fact that we have already seen that a crucial factor in the difference

---

[6] Heller (1976: p. 33) thinks the meaning of 'necessary needs' changes from 'natural' to 'historical' between *Grundrisse* and *Capital*, although the texts themselves betray some equivocation. Certainly Marx is explicit in *Capital* that there is such a thing as 'human nature in general' as well as historically modified in each 'epoch' (p. 608); on the bearing of this to his contextualism see Berry (1986: ch. 5).

between Smith and Hegel was their respective understanding of the relationship between Man and animals and whether or not needs are 'moralised'. Hence I will pursue that clue and look at what Marx has to say about this relationship.

Marx does distinguish between Man and animals. His criterion is productive activity. In the *German Ideology* he explicitly contrasts the fact that for humans, unlike for sheep or dogs, the production and satisfaction of needs is an historical process (tr. Dutt et al.: p. 89). Moreover, in that same work his contextualism is made clear. He openly regards productive activity as definitive or constitutive of humanity,

As individuals express their life, so they are. What they are therefore coincides with their production both with *what* they produce and *how* they produce. The nature of individuals thus depends on the material conditions determining their production. (Ibid.: p. 32)

History now becomes the history of the evolving productive forces but since Man *is* a producer then this history is also 'the history of the development of the forces of the individuals themselves' (ibid.: p. 90). In the *Grundrisse* (p. 44) this point is made with explicit, albeit passing, reference to needs,

Not only do the objective conditions change in the act of reproduction, for example, the village becomes a town, the wilderness a cleared field etc., but the producers change, too, in that they bring out new qualities in themselves, develop themselves in production, transform themselves, develop new powers and ideas, new modes of intercourse, new needs and new language.

The wording here is significant but to bring out the character of this significance we require a more detailed picture of what such 'new needs' might entail, if they are to represent a non-Smithian account. This picture can be found in his early writings. There Marx stresses that the Smithian 'new needs' which are developed serve only further to entrench estrangement (cf. *EW*: p. 358). An exchange economy is a system of mutual plunder and deceit seeking the satisfaction of 'selfish needs'. And, of course, the chief sufferer is the wage-labourer, who is determined by 'social needs alien to him', which 'act upon him with compulsive force' and to which he must submit 'from egoistic need' (*EW*: p. 269). However, Marx, here openly contradicting the political economists, does not regard this conjunction of need and egoism as a fixed 'natural' fact. Under capitalism, need is animalistic, selfish, egoistic and crude. Clearly these are all negative descriptions.

It is precisely one of the symptoms of alienation that the proletariat is *reduced* by capitalism to meeting merely animal needs (cf.: pp. 290, 327).

And following a familiar argument (intimated in Hegel) a further symptom is the distinction between the crude needs of the poor and the luxury and refined needs of the rich (*EW*: p. 363; Marx reiterates this distinction in his later writings, see, e.g., *Grundrisse* (p. 608), *Capital* (II, 403)). Marx was well aware of the disputed role of luxury in contemporary political economy – a dispute between those, like Malthus, who advocated luxury to produce labour and those, like Ricardo, who execrated luxury as the enemy of wealth (*EW*: p. 360). Marx thinks this dispute, like all the others, trivial in that it establishes a false dichotomy; luxury and privation are two sides of the same coin. Both are effects of the same cause – the system of private property. But when private property – the key premise of an exchange economy – has been positively superseded, selfish, animal need instead becomes a genuine human need. The hallmark of this genuine human need is the self-apprehension of humans that they are human so that even in their most putatively individual actions (like satisfying needs) they are simultaneously manifesting their true communal being.

One indication of Marx's meaning here would be the distinction he draws between the man/woman relationship as, on the one hand, expressive of human need and, on the other, as expressive of lust (*EW*: p. 347; cf. Berry, 1987). The latter is represented by the universal prostitution that crude communism would entail. This state of affairs Marx calls *tierische* (which is also translated here by our key term 'bestial' (*Frühschriften*: p. 233). Accordingly, it expresses crude animalistic need where the woman (typically) is seen as the object of selfish gratification (a sex-object in contemporary parlance). By contrast, when the female is regarded as another human being then that regard entails grasping oneself as human so that the need for the other 'has become a human need'. We can indeed judge from this relationship the level of development of mankind (*Bildungsstufe des Menschen*). Since, for Marx, to be human is to express one's 'communal essence' then this 'human need' transcends any selfish instrumentalism. This transcendence can, therefore, be interpreted, in an essentially Hegelian way, as a development from the expression of animal to the expression of human need or, alternatively, from basic egoistic need to basic communistic need.

Though it is perhaps not always unambiguously clear in these early writings, this transcendence is understood by Marx as the work of history. Indeed it is quite explicitly the 'historic destiny of capital' to make this transcendence possible. It is, furthermore, in this very context that Marx makes one of his best-known pronouncements on the historicity of needs. Capitalism has established the 'material elements' so that labour can become a need 'above and beyond necessity'. And, as such, it 'appears no longer as labour but as the full development of activity itself in which natural necessity in its direct form has disappeared; because a historically created need has taken the place of a natural one' (*Gundrisse*: p. 325). In addition Marx, with Hegelian echoes once again, explicitly criticises Smith's account of labour for not appreciating that it is properly a 'liberating activity' and an act of 'self-realisation' (ibid.: p. 611). Given such points then Marx can seem to subscribe to the Hegelian reading of history as the transformation of need-bearers in opposition to the Smithian economistic reading of history as the expansion of needed objects.

If that is true then does Marx's view fall into the same kind of over-all global perspective as Hegel's? Hegel's historicism rested on subsuming 'needs' within the moralised development of human (world) culture – it was part and parcel of the meaning of history itself. While Marx does, of course, make a great show of rejecting Hegel's Idealism, his own historicism appears to rest on subsuming 'need' within 'capacity' (cf. Springborg, 1981: p. 98; Elster, 1985b: pp. 71–4) whereby humans produce history and themselves. Herein lies the significance of that passage in the *Grundrisse* that referred to the 'producers' bringing out new qualities in themselves, developing new powers and transforming themselves. This same point recurs throughout the early work; hence, history is the 'true natural history of man' (*EW*: p. 391) in as much as, in the form of the development of 'industry', it is the 'open book of the essential powers of man (*menschlichen Wesenkräfte*)' (*EW*: p. 354), where such powers exist as 'dispositions and capacities' (*EW*: p. 389; cf. *Grundrisse*: p. 488).

Lest this be thought to be a characteristic of the 'young Marx's' work, we can take note of a well-known passage in *Capital* (1, 179) where Marx contrasts human and animal labour. Initially labour is an interaction within nature as Man sets in motion the 'natural forces of his body' in order to appropriate nature's products in a form to service his needs (ibid.). But this interaction 'develops his slumbering powers (*Potenzen*)' so that (he goes on) 'we are not now dealing with those primitive instinctive forms of labour that remind us of the mere animal'. The upshot is that 'by thus acting on the external world and changing it, he at the same time changes his own nature'. And given what we have already established, this change can be read as the development of new needs – no mere quantitative increase in needed objects but a qualitative alteration in need-bearers.

CONCLUSION

This discussion of Marx prompts two conclusions depending on which of the two interpretations of his notion of 'new needs' is adopted. The probability is that both are exegetically warranted in that Marx himself actually subscribed at some time to both. From our analytical perspective, however, the two interpretations bear divergent messages. The first interpretation reads Marx as, on this point, reprising Smith. The needs in question are those for new 'objects'. Over time, luxury goods as objects can lose that status and become needed as necessities. The needs here are instrumental but, as we saw in Chapter 1, that is no bar to the goods in question being at one time luxuries; a luxury good is an easily substitutable one, it is not a redundant or useless good. Since this is in line with Smith's account, then the conclusion drawn there concerning the de-moralisation of luxury will also hold good for Marx.

However this is not the case on the second interpretation. Here 'new needs' refer less to what is needed (the object) than to the needer (the subject). Just as Hegel's version of this argument moralised need and retained a place for luxury in a moral vocabulary, so too does Marx's. Seen in this light their arguments are assimilable to a long tradition. As we recalled in the opening paragraph of this chapter, in this tradition needs had served as a normative benchmark upon desire. Of course neither Hegel nor Marx simply repeats the traditional argument; rather they re-establish it. Classically, needs were an integral part of the rational/natural or teleological order of things. As part of the variously described overturn of that order (the rise of mechanism, the *Entzauberung* of the world, the dominance of *Zweck-* over *Wert-Rationalität* and the like), desire (passion, emotion) became not a threat to reason but its master, and needs became detached from 'reason' and assimilated to animal instinct. One consequence of this assimilation is the Collingwoodian view that basic needs have no history. It is here that the re-establishment that we have imputed to Hegel and Marx enters. If history itself is imbued with normative significance so that, rather than it being a (Humean) repeating record of human passions or a (Smithian) record of desire-driven technology, it becomes the bearer of value, then a temporal teleology becomes possible.

Once human nature is historicised then the human subject itself undergoes development to culminate in the rational State (Hegel) or communism (Marx). Since 'needs' are an ingredient in the subject, they too undergo development as 'new' ones emerge. And since this development is value-laden, it then becomes possible to use needs as a critical tool. Marx can criticise capitalism for fostering 'bestial degeneration' because that condition *ipso facto* is a perversion of human capacity – a thwarting and distorting of human needs, a corruption of the potential that humans possess to become fully human. While the formulations of this indictment may have changed, its grounding principles still license a criticism of luxury as a manifestation of that corruption within modern (capitalist) society. Luxury is not, all appearances to the contrary, innocent. This argument we shall examine in the next chapter.

Politics, needs and desires

CHAPTER 8

Luxury and the politics of needs and desires

A guiding principle of this study is that the issue of luxury – its meaning and definition – is deeply implicated in the broadly political question of the nature of social order and the definition of a good society. In Parts II and III we examined how, at various periods in Western history, this implication manifested itself. In this concluding Part, I return to more ostensibly conceptual concerns and, in so doing, pick up a number of the points adumbrated in Part I.

These concerns deal, again, with the relationship between needs and desires and the location/definition of luxury in those terms. The object of this Part is to bring the political aspect more directly to the front of the discussion. More precisely, I wish to discuss the ways in which the operant definitions of luxury and need indicate a society's conception of itself, that is, what it values or thinks important, what it regards as 'good and politic order'. The discussion in this chapter will focus on two topics – taxation and poverty – as two sides of the same coin. Taxation of consumption goods is a case where the definition of luxury is made socially explicit, when some goods are either exempted from or, conversely, specially selected for such a tax. Poverty is a case where it is the definition of need that is made socially explicit. It is necessary, however, to situate these topics within the more general conceptual picture. Hence I start by drawing that picture.

I

THE PRINCIPLE OF PRECEDENCE

The central proposition to be scrutinised is perhaps best encapsulated in what Frankfurt (1984) calls 'the Principle of Precedence' (cf. Braybrook, 1987). According to the principle, when Alan needs something that Brenda wants but does not need, then meeting Alan's need is prima facie morally preferable to satisfying Brenda's desire. This is explicitly a moral argument so that, more generally and loosely, the central proposition lends itself to the claim that needs ought to be met before luxuries. This claim can be understood both individually and societally. It might be claiming that an individual ought to allocate his or her own resources in such a way that their needs are met before they proceed to indulge themselves in the acquisition of luxuries. Or it might be claiming that a society (its political leaders) should ensure that the needs of its members are satisfied. Though there are differences between the two claims, some of which we shall address as we proceed, we can for the moment treat them together.

Two related issues are raised by the claim. First, there is the stringency of the precedence – should all needs be met before any desires are attended to? Or is there an indeterminate grey area, where a 'trade-off' might be permitted? Second, and implicit in the first issue, is the grounding of the precedence – are all needs morally more important or weighty than any desire? Or are there degrees of weight such that, on occasion, the realisation of desire can outweigh the satisfaction of some need? To resolve these issues two questions have to be answered; what is the moral base of need? And what is the moral case, if any, for desire?

THE MORALITY OF NEEDS

To ascertain the moral basis of need requires that the range of meaning covered by the term be elucidated. In Chapter 1 we noted, citing Wiggins's representative analysis, that 'need' can be held to possess a logical form distinct from that possessed by 'want' or 'desire'. In that analysis the non-intentionality of needing was stressed but, as we also observed in Chapter 1, in many uses of the term, 'need' refers to the instrumental attainment of some intended goal. It will be worthwhile to pursue this discussion more systematically.

One analysis of need regards all its uses as instrumental. According to White, any correct statement about needs is reducible to a triad: A needs V in order to F (White, 1975: p. 105; cf. (*inter alia*) Barry, 1965; Griffin, 1986; Galston, 1980). Implicit here is the claim that any dyadic statement to the effect that A needs to V or A needs X is elliptical. That White expresses his point by means of a formula is symptomatic of his argument that the triad applies regardless of the subject-matter. Hence he is able to declare that 'a man can need a drink or to know what to do, an engine can need more oil or to be overhauled, and a triangle can need at least two acute angles or to be revolved on its axis' (White, 1975: p. 104). As this last example makes plain, for White, the language of need is not necessarily normative. This position is the target of a criticism. White's analysis, with its emphasis on logical *form*, is criticised because it omits the significant *content* of needs-language, which is precisely concerned with normative issues.

This criticism does not of itself undermine the triadic formula since it can be argued that any normativity possessed by needs resides in the final leg 'F'. Accordingly, the triadic approach leaves room for discrimination. Hence, to use an earlier example, to say I(A) need a pen(V) to complete my pools coupon(F) is not to make a claim of much moral significance. It follows from this that the precedence claimed by needs over the 'mere' satisfaction of wants depends upon the moral seriousness of the need in question. However, this recognition of degrees of seriousness brings us back to the discussion of basic (or fundamental or absolute) needs undertaken in Chapter 1.

The argument put forward by, for example, Thomson (1987) and Braybrooke (1987) as well as Wiggins (1985) is that in the case of these needs the triadic formula is supererogatory. The pivot of the argument is that these needs differ significantly from instrumental needs. Thomson (1987: p. 21) identifies the distinguishing criterion as follows,

in normal circumstances the questions 'Do you need to survive?' and 'Do you need to avoid serious harm?' are logically inappropriate, because they involve a category mistake akin to the category mistake involved in questions 'Is death fatal?' and 'Is harm harmful?'

This last example is not fortuitous. Harm has a direct role to play in this context because it is central to the *moral* force of needs. Fundamental needs are practically necessary and indispensable (cf. Thomson, 1987: p. 27); there is no alternative, on pain of suffering serious harm, but to obtain what we need fundamentally. Desires, by contrast, and luxuries *a fortiori* lack that force. The underlying argument seemingly relies on standard intuitions. Indeed it might be claimed that it is built into the fabric of human nature that harm is to be avoided and where the befalling of harm is virtually certain then that avoidance constitutes an imperative. Needs compel – they must be met or harm will ensue.

It is worth spelling out the link between these intuitions and the analysis of the difference between needs and wants. Clearly it is these basic needs that we can genuinely say are universal and objective – we all have these needs whether we desire them (have them as objects of intention) or not. In Chapter 1 we drew attention to a further feature of these basic needs, namely, their abstractness. What is less clear, but as we shall see is crucial, is how this feature bears upon the difference between needs and wants. If it is the essence of desires that they embody intentions then they are open to amendment. At a trivial level my desire for a pint of beer can be amended upon learning that it is flat or upon perceiving cider or upon recalling my resolution to forgo alcohol and so on. (There is a non-trivial dimension to this to which we shall turn when we discuss the moral base of desire.) However, the use of the possibility of amendment as a criterion is not as clear-cut as these remarks suggest.

The source of this indeterminacy lies in the abstractness of the basic needs. As we outlined in Chapter 1, to identify a need for sustenance says nothing specific about what foods are thought to be edible or liquids potable. The crux here is the direct link between edibility and potability on the one hand and what is 'thought to' possess those attributes on the other. Once 'thought' is introduced then the 'necessity' attached to needs, and from which intuitively their moral importance and consequent obligatoriness arise, is also affected. As Hegel had argued, once needs are understood as *geistig* then the necessity in question is open to individual (and cultural) self-determination. Clare as a vegetarian will only consume foodstuffs that meet her criteria of appropriateness; David, as a Jew, will only eat such meat as is deemed kosher. What matters, as Leiss (1978: p. 72) has pointed out, is 'What kinds of foods? In what forms? With what *qualities*? And how does the perceived need for certain kinds of foods stand in relation to other perceived needs?' (author's emphasis).

This bears upon the arguments outlined above. If indeed all needs, even a 'basic' one like sustenance, are always defined by human practices or conventions then it means that the triadic formula is not supererogatory. It always remains pertinent to inquire further as to just how indispensable or practically necessary the satisfaction of the need is. While food is a need, indeed is a basic need for without it we suffer harm and eventually die and this is true regardless of any belief or intentions we might entertain, nonetheless this is an 'abstract' truth. The requirements of a kosher diet in David's case can possess all the necessity that the abstract need for food possesses: he doesn't simply need food; he(A) needs kosher food(V) in order to comply with the prescriptions of his faith(F). It is perfectly conceivable that if confronted with pork or starvation David might *choose* the latter.

We need to be clear about the meaning of 'choice' here. On one dimension the following of a kosher diet is *not* an option; it is, as some communitarian critics of liberalism like to term it, a question of identity not choice (cf., e.g., Sandel, 1982; MacIntyre, 1985; Taylor, 1979). Identity is discovered through participation in some conceptually prior way of life, it is not self-determined.[1] However, there is another dimension to the meaning of choice. The abstract need for food, the imperative attached to the satisfaction of basic needs, is overridden by an act of will. This latter dimension demonstrates that for humans this abstract need is always made concrete by certain judgments about what is edible. These judgments can, as in David's case, be glossed as supra-individualistic conventions that possess all the exigency and imputed objectivity of 'needs'. They can also be individualistic, as when I choose to go on hunger-strike to protest my innocence or to keep faith with my conscience.

The upshot of this is that the moral significance or weight of human needs cannot be read off automatically from certain postulates about indispensability and the like. Human needs are never brute and are always, in principle, open to question. It follows that their imperativeness is short of direct unmediated compliance and the stringency of their obligatoriness does devolve, as the supporters of the triadic formulation claim, upon the 'end' in question. Further, if this significance is conceptually connected to the avoidance of harm then there is no automatic prima facie reason why the frustration of desires might not also be harmful. Once we allow the connexion between desires and harm then the principle of precedence, whereby needs trump desires, cannot necessarily hold across the board.

As a result of this analysis we can now identify clearly the locus of luxury. Luxury is dissociable from harm. It is this dissociation, and here is the justification for this preliminary analysis, that underwrites the case for taxing some goods exceptionally. But before taking up that case directly we need to examine further the relationship between desire and harm. This examination will arrive at this same rationale for exceptional taxation but it will also suggest reasons, that

---

[1] Cf. Berry (1989a: ch. 5) for further discussion of this supposed link between identity, community and choice.

echo some of the discussion in Chapter 1, why it requires the exercise of political judgment.

It is not difficult to argue that desires and their satisfaction can enjoy moral status. Certainly those who argue for the priority of needs over desires would not deny that; indeed, it is implicit in the very notion of 'precedence' that desires do have independent value. Hence Frankfurt (1984: p. 1) gives the example that 'it might be quite sensible for a seriously ill person to use his limited financial resources for the pleasure cruise he has long wanted to take than for the surgery he needs to prolong his life'. It is worth noting the force of the fact that the cruise has been *long* wanted since this is indicative of some conceptual refinement of the notion of 'desire'. Hume, for example, distinguished between calm and violent passions and, in general terms, there is a significant distinction between settled or informed desire, on the one hand, and caprice or whim, on the other. In Frankfurt's example the cruise is not undertaken on a whim, on the 'spur of the moment', but is the realisation or fulfilment of a long-held desire. To say that desire is calm or settled is to say that the desirer has some aim or goal in terms of which day-to-day life can be led, or which can serve to establish a 'point' to various activities and enterprises.

It is now relatively easy to make such desires carry moral weight. One favourite way of making that move is to declare that in having goals, in terms of which individuals direct their energies, these individuals are pursuing their conception of the 'good'. Rawls (1972: pp. 92–3, *et passim*), for example, encapsulates this point in his notion of a 'plan of life', whereby individuals pursue a conception of the good which should be respected by others. To be a moral agent entails not only being capable of having a conception of the good, with the right to pursue it, but also respecting the equal right of others to pursue their life-plan and its conception of the good. This paints a typical 'liberal' picture of morality; indeed, some writers define liberalism in these terms (cf. Dworkin, 1978). A fundamental moral pluralism is being underwritten. Since desires generically are specific, and since the conception of the good is (on this model) a settled or, as Rawls typifies it, a 'rational' desire, then what one individual views as a good, will not necessarily coincide with another's view. Hence Eric might desire to run a four-minute mile and so he undertakes a rigorous physical training programme and strict diet (a high protein intake is an instrumental need), while Fred might desire a place in graduate school so he directs his energy into study (a well-stocked library is an instrumental need).

We can relate this analysis to the taxonomy of goods outlined in Chapter 1. Desires conceived of as settled, as embodying an individual's view of the good and as thereby motivating that individual's actions, are what we labelled 'fervent desires'. The example of the book collector in search of the First Edition of *De Cive* conforms to this model. The ownership of books for this person is not some incidental aspect of her life but a matter of importance. This 'importance' can be gauged by the sacrifices and trouble that she would go through to obtain a particularly prized object like the *De Cive*. While I might think she is foolish to miss her summer holidays because the purchase of the book exhausts her savings, I can still appreciate why she has done what she has done and, more strongly, it would have been morally reprehensible of me to prevent her from spending her money on that object. The upshot is that she could properly be said to suffer harm if she should be prevented from pursuing her collection. This reinforces the earlier point that it is untenable to argue that needs necessarily enjoy moral superiority over desires. Harm can befall a human agent as a consequence of a failure both to have needs met and desires satisfied. And, as Frankfurt's example illustrated, on occasion more harm might follow the latter than the former.

Since, as the taxonomy indicated, luxury goods are distinct from those that are fervently desired, then the conclusion reached earlier about the nature of luxury is reiterated. That is, no harm ensues if individuals do not enjoy luxuries. It does not, of course, follow that it is morally legitimate to prevent that enjoyment but it does provide the rationale for levying extra taxes upon them. However, we need to recall a further aspect of the earlier discussion. We remarked in Chapter 1 that the *content* of the various categories was indeterminate. While for the collector the *De Cive* is the object of a fervent desire, for me it could be a luxury good in as much as I would like to possess that book but not at the cost of forgoing my summer holidays. The issue that is now raised is that the determination of what is a luxury, and thus susceptible to exceptional taxation, is not necessarily uncontroversial. Suppose, here, that books over £500 were deemed luxuries and thus subjected to taxation, while holidays were not, then my preference, my view of what is a luxury, is socially favoured. The reverse situation is equally possible when holidays over £500 are surcharged and books are not. This means that the taxation of 'luxuries' is as much a question of political decision as any other form of taxation.

II

Taxes are levied for two reasons. The first and most obvious is to raise revenue in order to provide (at least minimally) 'public goods' such as defence and law and order. (This also serves to reduce private expenditure (Allen, 1971: p. 23).) The second is to act discriminately as a tool of social policy. Luxury can be involved on both counts.

DIRECT AND INDIRECT TAXATION

Revenue can be raised directly or indirectly. In contemporary societies the former comes in the guise of an income tax, while the latter can appear variously as some form of purchase tax as well as excise duties. Historically, consumption taxes of differing sorts were the major source of revenue. As late as the mid-eighteenth century in Britain out of a total revenue of £6.75 million, customs and excise contributed £5.5 million (Sabine, 1966: p. 16). Almost every conceivable comestible and utensil from raisins to vinegar to stone bottles to candles has at some time been imposted (Dowell, 1884: vol. IV). The reasons for this dominance and breadth of incidence are reasonably straightforward. The most important is negative. The computation of the amount of income was beyond the capacity of a taxing authority. It was not until 1798 that something approaching an income tax was levied in Britain. Its imposition then was because of the time-honoured need to raise funds to support military action – in this case the expense of the Napoleonic Wars – but even then its contribution was less than that derived from excise.

However, with the increased demand for revenue the drawbacks to reliance on indirect taxes became evident. By its very nature the 'return' of these taxes was open to fluctuations caused by the ability to forgo consumption of the good in question. Here the determination of what is to count as a 'luxury' becomes relevant. If 'luxuries' were targeted for tax then, because of elasticity or substitutability, revenue might well diminish as consumption of these goods declined. To offset this fluctuation by taxing the relatively inelastic 'necessities' itself runs into problems. These are problems partly of a moral sort. Luxuries, because they can be forgone without harm, may be judged to be a morally more appropriate object of taxation than necessities, which by definition are not forgoable and not dissociable from harm. In addition, a tax on necessities means that the poor, because the percentage of their total expenditure devoted to necessities is high, would be contributing disproportionately more than the rich (I will return to this in the next section). Even if the moral considerations do not weigh heavily – and historically they are not conspicuous – there are also practical problems. Any taxation of necessities will be inefficient since a premium will be placed upon evasion.

For these reasons once the collection of income tax became feasible it was adopted. Once adopted it assumed its current dominance since it could simultaneously raise revenue in sufficient quantities and meet the increasingly expressed moral case of equity because it could be levied relative to income, either as a proportion or (later) on a progressive scale. Yet despite these advantages contemporary states have not abolished indirect taxes. A number of explanations can be given for this, even apart from institutional inertia and difficulties in overturning long-established practices.

Negatively, indirect taxes provide a back-up so that even those who have no income nevertheless contribute to the public purse. Also negatively, in their absence the revenue they do raise would have to be obtained directly and the increased burden that this would entail is often regarded as having serious disincentive effects upon effort. There are also positive reasons for their continuance. It is here that the second reason for levying taxes comes into focus. Taxes, as well as raising revenue, can also be used as an instrument of social policy. For example, they can help police 'externalities' – taxing goods made in atmospherically polluting factories can help not only meet the costs of such pollution but also act as an incentive to remove the cause of the pollution in the first place. The converse is also possible, by subsidising environmentally 'friendly' production. A further example is, in a version of mercantilism, the placing of duties on foreign goods in order to protect or nurture domestic industry.

In these examples the role of deliberate political decision is clear. This role is also discernible in other positive reasons for indirect taxes. These are the reasons that are of concern to us. What indirect taxes enable the government to do is discriminate between activities. The discrimination can be based on judgments about the quality of life of its citizens, for example, duties on tobacco, extra duty on leaded over unleaded petrol. Implicit in these judgments are assumptions about what constitutes social necessities and what constitutes luxuries.

Before proceeding we should ask why governments should wish to discriminate between necessity and luxury. This is an important question to ask because it would be administratively simpler and cheaper to collect it (an obviously relevant point when the object is to gather, not expend, revenue) if the rate of tax was uniform and applied to all goods. It is, therefore, reasonable to suppose that there must be other factors at work. Indeed this is why there are *positive* reasons for indirect taxes. While they can be criticised for lack of 'neutrality' or the distortion of consumer choices, and thus (so the criticism runs) inhibiting an efficient economy, they are favoured precisely for their impact upon choice.[2] Since a tax system is designed then the impact is intended, though that is not to say the actual consequences match the intentions. Nevertheless those intentions reveal much about a society (or about an elite portion thereof) and its sense of priorities. It seems to be a truth about society that it is impossible not to make priorities. Hence, aside from the specific items identified as 'luxuries', there is the conceptually prior question of why the division between them and necessities is made in the first place. That question will occupy us in the concluding chapter.

HUME AND SMITH ON TAXATION OF LUXURIES

Unsurprisingly, given the earlier discussion, the justifications for taxing luxuries at a special rate depend on whether the chief object is to garner income, that is, whether they are made before or after the systematic levying of an income tax. Writing prior to that levy, the author of *An Essay on the Causes of the Decline of Foreign Trade* [1744], for example, developed an elaborate list of some eighteen categories of articles of luxury, ranging from keeping two coaches to drinking tea, graded so that the tax paid was consistent with the 'station of life they voluntarily place themselves in' (in McCulloch, 1859: p. 218). Smith was familiar with this work, which he attributes to Mathew Decker ('an excellent authority' (*WN*: p. 514)), and he too advocated taxing luxury as a means of raising revenue. Smith closely followed Hume,

[2] Cf. Allen (1971: p. 92) for the economists' version, 'one of the functions of government is to manipulate the consumption of merit and demerit goods by taxes and subsidies (negative taxes)'.

who had declared that taxes levied upon consumption are 'best' and he singled out those upon luxury for special merit (*Essay*, 'Of Taxes': p. 345). The reasons he gives for this judgment are that they are 'least felt' and are paid 'gradually and insensibly'. Because of this, he believes, they seem to be in some measure voluntary since how much of the commodity is consumed is open to choice. In addition, he maintains that they 'naturally produce sobriety and frugality'. Their chief drawback is that they are expensive to levy. Given Smith's indebtedness to Hume we find, consistent with this analysis, that taxes on luxuries pass three of his four 'canons' of taxation – they are equitable, certain and convenient and only fall foul of the criterion of economy (*WN*: pp. 896–7, cf. p. 825).

The link made by Hume and Smith (and Decker) between a tax on luxury and its voluntary character raises the question of the 'place' of necessity in their schema. To advocate a differential tax on luxuries is, at least in part, implicitly to criticise a policy that fails to discriminate between luxury and necessity. Smith gives a mixture of arguments to underwrite that advocacy. He supplies an economic argument to the effect that a tax on necessities is in practice a tax on wages which will be displaced or translated into higher prices generally, whereas a tax on luxuries only raises the prices of those specific goods and is not displaced more generally (*WN*: p. 873). This argument is supported by more overtly moral ones. Smith declares that a 'window-tax' is an inequity of the 'worst kind' since it falls more heavily upon the poor than the rich (p. 846). A tax on houses on the contrary would fall more heavily upon the rich because the 'luxuries and vanities of life' are frequently manifested in magnificent dwellings (p. 842). This same line of reasoning leads Smith to advocate levying higher tolls on private carriages than on commercial traffic. The former are an expression of the 'indolence and vanity of the rich', who will, via their tolls, thus contribute 'in a very easy manner' to the relief of the poor by reducing transportation costs and thereby keeping down the cost of necessities (p. 725).

As this example testifies, Smith is well aware that the poor spend more of their income on necessities than do the rich. This in itself says little, but Smith is more forthcoming. As we saw in Chapter 7, Smith did not accept Mandeville's rigorous definition of luxury. Instead he adopted a sociologically more sensitive notion. He introduced the notions of 'decency' and 'shame', the definitions of which were relative to customs of the country (*WN*: p. 870). Smith's examples were a linen shirt and leather shoes. Although unknown to the Romans, these are now 'necessities' because their non-possession by a day-labourer is a source of shame. This should mean, though Smith does not explicitly make the point, that these articles should not be taxed (or should be taxed at a lesser rate than luxuries). Smith defines 'luxuries' negatively as everything not accounted a necessity *on his extended definition.* He mentions beer and ale because it is possible to abstain from their consumption by choice, both because there are alternative sources of liquid refreshment and because to be abstemious is not a source of shame. Smith actually goes on to remark that taxes on these beverages act 'as sumptuary laws' upon the 'sober and industrious poor' because they cause them to moderate their consumption of what are in fact 'superfluities which they can no longer easily afford' (p. 872).

We should, perhaps, point out that Smith is not here contradicting his opposition to sumptuary law. He implicitly disavows a 'moralised' reading of 'luxury' by stating that he does not wish 'to throw the smallest degree of reproach upon their temperate use'. This is to adopt Hume's notion of 'excessive' luxury; in itself 'luxury' is not to be condemned. The merit in the form of an encouragement to sobriety that Smith sees in these taxes is crucially an indirect effect. The taxes act only *as* a sumptuary law unlike a sumptuary law proper which directly forbids particular behaviour and, as we observed above (p. 115), Smith is forthright in his denunciation of such prohibitions.

LUXURY, NECESSITY AND TAXATION

What is more generally informative here is that, although sumptuary legislation has indeed fallen into abeyance, the use of the fiscal system indirectly to affect behaviour is very much alive. Moreover, as we shall now see, this use distinguishes in a Smithian way between luxuries and necessities. However, with the implementation of income tax as the major source of revenue the justifications for a differential tax upon luxuries change their emphasis. When we turn to the detail of actual taxes, the two issues raised in Smith's amendment of Mandeville remain crucial, namely, the problem of defining necessity/luxury and the assumptions about a society's values and priorities that its definitions reveal.

To tax luxuries exceptionally is frequently criticised for its arbitrariness (cf. Silverman, 1931: p. 71; Kaldor, 1959: p. 22). There is some ambiguity here. It might mean that the tax requires such attention to detail that it leads to inconsistency. There are plenty of cases where the commitment to tax luxuries at a differential rate has produced hair-splitting. For example, when a special 'luxury' rate of Value-Added Tax (VAT) was introduced in Britain it produced the situation where irons were taxed as luxuries but ironing-boards were not (James & Nobes, 1978: p. 234). Luxury taxes can also be arbitrary because the category is in itself indeterminate. I will return to that point and its implications. Nevertheless it is a significant fact that tax systems do operate – sometimes explicitly sometimes implicitly – with notions of necessity and luxury. Hence, even if we allow for a due measure of arbitrariness in the first sense, when we look at what a society puts in what categories we can see its assumptions about what constitutes a necessity and what a luxury at work.

The best way to substantiate that claim is by means of some concrete cases. One such case is the United Kingdom's list (as of mid-1991) of zero-rated and exempt goods for VAT.

VAT IN THE UK

The following are zero-rated; food, water, books and newspapers, fuel and power, public transport, children's clothing, prescription drugs. The following are exempt; education, health, funeral and postal services, insurance, rent and land, betting and gaming. The difference between the two categories is that the trader can reclaim any tax charged on inputs for zero-rated goods but not for exempt goods (cf. Lee & Pashardes, 1988: p. 15). All other goods and services are taxed at 17.5 per cent.

These lists – with the apparent exception of the inclusion of betting and gaming[3] – provide us with a snapshot of what the UK government deems social necessities. Some reflect the exigencies of life in an industrial, late twentieth-century society – hence food, water, health and funeral services, clothing (though only children's).[4] 'Rent' reflects a mixture. It is both a testament to the basic need of shelter

---

[3] To explain the inclusion of betting and gaming by noting that these practices are subject to excise duties does not distinguish them from tobacco and alcohol on which both excise and VAT are levied.

[4] The restriction to children may conceivably be an expression of the fact that all societies think their youth important (although the other EC countries do not extend this expression to clothing). In addition, the exemptions upon education services are not confined to under-sixteen-year-olds. What might explain the specialness of clothing is that it is not, in general, purchased by the children themselves – they are a cost upon their parents/guardians. Once a certain maturity has been reached, then an independent economic life is possible and, with the resources that brings, comes the ability to give effect to choice.

and to the fact that in the UK home-owners receive other benefits from the tax system.

Any listings such as these are discriminatory and reflect, thereby, certain values and the exercise of political decision (they are also, therefore, liable to change). This is perhaps more obvious at the borderline. We can briefly examine two cases. These have been chosen because in different ways they reveal the implicit values.

Female sanitary wear

This is a case where a product is liable to VAT but for which there exists a strong lobby to exempt/zero-rate it (it has been part of the Labour Party's election manifestos). The premise of the argument for change is that the current practice, which should but does not apply in this case, manifests the political judgment that 'necessities' are not liable to VAT. The argument itself is that it is a physical fact that women menstruate, they have no choice in the matter. This absence of choice distinguishes this case from the frequently cited analogous case of razors. While the growth of facial hair is also a non-optional physical fact, men *do* have the choice of not shaving. The reason men have choice is because in the UK beards are socially respectable, whereas menstruation is still largely taboo (it is only recently that even very limited, somewhat coy, advertisements have been permitted on British television). Because of this difference then, so the argument goes, the fact that razors attract VAT is beside the point. Similarly irrelevant is the counter-argument that there are alternative measures, such as, according to one male MP, washable nappies (see *The Guardian* 3/4/90), because there exist products that are specifically designed for the purpose (in the same way that razors are) and are, as such, hygienic. The 'health angle' is also exploited by claiming that tampons etc. are health products (which are VAT-free) or that the extra cost of tampons (because of VAT) causes them to be used longer than medically advisable with proven fatal consequences in the form of toxic shock syndrome.

This case illustrates how the decision to levy different rates of tax on different goods is discriminatory in both the strict and pejorative senses of the word. If 'necessity' is indeed the criterion for the non-levying of VAT then some judgment is required to identify that criterion in particular cases. It is presumably one of the basic tasks of government to exercise that discrimination for the common good.

This case exemplifies just how disputable that exercise is. A protagonist for change could explain the presence of VAT on these products by the social fact that it is men who do the discriminating. It is the values of patriarchy that are manifest. Men who by definition have no direct experience of the product have used their power, whether wittingly or not is immaterial, to the detriment of women by taxing a necessity. Even if that explanation is not accepted in its entirety it does highlight the key point that definitions of necessity/need are importantly political. And since to define is also to exclude then the identification of the non-necessary (including the luxurious) is also a product of political decision. This relationship between necessity and luxury will be the focus of Chapter 9.

Food

This is a case where within one of the categories certain further specifications have been thought appropriate. Regarding 'food' there are exceptions to the zero-rating. Ice-cream, confectionery including chocolate products, crisps and prepared nuts are subject to VAT as are all drinks, except tea and coffee. The last two are excepted on the grounds that they are the commonest beverages. This fact has not been offset by any doubts (especially regarding coffee) over their innocuousness.

What this discrimination between foodstuffs reveals is certain low-level nutritional judgments. The exceptions fall into the realm of 'snacks' and possess a high sugar content (though they are scarcely alone in that). By identifying them through these features the judgment appears to be that if not taxed their consumption would increase to the detriment of a healthy diet. It is a mark of 'modern' governance that it interprets its concern with the common good to include a concern with its citizens' 'health'; hence the zero-rating of drugs and exemption of health services. This is an area where the government can draw upon the 'objectivity' of needs – a point we shall shortly meet again – you might want more sugar but you don't need it. Yet it is not difficult to detect here an aspect of what has been called 'food ideology'. The very term 'snack', meaning something eaten between 'main meals', is itself indicative of the 'social and ideological values attached to food [that] are . . . crucial in defining what is meant by proper eating' (Charles and Kerr, quoted in Veit-Wilson, 1987: p. 185).

Once again there is no need to accept this position in its entirety for it to highlight that, notwithstanding this appeal to objective facts, it is judgments or assessments that are decisive. These judgments discriminate, but once discrimination is made in this way then it opens the way to the same charge of arbitrariness that had been laid against luxury tax. When is a snack a snack and not 'food'? This question has been put to the test. The manufacturer of one particular brand of confectionery argued that because their product contained essentially the same ingredients as breakfast cereal, which was zero-rated, their 'chewy-bar' should be similarly judged. Moreover, since it contained less sugar than the average 'sweet' it did not qualify as 'confectionery' under the Act. The judgment was made in favour of the manufacturer (see Law Report, *The Times* 15/10/87). Interestingly the law was subsequently changed to make the product liable.[5]

Having once made some discrimination, the absence now in the UK of a special luxury rate of VAT is, comparatively speaking, noticeable. Not only, as we saw, was food a major target of sumptuary laws but also in modern societies we find that, for example, the Italian government in 1991 levied an extra tax on expensive food like lobsters (see *The Times* 13/5/91) and the French government levied a high luxury tax rate of 33.3 per cent on caviar and *pâté de foie gras* (Sullivan, 1965: p. 91).

The most plausible explanation for the absence of a special luxury rate is the pragmatic one of practicality. It is possible to provide speculatively an explanation in line with the principles spelt out above. What the two lists of zero-rated and exempt goods signify is an illustration of the precedence principle. That is, it is deemed more important to itemise goods and services that are essential to (British) social life than to attempt to discriminate between necessities and luxuries. In its turn this reflects the judgment that there is more likely to be a social consensus over the contents of these lists than over one which separated out luxuries from other non-essential goods. I will discuss this point further in the next section. However, it bears repeating that this is speculative. More realistically, the exclusion of a special 'luxury' rate is to be put down to administrative convenience.

---

[5] This case is not unique. A later example is the status of the product called (in the UK) a 'Jaffa Cake'. The Customs and Excise claimed that because the product was packaged like biscuits and sold on biscuit shelves it was a confection liable to VAT. The manufacturer claimed it was cake because its chief ingredient was sponge and was therefore not eligible for VAT rating. The VAT tribunal found in favour of the manufacturer. See *Financial Times* 29/8/91.

It seems a fair presumption that if for political/economic reasons it was thought worthwhile to levy an extra tax on luxuries it would be done. The US government did precisely that in 1990.

We can take this US action as a second concrete case. In the 1990 Budget, as part of a package designed as an initial step to eliminate the federal deficit, the US government explicitly introduced a new luxury tax of 10 per cent. The tax applied to private transport (aircraft, boats and cars) and to jewels and furs. The tax was only levied when the goods were already highly priced, for example, on cars above $30,000 (see *Financial Times* 31/10/90).

The implicit justification for this new rate is (we may hazard) two-fold. Firstly, these goods are not necessities in the sense that cheaper versions, or alternatives in the case of furs, exist. The non-necessitarian element is further supported by the fact that vehicles that are used for business are not eligible for the tax. Accordingly, and secondly, if consumers persist in purchasing $50,000 cars (which will now cost them $55,000) it means that it provides a good index of ability to pay (cf. Silverman, 1931: p. 19). This also means, as Hume and Smith had observed, that these consumers are deliberately choosing to incur this tax. But, of course, the reasons for that choice can be diverse and certainly, from an individual's point of view, are not conterminous with it being a luxurious indulgence (see the discussion of the Rolls-Royce in Chapter 1). What the US government has done is to take a cut-off point and say that, *for its purposes*, goods bought at above that level are 'luxury goods'.

This tells us two things. One that it confuses 'luxury' with 'expensive' but, two, that that confusion is the seemingly inevitable outcome of having to adopt a uniform social definition. A society (its government) has to assume a certain schedule of needs and desires and a certain prioritising of them. Regardless of how it concretely specifies them, a society will declare that needs should be met ahead of luxury. In practice, this can mean, as Walzer (1983: p. 67) cites, the ancient Athenians providing public baths and gymnasia but nothing like the social security provision of twentieth-century societies. (I will return to Walzer's argument in the next chapter.) As we pointed out in Chapter 1, and discerned as being present in the UK VAT legislation concerning confectionery, this social definition of need carries with it the objectivity or matter-of-factness characteristic of needs-language in general.

By virtue of this characteristic the government/taxing authority can ignore the subjective differences, such as the reasons for buying a Rolls-Royce, between its citizens. As a practical matter it has to assume that 'temperamentally all tax-payers are alike' (Pigou, quoted in Kaldor, 1959: p. 29n, cf. p. 205). But by invoking the language of needs it can utilise that language's 'objectivity' and 'universality' to underwrite the assumption. However, these same considerations should in all consistency preclude the tax system from making any judgments about luxury. By definition, as the US legislation testifies, luxuries are not needed, so the assumption of uniformity is not warranted. Any tax on luxuries is thus a tax on desires, on positive choices.[6]

To justify such a tax is to invoke some judgment about the desirability of the desires. And that judgment cannot but be indicative of the society's scale of values. While historically this was undoubtedly more overt and the relative infrequency of explicit 'luxury taxes' is some testament to modern sensibilities about the importance of individual choice, the point remains true. Hence even in the US case where revenue raising was the general aim (as well as, perhaps, representing a 'mercantilist' aim by making imported 'luxury cars' still more expensive) there is the implicit assumption that to target by price those three areas of consumption would be more acceptable than targeting, say, housing or holidays.

The fact that the US did, despite those sensibilities, levy a luxury tax confirms the argument that it is because indirect taxes in general rely on the mediation of choice that 'luxuries' have seemed well-suited to that mode of taxation. By the same token 'necessities' seem ill-suited. Any social policy, or set of priorities, that operates via a luxury tax must be in general terms sumptuary; it does not have a redistributive effect. Indirect taxes are regressive – someone with three times the income of another does not consume three times as much. As Smith had been well aware, the less the household income,

---

[6] Of course, it can be argued that all taxes, even direct ones, are taxes on choice, since I cannot spend at my discretion income the government has deducted. Libertarians automatically assume this is bad and wish to reduce the deduction to a minimum. In this context, Nozick (1974: p. 170) provides a good illustrative example of how taxation can impact differentially on desires. He gives the case of two individuals one of whom prefers the cinema and thus to pay for his ticket has to work overtime and pay tax on his extra earnings, the other's preferred pastime is watching sunsets, for which preference no extra work is required and no extra tax is levied.

the higher the percentage of that income devoted to meeting needs rather than realising desires. As we have seen and will meet again, there are analytical grounds for querying that contrast between needs and desires and for attributing an unqualified precedence to the former. Nevertheless, as we have also seen, the distinction is central to social policy. I now turn to that policy. In particular, I want to consider how the debate over the nature of poverty intersects with a society's view of luxury.

III

Rather than provide a comprehensive overview of the 'poverty debate', which would take us beyond the boundaries of this study, I adopt a selective approach. The criterion of selection is the light that some aspects of the debate throw upon certain central contentions. These include the supposed innocence of luxury, the transient quality of luxury as well as the general theme of this chapter, the connexions between notions of need, desire and broadly conceived social policy.

I argued in Chapter 1 (p. 19) that some goods in society become invested with the special status of being social necessities and, as such, they can have a prima facie claim upon the public purse. What underlies this claim is the belief that social necessities carry moral weight and impose obligations. That the government, as the controller of the public purse, is ultimately responsible for meeting those obligations is a prominent characteristic of the discussion of poverty. It has been argued that the 'term "poverty"' itself 'carries with it the implication and moral imperative that something should be done about it' and, further, that the study of poverty 'is only ultimately justifiable' if it influences individual and social attitudes and actions (Piachaud, 1987: p. 161; cf. Walker, 1987: p. 215). This is why studies of poverty are generally critical of current social policy in so far as this policy underestimates those in need or the depth of the deprivation.

One way (among several) to gauge the depth of that deprivation is to investigate if there is a public consensus as to what constitutes an unacceptable standard of living. One of the most thorough and thoughtful of such investigations was that undertaken by Mack and Lansley. Their book *Poor Britain* (1985) presents the findings of a survey that was designed to discover whether there was, in Britain in 1983, such a consensus. The survey took the form of a list of thirty-five household items (chosen after pilot studies) and asked those surveyed to distinguish, for each item, whether they possessed and could not do without it; possessed it but could do without it; did not have it and did not want it; did not have it but could not afford it (Mack & Lansley, 1985: p. 53). As the authors state, these questions are based on a 'simple binary distinction' between items that were 'necessities' and those that might be desirable but were not necessary (ibid.: p. 52).

The underlying rationale of Mack and Lansley's approach is captured in their judgment that 'items become "necessities" only when they are *socially* perceived to be so' (ibid.: p. 38, authors' emphasis). They then stipulate that 'poverty' is to be defined in terms of an 'enforced lack of socially perceived necessities' (ibid.: p. 39) and declare that those who lack three or more of these necessities are 'poor'.[7] As critics have pointed out (e.g. Piachaud, 1987: p. 150; Walker, 1987: p. 218), this definition is not an explicit finding of the survey but we can nevertheless usefully take note of some of their results.

What is particularly apt is what the survey revealed about what was thought to constitute 'necessity'. Over 90 per cent of the respondents regarded as necessities domestic heating; a non-shared toilet and bath; a damp-free home and beds for each inhabitant. An additional nine items were classified as necessities by more than two-thirds – enough money for public transport; a warm waterproof coat; three meals a day for children; self-contained accommodation; two pairs of all-weather shoes; bedroom for children of different sexes over ten years old; a refrigerator; toys for children; carpets; celebrations on special occasions like Christmas; roast meat (or equivalent) once a week and a washing-machine (Mack & Lansley, 1985: pp. 53–5).

Mack and Lansley themselves comment of these lists that they highlight the impact of labour-saving household goods. They note especially the inclusion of a refrigerator and a washing-machine and comment that 'even twenty years ago [they] would have been seen as a luxury' (ibid.: p. 55). Indeed in a follow-up survey, the percentage saying a refrigerator was a necessity rose to ninety-two.[8] As a further

___

[7] While there is little difference among the income deciles between households which forgo one necessity from choice (45 per cent in the lowest to 41 per cent in the highest), at three necessities the difference is 14 per cent to 4 per cent. They gloss this to mean that 'the rich do not choose lifestyles associated with lack of necessities' (Mack & Lansley, 1985: p. 96). They also observe that there is a tendency among 'the most intensely deprived' to say they do not want an item because they have already excluded that item from their range of choices (ibid.: p. 95). Cf. Elster's (1985a) notion of 'adaptive preferences'.

[8] Mack and Lansley (1985: pp. 56–7) gloss this to mean that these goods have become necessary 'because other aspects of life are planned and built on the very fact that these items are customary'. As we noted in Chapter 1, there has been a sharp decline in public wash-houses so that the choices of those without washing-machines are limited. A similar story can be told about refrigerators; food is sold on the assumption that it can be stored over a period of days.

testament to changing ideas of necessity, in this same survey 13 per cent stated that a video-recorder was a 'necessity' (14 per cent was the lowest of the thirty-five items deemed a necessity in 1983) (see *New Statesman & Society* 19/4/91).[9]

As the authors themselves note, their findings demonstrate empirically that luxuries have become necessities and Donnison (1988) even uses that demonstration as the basis for his concept of poverty. I wish now to explore that transition more systematically in order to draw out some further implications of the poverty debate for this study. There are two implications in particular that I wish to explicate. The first is the idea that poverty is a relative concept, and the second, which follows on from this, is that the 'innocence' of luxury may be questioned.

THE RELATIVITY OF POVERTY

The fact that 'luxuries' become 'necessities' has been taken as a vindication of the 'relativity' conception of poverty. The best-known exponent of this conception is Peter Townsend. At the beginning of his massive study *Poverty in the United Kingdom* (1979: p. 31) he stated that 'poverty can be defined objectively and applied consistently only in terms of the concept of relative deprivation'. If we leave aside for the moment the commitment to 'objectivism', at the heart of Townsend's enterprise is the conviction that 'need' must be understood sociologically. In other words, needs must be defined in terms of society and not in terms of some extra-societal criterion; as it was put in Chapter 1, needs are embedded in culture. Since axiomatically societies/cultures differ then, it follows, so too will the identification of needs. To be 'in need', to be 'in poverty', must therefore be relative to society. There are two dimensions to this relativity. Needs are relative across space – society A vis-à-vis society B – and time – society A at T vis-à-vis at T₁ – but, secondly, within society A at T₁ those who are in need are so relative to the standards of that society and that time (rather than society B or A at T).

Townsend emphasises the social, as opposed to the extra-social,

---

[9] This finding is redolent of the 'relativity' of luxury as discussed in Chapter 1. It also serves to reinforce the argument that 'luxury' is not some superadded category. Even those goods that almost everyone judges to be a necessity retain the element of choice. This retention is not itself open to choice. All goods, necessities included, are such under some description – they possess a qualitative aspect. This explains how it is possible for everyone to agree that a bathroom is necessary, is a basic need, while there are many manufacturers who market their product as a 'luxury bathroom'. The latter, as we argued in Chapter 1, is a qualitative/adjectival refinement, not a separate, superadded category – a luxury bathroom is still a bathroom.

because he associates the latter with the absolute conception of poverty. Beverly Shaw (1988: p. 29), a critic of the relative conception, is explicit that the reference in the absolute approach is to 'man as such' and not to a specific society or culture. She also makes it clear that 'man as such' refers principally to 'our biological nature'. Townsend (1985: p. 664), by contrast, is insistent that this is too narrow an understanding of needs. He believes absolutists – he has Amartya Sen (1983) explicitly in mind – underestimate the importance of needs other than those for food. He adopts a compendious conception that refers to needs (implicitly) as 'the conditions of life which ordinarily define membership of society'. These conditions comprise 'diets, amenities, standards, services and activities which are common or customary' (Townsend, 1979: p. 915). The poor are now identified, by Townsend, as those who lack the resources to participate in those customary conditions definitive of social member-ship, that is, they are 'excluded from ordinary living patterns' (ibid.: p. 31). (The references to 'custom' (ibid.: p. 32n; 1985: p. 666) deliberately evoke Smith.)

If luxuries become necessities and individuals are deprived by non-possession of these necessities it means that they are deprived by not having what were, at one time, luxuries. This strikes advocates of an absolutist approach as incongruous. It leads theoretically to a situation where there are more people who are 'relatively' poor in California than there are in Bangladesh. According to one theorist, poverty, like scarcity, is the 'invention of civilization. It has grown with civilization' (Sahlins, 1974: p. 37, cf. p. 4). Refrigerators, we might presume, remain a luxury good in Bangladesh but are a necessity in California so that non-possession of a luxury in the former country is an instance of poverty in the latter. Townsend is (consistently) unabashed by this presumption. He openly declares that 'despite continual economic growth over a period of years, the proportion of the population of an advanced industrial society which is found to be in poverty might rise' (Townsend, 1979: p. 31). It is because necessity is not a fixed or absolute state that it can accommodate one-time luxuries and the fact that while not having a refrigerator would have been no source of concern in the past, now it can be.

The idea that poverty is socially relative leads on to a further question once we consider what response is appropriate to deal with it. As we have seen, on Townsend's argument, in an affluent society the poor are those who are deprived of the consumer goods characteristic of such societies. They are deprived, that is to say, of the household items, the gadgets and the like, the leisure pursuits, the varied diet and the fashionable clothing that are presented by advertisers and others as the norm. By not possessing (say) a colour television, a household is made to feel ab- or sub-normal through the simple glib assumption that everyone has one.

Two responses are possible to this. The first, and consistent response, is to argue for a social arrangement so that everyone relative to everyone else should be 'normal'. The second is to criticise this whole emphasis upon consumer goods. In making this criticism the latter response questions the casual assumption that luxury is innocent.

POVERTY AND EQUALITY

While Townsend's 'logic' ought to make him adopt the first response, there are signs that he is resistant to it. In particular, he is critical of the approach adopted by Mack and Lansley because it fails to take properly on board the 'indoctrinated quality of our social perceptions' (1987: p. 477).[10] To judge perceptions as 'indoctrinated' is to adopt some standpoint other than that currently accepted. This is where Townsend's 'objectivism' comes forcefully into play. He is unequivocal that 'people may be in poverty when they believe they are not' (1985: p. 661; cf. 1979: p. 429). Such sentiments do, of course, chime in perfectly with the language of need. This is significant because Townsend's objective approach, like much of that concerned with poverty, is also openly prescriptive. In Townsend's case, in order to

[10] For their part, Mack and Lansley had deliberately focused on social perception to meet a standard criticism of Townsend's own 'objective' approach. In his 1979 study he had included not eating a cooked breakfast and not taking a holiday in his index of deprivation but, as critics pointed out, the failure to partake of these could be explained by individuals choosing to forgo them (cf. Piachaud, 1981; Ashton, 1984). Mack and Lansley (1985: p. 99) did therefore 'control' for taste and concluded that although it can be 'easily overestimated', their findings do 'suggest' it is worthwhile to exercise that control.

Nevertheless they criticised the argument that the poor are poor because, to a significant extent, their *choices*, such as whether or not to smoke, have cumulatively produced that outcome (cf. Joseph & Sumption, 1979: p. 27). Mack and Lansley deliberately used smoking to test for fecklessness as a cause of poverty. They did indeed find that those who lacked none of the standard-of-living necessities were the least heavy smokers (only 34 per cent buying a packet every other day), while of those who lacked eight necessities 50 per cent bought cigarettes with that frequency. They argued, however, that the difference is marginal – even if the money spent on cigarettes had been spent on necessities, these households would still have been deprived. They go further and claim that the causality is more likely to be the reverse, that is, the poor smoke because they are deprived not vice versa (Mack & Lansley, 1985: pp. 124–5).

remedy the 'bad' of poverty he advocates *inter alia* the abolition of 'excessive' income and wealth and the establishment of a more egalitarian society (1979: p. 926).

This egalitarianism is in line with the first of the two responses mentioned above. As we noted, the way to end 'relativity' is to enable all to enjoy the socially 'normal' pattern of consumption. As we shall see, the second response regards this as mistaken because it does not query the assumptions of consumption but simply its unequal distribution. Before turning to that response the connexion between poverty and equality merits a brief comment.

A clear distinction between the notions of absolute poverty and equality can be made. As Adam Smith held, universal poverty and equality were the conjoined experience of the first state of society but though there was inequality in a commercial society even the humblest there was far better provided for than in the first state. The underlying principle here has been made into a policy prescription. The claim is that the way to alleviate absolute poverty is to permit inequality in the form of wide income differentials so that the incentive to gain these high rewards produces the social wealth that enables even the relatively impoverished to escape poverty, absolutely understood. If the issue is indeed that of poverty then, as an advocate of the relativity of poverty like Townsend is aware, relativity and equality remain separate questions (e.g. Townsend, 1979: p. 57). Frankfurt crisply states the case for separation. He writes, 'what *is* important from the point of view of morality is not that everyone should have *the same* but that each should have enough. If everyone had enough it would be of no moral consequence whether some had more than others' (1988: pp. 134–5, author's emphases; cf. Raz, 1986: pp. 239–40). This same line of reasoning can be extended to include luxury. Both inequality and luxury are separable from poverty because the (morally salient) issue is not whether some enjoy comparatively more wealth but whether some have less than enough to lead a socially acceptable worthwhile life.

However, these separations can be challenged. Luxury and inequality can be connected to poverty by adopting some sort of a causal argument to the effect that *because* some in society are able to indulge in luxuries others are in poverty. But even leaving aside the tenability of such an argument it is confused in two ways. It is confused because by implication it equates luxury with a quantum of funds that makes expensive goods affordable but, as we have argued, such goods are not conterminous with luxury goods. It is confused, too, because it deals only with the quantum and not with the qualitative aspect of luxuries. Two individuals can have the same quantum but meet their needs and indulge in luxuries differently – Gerry eats fillet steak and goes youth-hostelling, Harry eats ox-tail and takes Caribbean cruises.

We move now to the second response, which takes the form of a general, principled critique of consumerism. At the heart of this response is the assertion that poverty and luxury are indeed connected and the denial, thereby, that luxury is innocent. The first response wanted to end relative poverty by ensuring that the social norms of consumption were enjoyed by all; in California but not in Bangladesh all should have a refrigerator. This acquiesces in, and thus validates, an ever-increasing accumulation of consumer goods. And given the dynamic of the transition from luxury to necessity it acquiesces in, and thus sees no inherent harm in, the role that luxury plays. The second response does detect harm; luxury is not 'innocent'.

We intimated the grounds of this response in Chapter 7. From Hegel there is extractable the idea that 'luxury' could be viewed as a symptom of the excesses of an unregulated Civil Society. His solution was Police action, that is, the action of the State in Civil Society. From Marx there is extractable the view that 'luxury' is a symptom of the ceaseless pursuit of exchange-value. His solution is not (illusory) neutral state action but the submission of the economy to conscious direction that would put use-value uppermost. Though very different, Hegel and Marx, by virtue of their retention of a place for luxury in a moralised vocabulary of needs, are both critical of the de-moralisation that we charted in Chapters 5 and 6, *in so far as* this was associated with the emergence of a liberal view of the economy.

Against this backcloth it is not surprising to discover that the contemporary criticisms of luxury's supposed innocence take the view that this innocence betrays a liberal celebration of desire in the form of the indefeasibility of 'free' choice in all aspects of life. These criticisms look upon this 'innocence' as an ideological construct that serves to underpin a capitalist economy and, increasingly, to underpin also a dangerously exploitative attitude to natural resources. A major ingredient in this argument is the claim that consumption is vital to the continuation and expansion of capitalism, with (as the 'Greens' would add) consequent deleterious effect on the environment. The capitalist emphasis on 'choice', and its associated freedom, is illusory because the choice is 'constructed'. Nor are 'needs' exempt from this process since they too are social constructions (recall the 'radical' thesis that I associated with Baudrillard in Chapter 1). Crucially for this second response the process is not neutral. In Marcuse's well-known (or notorious) version, this is expressed in his notion of 'false needs', that is, those that are repressive through being 'superimposed upon the individual by particular social interests'. Marcuse (1964: p. 5, cf. p. 245) includes in this category the need 'to behave and consume in accordance with the advertisements'. Consumption, though seemingly the sphere of subjective choice and judgment, occurs within an arena where goods have 'come to be defined as either "necessary" or "luxury" goods for differentially placed social groups and classes' and is thus (so the argument goes) inseparable from 'relations of privilege and power' (Tomlinson, 1990: p. 20). Marx himself defined luxury goods as those goods consumed by the capitalist class and not by the working class (except in freak conditions of prosperity and then only as a harbinger of crisis) (*Capital*: II, 410–11).

In the light of this argument luxury appears to be guilty on two related counts. Firstly it is associated with status or exclusiveness. This association, largely the creation of the advertising industry, serves as a goal for the mass of consumers who attempt to attain these goods and emulate those who already possess them. But, of course, once attained they no longer possess their original status and other goods have meantime taken on the cachet of 'luxury'. Luxury is thus a key element in the drive to consume and the effect of this is to generate profits and, thereby, maintain capitalism, while simultaneously, from the Green perspective, depleting the stock of sustainable resources.

On the second count, luxury is guilty because of its wastefulness. This accusation can take various forms. Luxury can be indicted because of its disutility – it absorbs labour that would be 'better' expended on more socially beneficial production (cf. Sidgwick, 1894). This can be given a more straightforwardly 'moral' twist in line with the classical and Christian tradition. Laveleye, for example, asserts within his general denunciation that luxury is unjustifiable because it leads men to squander on useless superfluities what ought to be given to the poor (*Luxury*: p. 59). Or, more recently with an argument amenable to the Green dimension, Hirsch (1977: pp. 66, 82, 84, *et passim*) decries the erosion of sociability and citizenship that follows from the self-interested and incessant desire to accumulate more consumer goods, especially luxuries which, on his understanding, ever escape the grasp. Finally, and chiefly from our current perspective, linking up with the first accusation, luxury is emblematic of capitalism's response not to 'need' but to effective purchasing power (cf. Soper, 1981: p. 65). Those who possess capital are able to use that capacity to ensure that their whims and indulgences are gratified. The effect of this, according to one critic, is that 'it shifts production from needs to luxuries and shapes the economy to protect the privileged' (Baker, 1987: p. 18).

The underlying theme in this second response is a connexion between luxury's lack of innocence and the 'fact' that capitalism is culpably responsible for the maintenance of poverty. This is guilt by association. That is, luxury's general role as a spur to increased consumption is a pathological symptom of capitalism, which has *already and on other grounds* been judged unacceptable. It would be too much of a detour to discuss these 'grounds' here. What is appropriate is a brief comment on the relationship between this 'modern' indictment and that supplied against *luxuria*.

It is possible to see in this second response what is in effect a reprise of some elements of the classical indictment. An important reason why this response to deprivation in affluent societies is thought better than the alternative of diffusing goods more equitably is because the lust after the latest gadget is indicative of what C.B. Macpherson (1962) pejoratively labelled 'possessive individualism'. Reinforcing the argument of Part III, this doctrine is, for Macpherson, and for those many writers who follow his lead, the key ingredient in 'liberal theory'. This criticism of the lust for the possession of the latest gadget echoes, though with an important difference, the old accusation that wants are insatiable. Whereas for the ancients this lust was straight-forwardly condemned because it corrupted the manly or truly Christian virtues, the moderns are criticising the defence of that insatiability that Barbon and the other 'de-moralisers' had put forward. It is a criticism of the legitimation of infinite desire that they see lying at the heart of liberalism (cf. Macpherson, 1973: pp. 18–21). The root of the criticism, as we have seen, is that this continuous stimulation is necessitated by the inner logic of capitalism.

To criticise this insatiability presupposes, as with Townsend's notion of 'indoctrination', some external reference point. For the ancients this was a teleologically ordered 'natural life' that is properly confined to meeting 'naturally' limited needs. We noted in the conclusion to Chapter 7 that Hegel and Marx could be interpreted to yield a re-formulated version of this position. In their case the teleology was given a historical cast. This survives in those contemporary accounts that look upon capitalism as a 'stage' on the way to a superior form of society. There are also attempts to resuscitate, or maintain, the 'classical' teleological (or theological)[11] approach. However, perhaps the most common modern approach is some sort of naturalism (Aristotle *sans* teleology, we might say). Cohen, for example, distinguishes between what an individual is disposed to seek and what 'in fact' affords satisfaction. Cohen (1978: pp. 310–20) himself uses this distinction to indict capitalism for inducing the pursuit of consumption while being indifferent to the quality of the satisfaction enjoyed (cf., e.g., Gibbs, 1976; Norman, 1982). But the same distinction can be used more generally to criticise a preoccupation with the social 'norm' of consumption rather than the intrinsic satisfaction afforded by goods.

In the last analysis the impact of this line of argument upon the status or assessment of luxury remains uncertain. Are we to suppose that in moving to a more 'rational' (as it is often termed) or less wasteful society 'luxury' will have no place? It could be held that nobody *needs* an electric carving knife with interchangeable blades and thus their non-manufacture will harm no-one. Those knives already in existence could be confiscated or allowed to complete their deliberately limited life-span or, perhaps, their owners in the new 'order' will be too ashamed to use them. These are, however, largely idle speculations. If the argument in Chapter 1 carries any weight it means that the notion of luxury is no more eliminable than are human desires *per se* and, *a fortiori*, than are those desires that are concrete specifications of basic needs. I shall return to this observation in the final chapter.

---

[11] Cf. the Archbishop of Canterbury's report *Faith in the City* (1985) which remarked 'a Christian is bound to feel [a profound unease] about the moral and spiritual effects of the modern consumer economy, depending as it does on the continual stimulation of all attainable desire' (quoted in Shaw, 1988: p. 33). A somewhat similar attitude is present in Schumacher's work (influential on the Green movement) where, for example, he remarks, 'It is more than likely, as Gandhi said, that "Earth provides enough to satisfy every man's need, but not for every man's greed." Permanence is incompatible with a predatory attitude which rejoices in the fact that "what were luxuries for our fathers have become necessities for us"' (Schumacher, 1973: p. 29). Schumacher's book is suffused with a concern for spiritual values and a critique of 'materialism' which he understands as a way of life based on 'permanent limitless expansion in a finite environment' (ibid.: p. 137, cf. 'Epilogue').

NEED, DESIRE AND POLITICS

In conclusion to this chapter I want to pursue one of the implications of the critique of luxury in the guise of consumerism. This pursuit will link up with the discussion on taxation. For the government (as a branch of deliberate social policy) to concern itself with luxury, to curb consumption of what it identifies as luxury goods, is to freeze the dynamic whereby luxuries turn into social necessities. Historically this is central to the passing of sumptuary laws and it also explains why that legislation is indicative of a hierarchical society. The limited incidence of a good (one currently enjoyed typically by the social elite) is stopped from becoming general by denying its possession to the mass.

Strictly, as the failure of these laws demonstrates, this should be expressed as an *attempt* at preventing general diffusion. A crucial factor in the explanation of the failure is that, on the one hand, the elite wants to keep the luxuries, often indeed wants to parade them as a mark of its power (recall from Chapter 1 (p. 31) McKendrick's comment on the political need for Elizabeth I's wardrobe to be extravagant), while, on the other, it wants to extirpate, or at least block, the aspiration to those goods on the part of the mass of the population.

Modern critics of consumerism do not usually advocate sumptuary legislation.[12] Their questioning of the 'innocence' of luxury is usually in the name of establishing more egalitarian, certainly anti-hierarchical, values. As Galliani (1989: p. 371) points out, even by the eighteenth century luxury was no longer being condemned because it confused ranks, but for its inequality. Typically the ideal of the contemporary critics is a co-operative society where (as the slogan has it) production is for need not greed. But that too is not without its problems. To curb the luxury-to-necessity dynamic, should it be successful, would be to head-off innovation. The diffusion of all those goods now thought to be luxuries would have to be forestalled and the current level of technology frozen. There is no inconsistency in judging this to be a 'good thing' – it would have been a better society if communal wash-houses had been retained rather than the spread to almost all households of their own private washing-machines. However, what

---

[12] Rosalind Williams (1982: pp. 398–410) is one who does think that a remedy for 'our corrosive individualism' is to revive 'the concept of sumptuary legislation' in order to 'control and direct consumption'.

this entails is the making of some decision to keep society (and thus its members) at some predetermined standard. Looked at in that way the distance from the attempt at sumptuary legislation narrows. Moreover, the reasons for the failure of that legislation could also be adduced to cast doubt on the viability of extirpating a desire for novelty. In Hume's phrase, such an attempt would do violence to the usual course of things, at least in so far as they have developed over the last three centuries. This development, we can suggest, is the major obstacle to Schumacher's (1973: pp. 48–56) notion of 'Buddhist economics' as an alternative to current (harmful) practices.[13]

The notion of decisions being made to predetermine social consumption is at the heart of a very familiar debate. Hence (to return to the slogan) 'production for need' can only mean production based on some assessment/decision of what individuals require. This is made prima facie justifiable by trading on the 'objectivity' of needs, by using it as a warrant to assume uniformity – everyone needs shelter for example. However, our analysis in Chapter 1 can be used to doubt the effective practicality of this. Shelter is an abstract need, it has to be specified by desire – I want a one-bedroomed flat, you want a villa with a garden, he wants a penthouse and so on. Townsend (1985: p. 668) nevertheless believes that his account releases the 'real potentialities which do exist of planning to meet need' (Townsend, 1985: p. 668). How this potential is, in practice, actualised remains problematic. It would seem consistent with this belief that the building of large blocks of uniform flats or housing-estates – regardless of how many, if any, want such dwellings – does indeed constitute an actualisation, and not a monstrous misapplication, of the potential.[14] Moreover, such uniformity could consistently be judged a 'good thing' – differential housing, including (perhaps especially) luxury apartments, is divisive and socially harmful.

Of course that judgment, as well as the underlying reliance on

[13] The same difficulty attends Sahlin's (1974: p. 2) 'Zen road to affluence' which is premised on finite wants.
[14] Cf. Leiss (1978: pp. 72–3) who comments that the demarcation between needs and wants affects 'practical issues of social policy' because it 'encourages us to regard the sphere of needs largely as a quantitative problem: each person needs a certain amount of nutrients, shelter, space and social services. The practical outcome of this statement of basic needs is reflected in some of the social policies of the existing welfare state: bulk foodstuffs for the poor, the drab uniformity of public housing projects, and the stereotyped responses of the bureaucracies. The qualitative aspects of needs are suppressed in these policies.' Also M. Cooper (1975: p. 20) who comments, '"Needs" are those demands which in the opinion of the doctor require medical attention.'

'needs', can be disputed and not only from the Right (cf., e.g., Flew, 1977) but also from those sympathetic to State welfare (cf., e.g., Goodin, e.g. 1988). These disputes I am not concerned to rehearse. Rather I want to interpret these disputes as an exemplification of the politics of need and desire. If social necessity or needs are objective facts (even if constituted by perceptions) then uniformity of action – as with the tax system – is underwritten. But if needs cannot automatically in all cases be given precedence over desires, and if desires are themselves sources of value, then how government should act is moot. One manifestation of this is the debate in social policy about the proper form that welfare provision should take (cf. Weale, 1983). The more needs are emphasised, the more direct State-financed (through taxation, direct and indirect) action is appropriate. The more individual ordering of preferences as to what is a necessity is emphasised, the more either indirect State provision, by means of vouchers or cash, or private insurance schemes can be thought appropriate. That these are indeed questions of 'emphasis' indicates that it is a practical, political decision to distinguish needs from choices or desires, and not a pre-existing (*kata phusin*) distinction that social policy simply reproduces.

This conclusion vindicates the hypothesis put forward in Chapter 1 and examined in subsequent chapters. That hypothesis proposed that different conceptions of political order were the result of different evaluations of desire and different identifications of need. Hence, in modern thought, liberalism emphasises indirect State action because of its willingness to accept desires as the authentic voice of individual preference, and by its distrust of much needs-talk. Conversely, socialism emphasises direct State action because of its willingness to assess individual desires for any self-deception or lack of authenticity, and by its commitment to needs as a basic distributive principle.

For our purposes, more important than the relative merits of the sides in this debate is the underlying assumption. The assumption is that government cannot be indifferent in these matters. This assumption transcends the modern preoccupation with welfare. Even for Plato the just city was one where all its components performed their proper functions in their proper place. As the hypothesis proposes, all governments, generally in the name of the common good, do in practice attempt some ordering between needs and desires; they draw up and implement a version of the 'principle of precedence'. However, once some Platonic insight into the Form of the Good is denied then this 'practice' has to rely on some form of Aristotelian *phronesis*. In its determination of priorities, the government gives effect to an idea of political order which itself is the result of an understanding as to what constitutes need and what luxury. What that presupposes is the subject of the concluding chapter.

CHAPTER 9

Luxury, necessity and social identity

The aim of this concluding chapter is not to provide a summing-up of the various elements in the earlier chapters. Aside from the suspicion of redundant repetition attendant on that exercise, it would also run the risk of imposing an unwarranted uniformity. There is not some grand synthesising theory of luxury waiting in the wings. I remain sceptical of the possibility, or even of the desirability, of any such theory. All that I have attempted to provide in the preceding discussion is a conceptual framework to serve heuristically as a means of giving some shape to an amorphous subject.

Positively, the aim of this chapter is to highlight and develop a little further a collection of ideas that have made a merely intermittent appearance thus far. These ideas are the linked notions of social identity and social order and I am concerned, at a more general and abstract level than heretofore, with the bearing that luxury has upon them. My concern principally is with 'luxury' as a conceptual category.

LUXURY AS RELATIONAL

The starting point is to re-address the question posed in Chapter 8: why is it that all societies make some categorical distinction between need/necessity and luxury? The first observation concerns the distinction itself. It is not paradoxical to assert that the distinction constitutes a unity, just as it is not mysterious to talk of two gloves, a right-hand and a left-hand, constituting *a* pair. Understood in that way, luxury is one component of a pair. As such it is a relational term. It follows that 'need' too is relational. Before elaborating upon this I want to clarify the usage of 'need' and 'necessity'. These terms can be used interchangeably, as I myself have done, but I now wish to make a stipulative distinction. 'Necessity' I will use in the specific sense of 'socially necessary', that is, those features that a particular society regards as indispensable. 'Need' is used more generally. Hence while everything necessary is needed not everything that can be needed is thought necessary.

To elaborate upon the meaning of luxury as 'relational' we can reinvoke the discussion of 'naturalism' in Chapter 1. There it was held that needs could be seen as pertaining to certain universal requirements of human life. It was also held, and this has been a recurrent theme, that 'needs' understood at that level of generality were abstract categories and, as a consequence, what occurred *in fact* was that these categories were embedded in concrete social practices. It is by virtue of this embedment that they became 'necessities'. Two dimensions are, therefore, revealed. There is, first, a ubiquity – rooted in certain universal propositions – so that questions of need and necessity occur in all societies and, second, a specificity – rooted equally in certain universal cultural facts – so that what counts as a necessity in one place is also understood in that place in terms of what counts as a luxury. Luxury serves to specify the necessity. We can be more precise.

The relation between necessity and luxury is negative or oppositional so that, in line with the maxim *omnis determinatio est negatio*, luxury specifies the necessity by indicating what it is not. Sexual determination provides an apt analogy. The notion of 'male' depends on its opposite – 'female'; it has no meaning without its negative counterpart. Hence it is that an hermaphrodite, which fuses male and female, is a sexless being. The following argument can now proceed. Needs are a given of the human condition; given also that sociality is part of the human condition, these needs (or a portion of them) are specified as necessities, and since needs/necessities are ineradicable then, because it stands in oppositional relation to these, luxury too is ineliminable.

In Western cultural history this formal categorical relationship has undergone a shift in evaluative significance as the content or substance of the categories has changed. We have charted this shift episodically in the earlier chapters. Up until the eighteenth century the needful, as an integral element in a rational purposive order, was the established normative benchmark – it was *kata phusin* – so that luxury, associated with the boundlessness of bodily desires, was, in some sense, a transgression. It is along these lines that Sekora (1977: p. xii) characterises luxury as a component in a theory of entropy, that is, in accounts of decline into depravity. From the late seventeenth century onwards this inter-relationship between need, desire and luxury changed. The crucial background condition was the displacement of final in favour of efficient causation. This meant that the 'nature' of a thing was no longer the fulfilment of its purpose but the 'material' that constituted it and the mechanism that moved it. One consequence of this displacement was that the link between luxury and desire could be retained without censure, even when what was desired was not needed or was unnecessary. To a culture premised upon the primacy of desire, luxury as a creature of desire no longer posed a threat.

RULES AND SOCIAL IDENTITY

The character of the threat had always been its unruliness. Although the threatening element changed, in the connexion with rules we have the next significant point. The categorical relation between necessity and luxury is a relation that helps to define certain basic rules of social life. But since social life is always concrete or specific it also means that this act of definition also defines the identity of the particular society in question, just as it is the rules that distinguish whist from bridge. Rules are in this sense constitutive. Accordingly, to know what a society thinks necessary, and what it thinks a luxury, is to know something important about that society. Of course, unlike card games, there are a number of rules that operate to constitute the definition of a society – its notions of law and punishment or piety and blasphemy for example. Nevertheless a good case can be made for regarding the necessary/luxury pairing as, at least, on a par with these. These rules should not be thought of as being discrete, they are intertwined, as indeed they must be if we are to talk of social *identity*. If the various contributory rules become too divergent then the effect is to put that identity in question. Certainly we should not take social identity as a fixed datum – there is plenty of evidence of social disintegration. The history of nationalism can be interpreted along these lines and the case of the split between India and Pakistan is one case where the rules of piety and blasphemy did not cohere with other rules.

Given this general picture, how does luxury/necessity bear more specifically on the rules constitutive of social identity? The answer to this question takes us into the realms of axiology. A number of interdependent issues are involved. The first issue is the basic assumption that questions of identity are themselves value-laden. Who a person is, what makes a society what it is, are not for those concerned indifferent issues. Being able to answer those questions affirmatively is a *sine qua non* of *action*, as the cases of schizophrenia and

Lebanon each testify. Since we have located the necessary/luxury pairing as a constitutive component of social identity then it too is value-laden. This is not meant to be a bold claim. All that is being claimed, without straying into the realm of moral epistemology, is that to say a state of affairs is socially necessary is to say something important, something which has (or should have) practical consequences. I will say something about those consequences later.

Douglas and Isherwood (1979: p. 26), for example, make the general claim that 'each culture cuts its slices of moral reality in a different way and metes out approval and disapproval to counterpoised virtues and vices according to the local views'. They then, relevantly for our purposes, exemplify that claim by noting how in different societies the ratio between income and consumption produces a situation where one culture's thrift is another's meanness, or where one's extravagance is another's magnificence. It is important to resist the full-blown 'contextualism' that can easily lurk here (cf. ibid.: p. 63). By contextualism I mean the notion that we introduced in Chapter 7 to the effect that human nature is completely defined by its cultural setting and has no transcultural or universalist dimension. The reason for the resistance is the presence of the other issues involved in the link between identity and necessity/luxury.

Simply to connect that link with values is insufficient. We need additionally to explain or, more modestly, to provide some indication as to why there should be this connexion. It is to the furtherance of that end that the naturalism of the pairing comes again into play. As we discussed in Chapter 1 in relation to Baudrillard, the social construction of 'needs' (necessity) has to be effected with some pre-existing building-blocks. For the same reason a deep contextualism is not self-sufficient, all societies contain certain practices or conventions around which, or in terms of which, their values and particular identities are formed.

NATURAL CONVENTIONS

To expand upon these points I wish to exploit some arguments of Stuart Hampshire. I say 'exploit' because I am using these arguments for my purposes; Hampshire himself is not concerned centrally with the issues that are here central.[1] In his essay 'Morality and Conflict',

---

[1] In a more recent work, Hampshire (1992: p. 62) does use the question, 'which kinds of products are considered luxuries?' as an example of the sort of question to be asked when investigating the extent to which abstract delineations of justice can be applied to any specific society.

Hampshire (1983: p. 155) argues that common human needs and capacities always underdetermine a way of life and an order of priority among the virtues. Echoing our earlier discussions, we can identify as a key factor in this underdetermination that these needs are *human* needs. Hampshire himself remarks that 'human nature' includes the capacity to evolve conventions. These conventions create a moral order within the natural order (ibid.). As he puts it elsewhere in the same collection of essays, 'we are unavoidably born into both a natural order and cultural order' (ibid.: p. 138). Natural phenomena are moralised by conventions.

It is central to Hampshire's own argument that the divergent character of these conventions not only is to be expected but also is important, given that a dominant strand in ethical thinking discounts this character in favour of a convergence upon a universal set of norms. The natural phenomena that he cites include old age, death, family, friendship, sex and, closest to our own concerns, clothing. Clothing, he argues, plays variations upon the human body and its shape in the sense that the embellishment and enhancement of nature occurs in accordance with variable conventions with their own history (ibid.: p. 163). As we observed in Chapter 1, Hampshire, too, remarks that much clothing is not primarily functional but is designed rather to be pleasing and to play a social role. Yet because of the relationship to the ineluctability of nature he also exclaims that 'one would be amazed if one found a people who had no conventions governing the covering or decoration of their bodies' (ibid.); here as in other spheres it is, in short, 'natural to be unnatural' (ibid.: p. 169).

Hampshire's linking of conventions, or rules, with morality reintroduces the issue of norms. In the same way that Adam Smith had accounted for the development of moral consciousness through living in society, so Hampshire holds that the conventions/norms are learnt by imitation. Children come to recognise normal (moral) conduct in the same way they learn their natural language (ibid.: p. 248). Hence, we may gloss, just as they learn irregular conjugations (that the past of 'see' is 'saw' not 'seed') so they learn that some clothes are 'Sunday best'. Of course, it is precisely because these are conventions that they can be manipulated say in poetry or to cock a snook. But this merely reinforces the point: poetry and teenage rebellion are themselves conventions (cf. Edgerton, 1985: p. 33).

Conventions bind; they have to. It is not feasible that 'anything goes' and the reason why it is not feasible is because there is no effective alternative. Recourse to a pristine 'state of nature', where all conventions as products of artifice are absent, is self-defeating and not only because, as Rousseau complained of Hobbes, the theoriser of this state transfers into it his own conventions. More importantly this 'state' is devoid of any demonstrable determinate content. There is no theoretical limit, as the Cynics demonstrated, even if against themselves, to what can be judged 'natural'. Consequently human social life has to be theorised in terms of conventions because such a life cannot be lived without them. Conventions establish the predictability and constancy without which social intercourse would be impossible. Part of what it means to be a stranger is an inability (remediable) to follow what is 'going on'.

The application of this line of thought to my argument lies in the claim that an ineliminable ingredient in this 'going on' is the categorical specification of what is necessary and what is, by the same token, unnecessary or a luxury. The distinction between the categories of 'necessity' and 'luxury' is indeed conventional but the presence of that convention is not; it is not a convention whether or not to have conventions. All societies manifest the distinction, just as they all manifest conventions into which are embedded those universal ('natural') processes like being born, procreating, growing old, and dying. In other words, to reinvoke our own basic categories, eating, wearing, dwelling and playing are processes of a similar sort.

And because the specifications of necessity and luxury are a non-optional convention, one instructive way to understand a society is to comprehend it by means of those specifications. In the sense in which we used the term in Chapter 1, these specifications could be said to constitute a 'social grammar'. For strangers to learn what is 'going on' they have to learn this grammar and, contrary to the full implications of contextualism, this learning is always in principle possible. But of course the native speakers too have learnt it. Just as ignorance of a language's grammar makes confident and accurate communication in that tongue extremely difficult and haphazard, so ignorance of social grammar makes comprehension of that society problematic. More importantly the members of a society, by virtue of their mastery of its grammar (their subscription to its rules, conventions or norms), give to their conduct not only a predictability but also, in so doing, the coherence that constitutes a vital ingredient in their own identity. Of course 'predictability' should not be confused with immutability – identity undergoes changes and faces challenges.

These remarks on identity are obviously skeletal but much of the discussion in the earlier chapters can be reinvoked to flesh them out. Recall, for example, the way in which the self-image of the Roman republic was manifest in its sumptuary laws; these laws, whatever their role in pressure-group politicking, ostensibly underlined the necessity of military virtue and the danger to the Republic of private wealth and indulgence. Or consider how Blair, in his sermons, voiced a generally felt disquiet about the increasing invasiveness of commercial values; 'the guid folk' of Edinburgh were disquieted because luxury was now being praised in some quarters as 'necessary' when they had been accustomed to regard it as a pernicious superfluity. Or again, think of how the identity of contemporary Britain is revealed when advertisers assume the presence of a widespread aspiration to possess a luxury penthouse or, as Mack and Lansley's survey revealed, when seven-eighths of the population think a refrigerator a necessity. And, as a final illustration, it is equally revealing that social critics of contemporary society can indict it for its 'shallow materialism' or 'commodity fetishism' since they are, in so doing, giving additional testimony to the fact that these values embody the character or identity of the society.

To develop a little further what is here at stake we can exploit another writer – Michael Walzer. In his argument for 'complex equality', Walzer (1983: p. 65) considers various 'spheres' of social life, each with their own characteristic 'goods'. One such sphere is 'security and welfare' or a system of communal provision. He claims that 'there has never been a political community that did not provide, or try to provide, for the needs of its members as its members understood those needs' (ibid.: p. 68). The last phrase is crucial. Walzer denies that the nature of need is self-evident and the reason he gives for that denial is that 'people don't just have needs, they have ideas about their needs' (ibid.: p. 66). And, although Walzer himself does not extend the point in this way, we can say that essential to these ideas is a (categorical) notion of the not-needed, the unnecessary or luxurious.

In line with this denial, and as an expression of his communitarianism, Walzer stresses how the determination of what is needed (necessary) or what should be provided communally is a question of that community's history and culture, as well as human nature in general. To exemplify his case he briefly discusses fifth-century BC Athens and medieval Jewish communes (ibid.: pp. 69–74). The former *inter alia* distributed public funds for political activity, the latter (in Valladolid) levied taxes to support teachers of the Scriptures. It is my contention that these particular decisions as to what was needed (was 'socially necessary' in my terminology) provide solid evidence as to what these two very different communities judged important and that these judgments reveal much of what made them distinctive, what made them what they were. In accord with the above argument we can also hypothesise that these communities would have had a view as to what constitutes luxury (as a category), which would itself have been equally revelatory of their identity.

As a test of this hypothesis, we can recall from Chapter 2 the discussion of Aristotle. Aristotle, who had noted the practice of political payment in democratic Athens (*Ath. Constit.*: 49.3), linked a life of luxury with oligarchy and regarded as corrupt a life given over to money-making. We can gloss this as follows. A democratic constitution can be defined/identified as one where political participation is regarded as a social necessity and, in accordance with the hypothesis, it is contrary to the democratic spirit when political activity is undertaken as a means to private wealth-creation and to the enjoyment of a life of luxury. ('Luxury' here is to be understood in both the substantive and categorical sense.) In the Jewish case, Walzer himself remarks that these communities had sumptuary laws. That is to say, in line with the hypothesis, they had a distinct view of what constituted 'luxury'. Walzer's explanation for the presence of these laws is that they were designed to prevent non-Jews in the dominant ambient culture from being envious and thus a threat to the community's well-being. But even if this prudentialism is the correct explanation it still means that these laws, just as much as their communal funding of religious education, reveal the identity-constituting values of these communities. They are a defence of *their* way of life.

THE GOOD LIFE

There is one final point made by Walzer that we can utilise. While he himself does not articulate the reasoning, he links together strongly the ideas of need and priority. Somewhat along the lines of Baudrillard's notion that the societal 'level of survival' is consequent upon a 'prededication' of 'luxury' (see Chapter 1, p. 35), Walzer (1983: pp. 75-6) remarks that 'socially recognised needs are the first charge against the social product; there is no real surplus until they have been met'. The crucial word in Walzer's statement is the qualifier 'real'. The reason why it is crucial is because, as Walzer himself puts it a little later, 'people's sense of what they need encompasses not only life itself but also the good life' (ibid.: p. 83).

The underlying point is that which Smith made against Mandeville. Mandeville's rigorous notion of luxury was unsustainable because his idea of a fixed minimal necessity was just as illusory or unrealistic as Epictetus' 'natural life'. For Smith, questions of shame were an inescapable component of 'necessity' as it is *experienced*. In line with the earlier account of the naturalness of conventions it is no surprise to discover that Smith's actual examples are articles of clothing. The category is rightly to be termed '*social* necessity' because individuals are social beings and their 'needs' are always embedded within the practices and conventions in terms of which they live their lives. To talk of needs as somehow external to this embedment is to de-humanise the possessors. It follows from this that the content of the category can differ between society and society and within the same society at different times. It is in this sense that needs are historical, though, as we have already discussed, this does not endorse the fully-fledged contextualist argument. It also follows, given our earlier argument, that as the content of the socially necessary changes so does that of its negative partner, luxury.

As relational items, the ideas of what is a necessity and what a luxury change together. But something more is involved than the logical/formal relationship. This distinctively additional factor lies in the fact that, as we have noted throughout this study, what substantively counts as a luxury is transient. This means that while the categories necessity/luxury remain constant, a particular good can, over time, appear in both. It is precisely such substantive changes that mark social change, but it is the placement of them into stable categories that enables societies to keep their grammar, and with it their identity while the vocabulary changes.

Of course, as Blair's sermons testify, this should not be thought of as a simple anxiety-free process, especially when it is recalled that questions of identity are value-laden. When Smith talks of 'shame' in the context of social necessity he is openly using moral language. The 'good life', in the general sense in which Walzer uses it, also clearly belongs to the same order of discourse. The consequence is that 'necessity' now incorporates expenditure upon that which is deemed by society to constitute the good life. The good life is always something specific and in contemporary Britain, as Mack and Lansley found, it is a matter of washing-machines and refrigerators. And over a longer time-scale it has been a question of the public provision of education and public health. As components of the good life they enter into the category of the socially necessary and thus the expenditure upon them cannot be deemed a 'luxury'. Yet, of course, as definitions of the good life have changed (to incorporate *inter alia* previous luxury goods like refrigerators and interior plumbing), so has the categorical realm of the luxurious.

Since the good life is always specific then one society's necessity can be another's luxury. What for one is not really surplus but part of its prededicated communal way of life can indeed be a luxury for another. In medieval Europe the splendour of the church was a fitting tribute to the glory and majesty of God (and His mundane servants, we might add) and the creation and maintenance of these buildings was a necessary and central aspect of life. And as testament to this necessity and centrality monies were found to create that splendour. If the construction of these churches was in this sense a 'necessity' then, conversely, concern for the living and working conditions of the peasantry was a 'luxury'. In the contemporary world a concern for the well-being of a state's citizens' bodies has a prior claim upon the public purse compared to any concern with its citizens' souls. It is symptomatic of this shift in values and perspective that the more splendid of these churches can become a charge on the public purse, not, however, to keep their religious function alive but to preserve the craftsmanship and aesthetic standards that the building embodies and/or to retain some substantive representation of tradition.

LUXURY AND POLITICS

The references here to the 'public purse' introduce the final set of remarks, which concern the way in which these questions of social identity are in practice dealt with. This is but another expression of the manner in which the ideas of luxury and 'good politic order' are linked. We have already observed that rules are never completely fixed and yet it is a *sine qua non* of social order that there be stable rules to create the predictability required for social intercourse. It is the task of politics, we can say, to co-ordinate these two conditions. Politics deals with the establishment, maintenance and amendment of these rules. Through its actions, either directly in the form of commands (laws, decrees and the like) or indirectly in the form of permissions, political activity supports a conception of social identity. And because identity is value-laden and requires a stable core then the activity involves some idea of what is necessary to its maintenance (funds to teach the Scriptures in medieval Valladolid, for example).

If politics is in this way concerned with the maintenance of social necessity (that which is required for the good life) then it is also concerned with threats to that maintenance. In earlier chapters we have presented this dual concern in the form of a hypothesis to the effect that a society's notion of political order is a result of its evaluation of desire and identification of need (that which is socially necessary). In the light of the discussion in this chapter we can add to this formulation. We have here argued that the identification of the socially necessary has a negative partner in the identification of the non-necessary, or luxury, as a category. By focusing on the changes in the assessment of 'desire' we are able to account for the change that overcame 'luxury' as a substantive issue. As desire was endorsed as the 'way of the world', so luxury substantively lost its position as a direct threat to the social order. And, as a consequence of this change, luxury as an issue began to lose its direct political salience.

The fate of sumptuary legislation can be explained in this way. In the classical and Christian traditions, luxury itself, that is, soft living, effeminacy and private indulgence, was perceived as a direct threat which must, therefore, be legislated against directly. Sumptuary laws embodied that imperative. We know from the various medieval statutes that the necessity of social hierarchy was deemed to require the support of legal sanction. Luxury was living beyond one's station. In later thinking, as luxury itself became assimilated into commercial society, then the concern to preserve hierarchy by legal means lost its impetus. Accordingly, these laws came to be judged as an illicit restraint upon the proper exercise of desire and the activities such as those of the Venetian *provveditori delle pompe* came to be judged as unwarranted intrusions on private liberty.

This does not mean that some idea of luxury as the non-necessary is absent. The presence of the idea is implicit within the whole idea of 'politics' as the ordering of priorities. Public resources – financial, administrative and legal – should be devoted to upholding what is socially necessary and letting the unnecessary look after itself. The practical 'business' of politics is (at least in part) about the specification of these terms: expenditure upon the upkeep of medieval churches should not be thought a luxury because of the importance of tradition, or it is a luxury that can be ill-afforded when there is a shortage of homes.

This example reinvokes the question of popular usage with which we began this study. From being regarded, because of its desirability, as a positive danger, a luxury has become a desirable object, which although unnecessary, is not to be condemned on those grounds. Hence to talk of a luxury as something one can ill-afford refers to potential folly, the mis-ordering of priorities, and not to corruption of virtue. This current usage is thus using 'luxury' categorically to refer to the non-necessary but in so doing it is exhibiting both its categorical continuity and substantive discontinuity with the older usage.

My hope is that this study has done something to bring out this duality. The historical investigation has sought to identify the differences between the classical and modern conceptions and to pinpoint, as a key factor in the explanation of that difference, the role played by changing evaluations of desire and need. The conceptual analysis has sought to account for the crucial role played by desire and need and also to have shown that the persistence of the term 'luxury' indicates that even its contemporary usage is not merely casual or peripheral to the large questions of social and political theory but, rather, provides an illuminating insight into those questions.

Bibliography

PRE-TWENTIETH-CENTURY SOURCES

Aquinas, T. *Summa Theologiae*, vol. XXVI; London: Blackfriars, 1956
Aristotle *The Athenian Constitution*, tr. H. Rackham; London: Loeb Library, 1952
  The Eudemian Ethics, tr. H. Rackham; London: Loeb Library, 1952
  Metaphysics, tr. J. Warrington; London: Everyman Library, 1956
  The Nicomachean Ethics, tr. H. Rackham; London: Loeb Library, 1934
    Tr. J. Thomson; Harmondsworth: Penguin Books, 1976
  Poetics, tr. T. Buckley; London: Bohn Library, 1910
  The Politics, tr. H. Rackham; London: Loeb Library, 1932
    Tr. E. Barker; Oxford: Clarendon Press, 1946
Augustine *The City of God*, tr. J. Healey (1620); London: Everyman Library, 1945
    Tr. M. Dods, in *Basic Writings of St Augustine*; New York: Random House, 1948
  'The Good of Marriage', in *Seventeen Short Treatises*; Oxford, 1858
  'On Marriage and Lust', in *Anti-Pelagian Writings*, vol. II, ed. M. Dods; Edinburgh: T. & T. Clark, 1884
  Opera Omnia; Paris: Gaume, 1838
Bacon, F. *Moral and Historical Works*, ed. J. Devey; London: Bohn Library, 1868
Barbon, N. *A Discourse concerning the Coining the New Money Lighter in Answer to Mr Lock's Considerations about raising the Value of Money*; London, 1696
  An Apology for the Builder (1685), reprinted in *A Select Collection of Scarce and Valuable Tracts on Commerce*, ed. J.R. McCulloch; London, 1859
  A Discourse of Trade (1690) (reprint edition), ed. J. Hollander; Baltimore: Johns Hopkins Press, 1905
Baudeau, N. *Principes de la Science Morale et Politique sur le Luxe et les Loix Sumptuaires* (1767), reprinted in *Collection des Économistes*, ed. A. Dubois; Paris: P. Geuther, 1912
Baudrillart, H. *Histoire du Luxe Privé et Public depuis l'antiquité jusqu'à nos jours*, 4 vols.; Paris: Hachette, 1880
Bentham, J. *An Introduction to the Principles of Morals and Legislation* (1789), ed. W. Harrison; Oxford: Basil Blackwell, 1948
Berkeley, G. *An Essay towards Preventing the Ruin of Great Britain* (1721), in

Works, ed. T. Jessop; Edinburgh: Nelson, 1953

Blair, H. *Sermons*, 5 vols.; London, 1794

Boswell, J. *The Life of Samuel Johnson LL.D* (1791); London: Routledge, n.d.

Brown, J. *An Estimate of the Manners and Principles of the Times* (7th edition); London, 1758

Carlyle, T. *Sartor Resartus* (1833); London: Chapman Hall, n.d.

Cassian, John *De Institutis Coenobiorum*; Paris: Patrologia Latina (Migne), vol. XLIX, 1874

Child, J. *A New Discourse of Trade* (5th edition); Glasgow, 1751

Cicero *Ad Familares*, tr. G. Williams; London: Loeb Library, 1927

   De Finibus, tr. H. Rackham; London: Loeb Library, 1931

   The Offices, tr. T. Cockman; London: Routledge, 1894

   Tr. W. Miller; London: Loeb Library, 1913

   Tr. E. Atkins; Cambridge: Cambridge University Press, 1991

   Pro Flacco, tr. C. MacDonald; London: Loeb Library, 1977

   Pro Murena, tr. C. MacDonald; London: Loeb Library, 1977

   The Republic, tr. C. Keyes; London: Loeb Library, 1928

   Tusculan Disputations, tr. J. King; London: Loeb Library, 1927

Clement, of Alexandria *The Writings of Clement of Alexandria*, tr. W. Wilson; Edinburgh: T. & T. Clark, 1857

Darwin, C. *The Voyage of the 'Beagle'* (1845); London: Heron Books, 1968

Davenant, C. *Works*, 5 vols., ed. C. Whitworth; London, 1771

Decker, M. *An Essay on the Causes of the Decline of Foreign Trade* (1744), reprinted in *A Select Collection of Scarce and Valuable Tracts on Commerce*, ed. J.R. McCulloch; London, 1859

Diogenes Laertius *Life of Zeno*, in *Essential Works of Stoicism*, ed. M. Hadas; New York: Bantam Books, 1961

   Lives and Opinions, tr. R. Hicks; London: Loeb Library, 1970

Epictetus *Manual*, in *Essential Works of Stoicism*, ed. M. Hadas; New York: Bantam Books, 1961

   Discourses, tr. G. Long; New York: A.L. Burt, n.d.

Erasmus, D. *Institutio Principis Christiani*, ed. O. Herding, *Opera Omnia*, vol. IV.1; Amsterdam: North Holland Publishing, 1974

   The Education of a Christian Prince, tr. N. Cheshire and M. Heath, *Collected Works*, vol. XXVII; Toronto: Toronto University Press, 1986

Ferguson, A. *An Essay on the History of Civil Society* (1767), ed. D. Forbes; Edinburgh: Edinburgh University Press, 1966

Fielding, H. *An Enquiry into the Late Increase of Robbers* (1751), ed. M. Zirker; Oxford: Clarendon Press, 1988

Fletcher, A. *Selected Writings*, ed. D. Daiches; Edinburgh: Scottish Academic Press, 1979

Florus *Epitome of Roman History*, tr. E. Foster; London: Loeb Library, 1943

Gellius, Aulus *Attic Nights*, tr. J. Rolfe; London: Loeb Library, 1927

Goldsmith, O. *Works*, 5 vols.; London: Bohn Library, 1885

Gregory, the Great *Moralia*; Paris: Patrologia Latina (Migne), vol. LXXXVI, 1878

Hegel, G.W.F. *Philosophy of Right* (1821), tr. T.M. Knox; Oxford: Clarendon Press, 1942
  Philosophie des Rechts (4th edition), ed. J. Hoffmeister; Hamburg: F. Meiner, 1955
Hobbes, T. *Leviathan* (1651), ed. R. Tuck; Cambridge: Cambridge University Press, 1991
Homer *The Iliad*, tr. E.V. Rieu; Harmondsworth: Penguin Books, 1950
Horace *Collected Works*, ed. Ld Dunsany and M. Oakley; London: Everyman Library, 1961
Hume, D. *Essays Moral, Political and Literary* (1779 edition), ed. E. Miller; Indianapolis: Liberty Classics, 1987
  The History of England (1786 edition), 3 vols.; London: Geo. Routledge, 1894
  An Inquiry concerning Human Understanding (1748), ed. C. Hendel; Indianapolis: Library of Liberal Arts, 1955
  An Inquiry concerning the Principles of Morals (1751), ed. C. Hendel; Indianapolis: Library of Liberal Arts, 1957
  Letters, 2 vols., ed. J. Greig; Oxford: Clarendon Press, 1932
  A Treatise of Human Nature (1739/40), ed. L. Selby-Bigge; Oxford: Clarendon Press, 1888
Hutcheson, F. *Observations on the Fable of the Bees* (1758 edition); Bristol: Thoemmes Reprint, 1989
Juvenal *Satires*, tr. W. Gifford; London: George Bell, 1895
Kames, Ld. *Historical Law Tracts* (3rd edition); Edinburgh, 1776
  Sketches on the History of Man (3rd edition); Dublin, 1779
Kant, I. *The Moral Law: Kant's Groundwork of the Metaphysics of Morals* (1785) (3rd edition), tr. H. Paton, London: Hutchinson, 1956
Laveleye, E. *Luxury* (2nd edition); London: Swan Sohnenschein, 1891
Livy *History of Rome*, tr. D. Spillan; London: Bohn Library, 1854
  Tr. E. Sage; London: Loeb Library, 1934
Locke, J. *Consequences of the Lowering of Interest and Raising the Value of Money* (1691), in *The Works of John Locke*; London: Ward Lock, n.d.
  Essay concerning Human Understanding (1690), in *The Works of John Locke*; London: Ward Lock, n.d.
  Two Treatises of Government (1689/90), ed. P. Laslett; New York: Mentor Books, 1965
Mackenzie, G. *The Moral History of Frugality*; London, 1711
Macrobius *Saturnalia*, ed. J. Willis; Leipzig: Teubner, 1970
Mandeville, B. *An Enquiry into the Origin of Honour and the Usefulness of Christianity in War* (1732), ed. M. Goldsmith; London: F. Cass, 1971
  The Fable of the Bees or Private Vices, Publick Benefits (1732 edition), 2 vols., ed. F. Kaye (1924); Indianapolis: Liberty Classics, 1988
Marx, K. *Capital* (1857[1885/1894]), 3 vols., tr. S. Moore and S. Aveling; New York: International Publishers, 1967
  Early Writings (1843/4), tr. R. Livingstone and G. Benton; Harmondsworth: Penguin Books, 1975

Die Frühschriften (1843/5), ed. S. Landshut; Stuttgart: Kroner, 1971
German Ideology (1844), tr. C. Dutt et al.; London: Lawrence & Wishart, 1965
Grundrisse (1857), tr. M. Nicolaus; Harmondsworth: Penguin Books, 1973
Melon, J-F. *Essai Politique sur le Commerce* (1734), reprinted in *Economistes Financiers du XVIIIe Siècle*, ed. E. Daire; Paris: Guillaumin, 1843
Montesquieu, C-L. S. *De l'Esprit des Lois* (1748), 2 vols., ed. G. Truc; Paris: Garnier, 1971
Lettres Persanes (1721), ed. E. Faguet; Paris: Nelson, 1951
Mun, T. *England's Treasure by Forreign Trade* (1664), reprinted in *Early English Tracts on Commerce*, ed. J.R. McCulloch; Cambridge: Economic History Society Reprint, 1952
North, D. *Discourses upon Trade* (1691), reprinted in *Early English Tracts on Commerce*, ed. J.R. McCulloch; Cambridge: Economic History Society Reprint, 1952
Plato *The Dialogues of Plato*, 4 vols., tr. B. Jowett; New York: Scribner, 1895
Politeia, ed. J. Burnett (1902); Oxford: Clarendon Press, 1968
The Republic, tr. F. Cornford; Oxford: Clarendon Press, 1941
Tr. H. Lee; Harmondsworth: Penguin Books, 1955
Pliny *Natural History*, tr. H. Rackham; London: Loeb Library, 1945
Plutarch *Lives*, tr. B. Perrin; London: Loeb Library, 1928
Polybius *The Histories*, tr. W. Paton; London: Loeb Library, 1925
Prudentius *Psychomachia*, tr. H. Thomson; London: Loeb Library, 1949
Rousseau, J-J. *Emile or Education* (1762), tr. B. Foxley: London: Everyman Library, 1911
Discours de l'Inégalité parmi les Hommes (1755), in *Du Contrat Social etc.*; Paris: Garnier, 1962
Discours sur les Sciences et les Arts (1750), in *Du Contrat Social etc.*; Paris: Garnier, 1962
St Lambert, C. 'Luxury' (1765), in *Encyclopedia Selections*, ed. and tr. N. Hoyt and T. Cassirer; Indianapolis: Library of Liberal Arts, 1965
Sallust *De Coniuratione Catilinae*, ed. W. Summers; Cambridge: Cambridge University Press, 1930
The Conspiracy of Catiline, tr. S. Handford; Harmondsworth: Penguin Books, 1963
Seneca *Letters to Lucilius*, tr. E.P. Barker; Oxford: Clarendon Press, 1932
Tr. R. Gummere; London: Loeb Library, 1932
Ed. and tr. R. Campbell; Harmondsworth: Penguin Books, 1969
'De Consolatione ad Helviam', 'De Vita Beata', 'De Tranquillitate Animi', 'De Brevitate Vitae', in *Moral Essays*, vol. II, tr. J. Basore; London: Loeb Library, 1932
Shaftesbury, 3rd Earl *Characteristics of Men, Manners, Opinions, Times etc.* (1710), 2 vols., ed. J.M. Robertson; London: Grant Richards, 1900
Smith, A. *Essays on Philosophical Subjects* (1795), ed. W. Wightman; Indianapolis: Liberty Classics, 1982
An Inquiry into the Nature and Causes of the Wealth of Nations (1776), eds. A.

Skinner and R. Meek; Indianapolis: Liberty Classics, 1981
Lectures on Jurisprudence, eds. R. Meek, D. Raphael and P. Stein; Indianapolis:
 Liberty Classics, 1982
The Theory of Moral Sentiments (6th edition, 1790), eds. A. Macfie and D.
 Raphael; Indianapolis: Liberty Classics, 1982
Steuart, J. *An Inquiry into the Principles of Political Oeconomy* (1767), 2 vols., ed.
 A. Skinner; Chicago: University of Chicago Press, 1966
Tacitus *Agricola*, tr. W. Peterson; London: Loeb Library, 1924
 Complete Works, tr. W. Church and W. Jackson; New York: Modern
 Library, 1942
Temple, W. *Works*, 4 vols.; Edinburgh, 1754
Tertullian *On Female Dress*, tr. S. Thelwall, Ante-Nicene Christian Library,
 vol. XI; Edinburgh: T. & T. Clark, 1869
 Opera Corpus Christianorum; Turnholti, 1954
Thucydides *History of the Peloponnesian War*, tr. C. Smith, London: Loeb
 Library, 1929
Valerius Paterculus *History of Rome*, tr. F. Shipley; London: Loeb Library, 1924
Veblen, T. *The Theory of the Leisure Class* (1899); London: Unwin Books, 1970
Xenophon *Oeconomicus*, in *Minor Works*, tr. J. Watson; London: Bohn
 Library, 1878
 On the Athenian Government, in *Minor Works*, tr. J. Watson; London: Bohn
 Library, 1878

TWENTIETH-CENTURY SOURCES AND SECONDARY MATERIAL

Abbott, F.F. (1963) *A History and Description of Roman Political Institutions*
 (reprint of 3rd edition, 1910); New York: Biblo & Tennen
Adam, J. (1965) *The Republic of Plato* (2nd edition, introd. D. Rees);
 Cambridge: Cambridge University Press
Adcock, F.E. (1964) *Roman Political Ideas and Practice*; Ann Arbor: University
 of Michigan Press
Allen, C. (1971) *The Theory of Taxation*; Harmondsworth: Penguin Books
Andersson, T.J. (1971) *Polis and Psyche: A Motif in Plato's 'Republic'*;
 Stockholm: Almqvist & Wiksell
Appleby, J.O. (1978) *Economic Thought and Ideology in Seventeenth Century
 England*; Princeton: Princeton University Press
Arnold, R.V. (1958) *Roman Stoicism* (reprint of 1911 edition); New York:
 Humanities Press
Ashcraft, R. (1980) 'The Two Treatises and the Exclusion Crisis', in his *John
 Locke*; Los Angeles: Clark Memorial Library
Ashley, W.J. (1900) 'The Tory Origin of Free Trade Policy', in his *Surveys:
 Historic and Economic*; London: Longmans Green
Ashton, P. (1984) 'Poverty and its Beholders', *New Society* (18 October)
Astin, A.E. (1978) *Cato the Censor*; Oxford: Clarendon Press
Baker, J. (1987) *Arguing for Equality*; London: Verso

Balsdon, J. (1969) *Life and Leisure in Ancient Rome*; London: The Bodley Head
Barker, E. (1959) *The Political Thought of Plato and Aristotle*; New York: Dover
Barry, B. (1965) *Political Argument*; London: Routledge & Kegan Paul
Baudrillard, J. (1981) *For a Critique of the Political Economy of the Sign*, tr. C. Levin; St Louis: Telos Press
   (1988) *Selected Writings*, ed. M. Poster; Cambridge: Polity Press
Bell, Q. (1976) *On Human Finery* (new edition); London: Hogarth Press
Berry, C.J. (1977) 'On the Meaning of Progress and Providence in the Fourth Century', *The Heythrop Journal*, 18, 257–70
   (1982) *Hume, Hegel and Human Nature*; The Hague: M. Nijhoff
   (1986a) *Human Nature*; London: Macmillan
   (1986b) 'The Nature of Wealth and the Origins of Virtue: Recent Essays on the Scottish Enlightenment', *History of European Ideas*, 7, 85–99
   (1987) 'Need and Egoism in Marx's Early Writings', *History of Political Thought*, 8, 461–73
   (1989a) *The Idea of a Democratic Community*; Hemel Hempstead: Harvester Wheatsheaf
   (1989b) 'Adam Smith; Commerce, Liberty and Modernity', in *Philosophers of the Enlightenment*, ed. P. Gilmour, pp. 113–32
Bloomfield, M. (1952) *The Seven Deadly Sins*; East Lansing: Michigan State College Press
Boucher, F. (n.d.) *20,000 Years of Fashion: The History of Costume and Personal Adornment*; New York: H. Abrams
Bourdieu, P. (1979) *La Distinction: Critique sociale du jugement*; Paris: Les éditions de Minuit
Bowley, M. (1973) *Studies in the History of Economic Theory Before 1870*; London; Macmillan
Braudel, F. (1981) *Civilisation and Capitalism, vol. I The Structures of Everyday Life*, tr. S. Reynolds; London: Collins
Braybrooke, D. (1987) *Meeting Needs*; Princeton: Princeton University Press
Brown. P. (1989) *The Body and Society: Men, Women and Sexual Renunciation in Early Christianity*; London: Faber & Faber
Burrow, J.W. (1988) *Whigs and Liberals: Continuity and Change in English Political Thought*; Oxford: Clarendon Press
Burtt, S. (1992) *Virtue Transformed: Political Argument in England 1688–1740*; Cambridge: Cambridge University Press
Calvert, B. (1987) 'Slavery in Plato's Republic', *Classical Quarterly*, 37, 367–72
Campbell, C. (1987) *The Romantic Ethic and the Spirit of Modern Consumerism*; Oxford: Blackwell
Castiglione, D. (1986) 'Considering Things Minutely: Reflections on Mandeville and the Eighteenth Century Science of Man', *History of Political Thought*, 7, 463–88
Chadwick, H. (1966) *Early Christian Thought and the Classical Tradition: Studies in Justin, Clement and Origen*; Oxford: Clarendon Press
Chadwick, H. and Oulton, J. (eds.) (1954) *Alexandrian Christianity: Selected*

Translations of Clement and Origen; London: SCM Press

Chamley, P. (1965) 'Les origines de la Pensée Economique de Hegel', *Hegel Studien*, 3, 225–61

Chanteur, J. (1980) *Platon, le désir et la cité*; Paris: Editions Sirey

Cherry, G. (1953) 'The Development of the English Free Trade Movement in Parliament 1698–1702', *Journal of Modern History*, 25, 103–19

Clark, G.N. (1949) *The Cycle of War and Peace*; Cambridge: Cambridge University Press

Cohen, G.A. (1978) *Karl Marx's Theory of History: A Defence*; Oxford: Clarendon Press

Cohn, N. (1970) *The Pursuit of the Millennium*; London: Paladin Books

Coleman, D.C. and John, A.H. (eds.) (1976) *Trade, Government and Economy in Pre-Industrial England*; London: Weidenfeld & Nicolson

Collingwood, R. (1961) *The Idea of History*; London: Oxford University Press

Collini, S., Winch, D. and Burrow, J. (1983) *That Noble Science of Politics: A Study in Nineteenth Century Intellectual History*; Cambridge: Cambridge University Press

Colman, J. (1972) 'Bernard Mandeville and the Reality of Virtue', *Philosophy*, 47, 125–39

Cooper, M. (1975) *Rationing Health Care*; London: Croom Helm

Cunningham, W. (1910) *The Growth of English Industry and Commerce*, 3 vols. (5th edition); Cambridge: Cambridge University Press

Davie, G.E. (1981) *The Scottish Enlightenment*; London: Historical Association pamphlet no. 99

Davis, J.H. (1973) *Venice: Art and Life in the Lagoon City*; New York: Newsweek Books

Deaton, A. and Muellbauer, J. (1980) *Economics and Consumer Behaviour*; Cambridge: Cambridge University Press

Dickey, L. (1986) 'Historicizing the "Adam Smith Problem"', *Journal of Modern History*, 58, 579–609

(1987) *Hegel: Religion, Economics and the Politics of Spirit 1770–1807*; Cambridge: Cambridge University Press

Dickson, P.G.M. (1967) *The Financial Revolution in England*; London: Macmillan

Donnison, D. (1988) 'Defining and Measuring Poverty' *Journal of Social Policy*, 17, 367–74

Douglas, M. and Isherwood, B. (1979) *The World of Goods: Towards an Anthropology of Consumption*; London: Allen Lane

Dowell, S. (1884) *A History of Taxation and Taxes in England*, 4 vols.; London: Longmans Green

Doyal, L. and Gough, I. (1984) 'A Theory of Human Needs', *Critical Social Policy*, 4, 6–35

Duesenberry, J. (1949) *Income, Saving and the Theory of Consumer Behavior*; Cambridge, MA: Harvard University Press

Dunn, J. (ed.) (1990) *The Economic Limits of Politics*; Cambridge: Cambridge University Press

Dworkin, R. (1978) 'Liberalism', in *Public and Private Morality*, ed. S. Hampshire, pp. 113–43

Dwyer, J. (1987) *Virtuous Discourse: Sensibility and Community in Late Eighteenth Century Scotland*; Edinburgh: John Donald

Dwyer, J., Mason, R. and Murdoch, A. (eds.) (1983) *New Perspectives on the Politics and Culture of Early Modern Scotland*; Edinburgh: John Donald

Dwyer, J. and Murdoch, A. (1983) 'Paradigms and Politics: Manners, Morals and the Rise of Henry Dundas, 1770–1784', in *New Perspectives on the Politics and Culture of Early Modern Scotland*, eds. J. Dwyer, R. Mason and A. Murdoch, pp. 210–48

Earl, D.C. (1961) *The Political Thought of Sallust*; Cambridge: Cambridge University Press

(1967) *The Moral and Political Tradition of Rome*; London: Thames & Hudson

Edgerton, R. (1985) *Rules, Exceptions and Social Order*; Berkeley and Los Angeles: University of California Press

Ellis, A. and Kumar, K. (eds.) (1983) *Dilemmas of Liberal Democracies*; London: Tavistock

Elster, J. (1985a) *Sour Grapes: Studies in Subversive Rationality*; Cambridge: Cambridge University Press

(1985b) *Making Sense of Marx*; Cambridge: Cambridge University Press

Emerson, R. (1985) 'Conjectural History and the Scottish Philosophers', *Historical Papers of the Canadian Historical Association*, 63–90

Eversley, D.C. (1959) *Social Theories of Fertility and the Malthusian Debate*; Oxford: Clarendon Press

Fitzgerald, C.P. (1974) *A Concise History of East Asia*; Harmondsworth: Penguin Books

Fitzgerald, R. (ed.) (1977) *Human Needs and Politics*; Rushcutter Bay, NSW: Pergamon Press

Flew, A.G.N. (1977) 'Wants or Needs, Choices or Commands', in *Human Needs and Politics*, ed. R. Fitzgerald, pp. 213–28

Fontana, B. (1985) *Rethinking the Politics of Commercial Society*; Cambridge: Cambridge University Press

Forbes, D. (1975a) *Hume's Philosophical Politics*; Cambridge: Cambridge University Press

(1975b) 'Sceptical Whiggism, Commerce and Liberty', in *Essays on Adam Smith*, eds. A. Skinner and T. Wilson, pp. 179–201

Forde, N. (1975) *Cato the Censor*; Boston: Twayne

Frankfurt, H. (1984) 'Necessity and Desire', *Philosophy and Phenomenological Research*, 45, 1–13

(1988) 'Equality as a Moral Ideal', in his *The Importance of what we Care About*; Cambridge: Cambridge University Press, pp. 134–58

Fraser, W.H. (1981) *The Coming of the Mass Market 1850–1914*; London: Macmillan

Freudenberger, H. (1963) 'Fashion, Sumptuary Laws and Business', *Business History Review*, 37, 37–48

Fritz, P. and Williams, D. (eds.) (1973) *City and Society in the Eighteenth Century*; Toronto: Hakkert

Galbraith, J.K. (1962) *The Affluent Society*; Harmondsworth: Penguin Books (1985) *The New Industrial State*, 4th edition; Boston: Houghton Mifflin

Galliani, R. (1989) *Rousseau, le luxe et l'idéologie nobiliaire*; Oxford: Voltaire Foundation, Studies in Voltaire & Eighteenth Century no. 268

Galston, W.A. (1980) *Justice and the Human Good*; Chicago: University of Chicago Press

Garland, M. (1975) *A History of Fashion*; London: Orbis

Gelzer, M. (1968) *Caesar: Politician and Statesman*, tr. P. Needham; Oxford: Blackwell

Gershuny, J. (1983) 'Technical Change and "Social Limits"', in *Dilemmas of Liberal Democracies*, eds. A. Ellis and K. Kumar, pp. 23–44

Gibbs, B. (1976) *Freedom and Liberation*; Brighton: Sussex University Press

Gilmour, P. (ed.) *Philosophers of the Enlightenment*; Edinburgh: Edinburgh University Press

Glass, D.V. (1973) *Numbering the People: The Eighteenth Century Population Controversy and the Development of Census and Vital Statistics in Britain*; Farnborough: Saxon House

Goldsmith, M.M. (1985) *Private Vices, Public Benefits: Bernard Mandeville's Social and Political Thought*; Cambridge: Cambridge University Press (1987) 'Liberty, Luxury and the Pursuit of Happiness', in *Languages of Political Theory in Early Modern Europe*, ed. A. Pagden, pp. 225–51

Gooch, G.P. (1915) *Political Thought in England: Bacon to Halifax*; London: Oxford University Press

Goodin, R.E. (1988) 'Reasons for Welfare', in *Responsibility, Rights and Welfare: The Theory of the Welfare State*, ed. J.D. Moon, pp. 19–54

Gosling, J.C.B. (1969) *Pleasure and Desire: The Case for Hedonism Reviewed*; Oxford: Clarendon Press

Gould, C. (1980) *Marx's Social Ontology*; Cambridge, MA: MIT Press

Graham, K. (ed.) (1982) *Contemporary Political Philosophy*; Cambridge: Cambridge University Press

Griffin, Jasper (1976) 'Augustan Poetry and the Life of Luxury', *Journal of Roman Studies*, 66, 87–105

Griffin, John (1986) *Well-Being: Its Meaning, Measurement and Moral Importance*; Oxford: Clarendon Press

Griffin, M.T. (1976) *Seneca: A Philosopher in Politics*; Oxford: Clarendon Press

Gunn, J.A.W. (1969) *Politics and the Public Interest in the Seventeenth Century*; London: Routledge & Kegan Paul (1983) *Beyond Liberty and Property: The Process of Self-recognition in Eighteenth Century Political Thought*; Kingston and Montreal: McGill-Queen's University Press

Haakonssen, K. (1981) *The Science of a Legislator*; Cambridge: Cambridge University Press (ed.) (1988) *Traditions of Liberalism*; St Leonards, NSW: Centre for Independent Studies

Hampshire, S. (1965) *Thought and Action*; London: Chatto & Windus

(ed.) (1978) *Public and Private Morality*; Cambridge: Cambridge University Press

(1983) *Morality and Conflict*; Oxford: Blackwell

(1992) *Innocence and Experience*; Harmondsworth: Penguin Books

Harte, N. (1976) 'State Control of Dress and Social Change in Pre-Industrial England', in *Trade, Government and Economy in Pre-Industrial England*, eds. D.C. Coleman and A.H. John, pp. 132–65

Hayek, F.A. (1967) 'Dr. Bernard Mandeville', *Proceedings of the British Academy*, 52, 125–41

Heckscher, E. (1955) *Mercantilism*, 2 vols., tr. M. Shapiro (first published 1931); London: G. Allen & Unwin

Heller, A. (1976) *The Theory of Need in Marx*; London: Allison & Busby

Herskovits, M.J. (1952) *Economic Anthropology: A Study in Comparative Economics*; New York: A. Knopf

Hill, B.W. (1976) *The Growth of Parliamentary Politics 1689–1742*; London: G. Allen & Unwin

Hinton, R.W.K. (1955) 'The Mercantile System in the Time of Thomas Mun', *Economic History Review*, 7, 279–90

Hirsch, F. (1977) *Social Limits to Growth*; London: Routledge & Kegan Paul

Hirschman, A.O. (1977) *The Passions and the Interests: Political Arguments for Capitalism before its Triumph*; Princeton: Princeton University Press

Hollander, A. (1988) *Seeing Through Clothes*; Harmondsworth: Penguin Books

Holmstrom, N. (1982) 'Do Women have a Distinct Nature?'; *The Philosophical Forum*, 14, 25–42

Honderich, T. (ed.) (1985) *Morality and Objectivity*; London: Routledge & Kegan Paul

Hont, I. (1990) 'Free Trade and the Economic Limits to National Politics: Neo-Machiavellian Political Economy Reconsidered', in *The Economic Limits to Modern Politics*, ed. J. Dunn, pp. 41–120

Hont, I. and Ignatieff, M. (eds.) (1983) *Wealth and Virtue: The Shaping of Political Economy in the Scottish Enlightenment*; Cambridge: Cambridge University Press

Hooper, W. (1915) 'Tudor Sumptuary Laws', *English Historical Review*, 30, 433–49

Höpfl, H. (1978) 'From Savage to Scotsman: Conjectural History in the Scottish Enlightenment', *Journal of British Studies*, 7, 20–40

Hopkins, J. (1975) 'The Cant of Compromise: Some Observations on Mandeville's Satire', in *Mandeville Studies*, ed. I. Primer, pp. 168–92

Horne, T.A. (1978) *The Social Thought of Bernard Mandeville*; London: Macmillan

Huizinga, J. (1949) *Homo Ludens*, tr. C. Hull; London: Routledge & Kegan Paul

Hurlock, E. (1965) 'Sumptuary Law', in *Dress, Adornment and the Social Order,* ed. M. Roach and J. Eicher, pp. 295–301

Ignatieff, M. (1984) *The Needs of Strangers*; London: Chatto & Windus

Inwood, B. (1985) *Ethics and Human Action in Early Stoicism*; Oxford: Clarendon Press

Irwin, T.H. (1991) 'Aristotle's Defense of Private Property', in *A Companion to Aristotle's Politics*, eds. D. Keyt and F. Miller, pp. 200–25

James, S. and Nobes, C. (1978) *The Economics of Taxation*; London: Philip Alan

Johnson, E.A.J. (1937) *Predecessors of Adam Smith*; London: P. King

Joseph, K. and Sumption, J. (1979) *Equality*; London: John Murray

Kaldor, N. (1959) *An Expenditure Tax*; London: G. Allen & Unwin

Kelly, P. (1991) *Locke on Money*, 2 vols.; Oxford: Clarendon Press

Keyt, D. and Miller, F. (eds.) (1991) *A Companion to Aristotle's Politics*; Oxford: Blackwell

Kienast, D. (1954) *Cato der Zensor: Seine Persönlichkeit und Seine Zeit*; Heidelberg: Quelle & Meyer

Kontos, A. (ed.) (1979) *Powers, Possessions and Freedom*; Toronto: University of Toronto Press

Kramnick, I. (1968) *Bolingbroke and His Circle: The Politics of Nostalgia in the Age of Walpole*; Cambridge, MA: Harvard University Press

Kropotkin, P. (1906) *The Conquest of Bread*; London: Chapman & Hall

Kybalova, L. (1968) *The Pictorial Encyclopedia of Fashion*, tr. C. Rosoux; London: Paul Hamlyn

Kyrk, H. (1976) *A Theory of Consumption* (first published 1923); New York: Arno Press

Labriolle-Rutherford, M. (1963) 'L'Evolution de la notion du luxe depuis Mandeville jusqu'à la Révolution', *Voltaire Studies*, 26, 1025–36

Lancaster, K. (1971) *Consumer Demand*; New York: Columbia University Press

Landreth, H. (1975) 'Economic Thought of Mandeville', *History of Political Economy*, 7, 192–208

Le Corbusier (1975) *Almanach d'Architecture Moderne* (1925); Torino: Bottege d'Erasmo

Lee, C. and Pashardes, P. (1988) *Who Pays Indirect Taxes?*; London: Institute of Fiscal Studies, Report no. 32

Leibenstein, H. (1950) 'Bandwagon, Snob and Veblen Effects in the Theory of Consumers' Demand'; *Quarterly Journal of Economics*, 64, 183–207

Leiss, W. (1978) *The Limits to Satisfaction: On Needs and Commodities*; London: Marion Boyars

Letwin, W. (1963) *The Origins of Scientific Economics: English Economic Thought 1660–1776*; London: Methuen

Levine, D. (1988) *Needs, Rights and the Market*; Boulder and London: Lynne Rienner

Lévi-Strauss, C. (1968) *Structural Anthropology*, vol. I, tr. C. Jacobson and B. Schoef; London: Allen Lane

(1977) *Structural Anthropology*, vol. II, tr. M. Layton; London: Allen Lane

(1978) *The Origin of Table Manners*, tr. J. and D. Wightman; London: Jonathan Cape

Lewis, C.S. (1936) *The Allegory of Love*; Oxford: Oxford University Press

Lintott, A.W. (1972) 'Imperial Expansion and Moral Decline in the Roman Republic', *Historia*, 21, 626–38

McCulloch, J.R. (ed.) (1859) *A Select Collection of Scarce and Valuable Tracts*, 4 vols.; London

(ed) (1952) *Early English Tracts on Commerce* (1856); Cambridge: Economic History Society reprint

MacIntyre, A. (1985) *After Virtue*, (2nd edition); London: Duckworth

(1988) *Whose Justice? Which Rationality?*; London: Duckworth

Mack, J. and Lansley, S. (1985) *Poor Britain*; London: G. Allen & Unwin

McKendrick, N. (1983) *The Birth of a Consumer Society: The Commercialization of Eighteenth Century England*; London: Hutchinson

McNally, D. (1988) *Political Economy and the Rise of Capitalism*; Berkeley and Los Angeles: University of California Press

Macpherson, C.B. (1962) *The Political Theory of Possessive Individualism*; Oxford: Clarendon Press

(1973) *Democratic Theory: Essays in Retrieval*; Oxford: Clarendon Press

Mâle, E. (1958) *The Gothic Image: Religious Art in France of the Thirteenth Century* (3rd edition 1913), tr. D. Nussey; New York: Harper Row

Malinowski, B. (1960) *A Scientific Theory of Culture*; New York: Oxford University Press

Mandel, E. (1968) *Marxist Economic Theory*, tr. B. Pearce; London: Merlin Press

Marcuse, H. (1964) *One Dimensional Man*; Boston: Beacon Press

Marly, D. (1985) *Fashion for Men: An Illustrated History*; London: Batsford

Mason, R. (1981) *Conspicuous Consumption: A Study of Exceptional Consumer Behaviour*; Farnborough: Gower

Meek, R.L. (1962) *The Economics of Physiocracy*; London: G. Allen & Unwin

(1967) 'The Scottish Contribution to Marxist Sociology', in his *Economics and Ideology*; London: Chapman & Hall

(ed.) (1973) *Precursors of Adam Smith 1750–1775*; London: Everyman Library

(1976) *Social Science and the Ignoble Savage*; Cambridge: Cambridge University Press

Meikle, S. (1979) 'Aristotle and the Political Economy of the Polis', *Journal of Hellenic Studies*, 99, 57–73

Melden, A. (1961) *Free Action*; London: Routledge

Melling, D.J. (1987) *Understanding Plato*; Oxford: Oxford University Press

Meszaros, I. (1990) 'The Decreasing Rate of Utilization under Capitalism', *Critique*, 22, 16–58

Miller, D. (1976) *Social Justice*; Oxford: Clarendon Press

Minogue, K. (1963) *The Liberal Mind*; London: Methuen

Monro, H. (1975) *The Ambivalence of Bernard Mandeville*; Oxford: Clarendon Press

Moon, J. (ed.) (1988) *Responsibility, Rights and Welfare*; Boulder and London: Westview Press

Moore, J. (1977) 'Hume's Political Science and the Classical Republican Tradition', *Canadian Journal of Political Science*, 10, 809–39

Morizé, A. (1909) *L'Apologie du Luxe au XVIIIe siècle et 'Le Mondain' de Voltaire; Etude critique sur 'Le Mondain' et ses sources*; Paris: H. Didier

Mossé, C. (1979) *La Fin de la Démocratie Athénienne*; New York: Arno Press

Nettleship, R.L. (1962) *Lectures on the Republic of Plato* (reprint of 2nd edition 1901); London: Macmillan

Norman, R. (1982) 'Does Equality destroy Liberty?', in *Contemporary Political Philosophy*, ed. K. Graham, pp. 113–37

Novak, M. (1962) *Economics and the Fiction of Daniel Defoe*; Berkeley and Los Angeles: University of California Press

Nozick, R. (1972) *Anarchy, State and Utopia*; Oxford: Blackwell

Oestreich, G. (1982) *Neo-Stoicism and the Early Modern State*, tr. D. McLintock; Cambridge: Cambridge University Press

Packard, L.B. (1923) 'International Rivalry – Free Trade Origins 1660–78'; *Quarterly Journal of Economics*, 37, 412–35

Pagden, A. (ed.) (1987) *Languages of Political Theory in Early Modern Europe*; Cambridge: Cambridge University Press

Pagels, E. (1990) *Adam, Eve and the Serpent*; Harmondsworth: Penguin Books

Parker, S. (1972) *The Future of Work and Leisure*; London: Paladin Books

Pascal, R. (1938) 'Property and Society', *Modern Quarterly*, 1, 167–79

Perkin, H. (1985) *Origins of Modern English Society*; London: Ark Books

Pesciarelli, E. (1978) 'Italians and the Four Stages', *History of Political Economy*, 10, 596–607

Phillipson, N. (1973) 'Towards a Definition of the Scottish Enlightenment', in *City and Society in the Eighteenth Century*, eds. P. Fritz and D. Williams, pp. 125–47

(1981) 'The Scottish Enlightenment', in *The Enlightenment in National Context*, eds. R. Porter and M. Teich, pp. 19–40

Piachaud, D. (1981) 'Townsend and the Holy Grail', *New Society* (10 September)

(1987) 'Problems in the Definition and Measurement of Poverty', *Journal of Social Policy*, 16, 147–64

Plant, R. (1983) *Hegel: An Introduction* (2nd edition); Oxford: Blackwell

(1991) *Modern Political Thought*; Oxford: Blackwell

Plumb, J.H. (1967) *The Growth of Political Stability in England 1675–1715*; London: Macmillan

Pocock, J.G.A. (1972) 'Languages and their Implications', in his *Politics, Language and Time*; London: Methuen

(1975) *The Machiavellian Moment: Florentine Political Thought and the Atlantic Republican Tradition*; Princeton: Princeton University Press

(1985) *Virtue, Commerce and History*; Cambridge: Cambridge University Press

Porter, R. and Teich, M. (eds.) (1981) *The Enlightenment in National Context*; Cambridge: Cambridge University Press

Prétèceille, E. and Terrail, J-P. (1985) *Capitalism, Consumption and Needs*, tr. S. Mathews; Oxford: Blackwell

Priestley, M. (1951) 'Anglo-French Trade and the "Unfavourable Balance" Controversy 1660–85', *Economic History Review*, 4, 37–52

Primer, I. (ed.) (1975) *Mandeville Studies*; The Hague: M. Nijhoff

Prusak, B. (1974) 'Woman; Seductive Siren and Source of Sin?', in *Religion and Sexism: Images of Woman in the Jewish and Christian Traditions*, ed. R. Ruether, pp. 89–116

Rae, J. (1965) *Life of Adam Smith* (1895), ed. J. Viner; New York: Kelley Reprints of Economic Classics

Ranke-Heinemann, U. (1991) *Eunuchs for the Kingdom of Heaven*, tr. P. Heinegg; Harmondsworth: Penguin Books

Raphael, D.D. (1967) 'Human Rights, Old and New', in his *Political Theory and the Rights of Man*; London: Macmillan, pp. 54–67

Rawls, J. (1972) *A Theory of Justice*; London: Oxford University Press

Rawson, E. (1969) *The Spartan Tradition in European Thought*; Oxford: Clarendon Press

Raz, J. (1986) *The Morality of Freedom*; Oxford: Clarendon Press

Ribeiro, A. (1986) *Dress and Morality*; London: B.T. Batsford

Rist, J.M. (1969) *Stoic Philosophy*; Cambridge: Cambridge University Press

Roach, M. and Eicher, J. (eds.) (1965) *Dress, Adornment and the Social Order*; New York: J. Wiley

Robertson, J. (1983) 'Scottish Political Economy Beyond the Civic Tradition: Government and Development in the "Wealth of Nations"', *History of Political Thought*, 4, 451–82

Robinson, D. (1961) 'The Economics of Fashion Demand', *Quarterly Journal of Economics*, 75, 376–98

Ross, E. (1976) 'Mandeville, Melon and Voltaire: The Origins of the Luxury Controversy in France', *Voltaire Studies*, 155, 1897–1912

Rousselle, A. (1988) *Porneia: On Desire and the Body in Antiquity*, tr. F. Pheasant; Oxford: Blackwell

Ruether, R. (ed.) (1974) *Religion and Sexism: Images of Woman in the Jewish and Christian Traditions*; New York: Simon & Schuster

(1974) 'Misogynism and Virginal Feminism in the Fathers of the Church', in *Religion and Sexism: Images of Woman in the Jewish and Christian Traditions*, ed. R. Ruether, pp. 150–83

Rybczynski, W. (1988) *Home: A Short History of an Idea*; London: Heinemann

Sabine, B.E.V. (1966) *A History of Income Tax*; London: G. Allen & Unwin

Sahlins, M. (1974) *Stone Age Economics*; London: Tavistock

Sandel, M. (1982) *Liberalism and the Limits of Justice*; Cambridge: Cambridge University Press

Schama, S. (1987) *The Embarrassment of Riches: An Interpretation of Dutch Culture in the Golden Age*; London: Collins

Schapiro, M. (1985) *The Sculpture of Moissac*; London: Thames & Hudson

Schumacher, E.F. (1973) *Small is Beautiful: A Study of Economics as if People Mattered*; London: Blond & Briggs

Schumpeter, J. (1954) *History of Economic Analysis*, ed. E. Schumpeter; London: G. Allen & Unwin

Scitovsky, T. (1976) *The Joyless Economy: An Inquiry into Human Satisfaction and Consumer Dissatisfaction*; New York: Oxford University Press

Scullard, H. (1951) *Roman Politics 220–150 BC*; Oxford: Clarendon Press (1982) *From the Gracchi to Nero* (5th edition); London: Methuen

Sekora, J. (1977) *Luxury: The Concept in Western Thought, Eden to Smollett*; Baltimore: Johns Hopkins University Press

Sen, A. (1983) 'Poor, Relatively Speaking', *Oxford Economic Papers*, 35, 153–69 (1985) 'A Sociological Approach to the Measurement of Poverty: A reply to Professor Townsend', *Oxford Economic Papers*, 37, 669–76

Shaw, B. (1988) 'Poverty: Absolute or Relative?', *Journal of Applied Philosophy*, 5, 27–36

Sher, R. (1985) *Church and University in the Scottish Enlightenment*; Edinburgh: Edinburgh University Press

Sidgwick, H. (1894) 'Luxury', *International Journal of Ethics*, 5, 1–16

Silverman, H. (1931) *Taxation its Incidence and Effects*; London: Macmillan

Simmel, G. (1964) *The Sociology of Georg Simmel*, ed. and tr. K. Wolff; New York: Free Press

(1990) *The Philosophy of Money* (2nd edition), tr. T. Bottomore and D. Frisby; London: Routledge

Simpson, E. (1982) 'The Priority of Needs over Wants', *Social Theory and Practice*, 8, 95–112

Skinner, A. (1975) 'Adam Smith: An Economic Interpretation of History', in A. Skinner and T. Wilson (eds.) *Essays on Adam Smith*, pp. 154–78

Skinner, A. and Wilson, T. (eds.) (1975) *Essays on Adam Smith*; Oxford: Clarendon Press

Sombart, W. (1913) *Luxus und Kapitalismus*; München and Leipzig: Duncker & Humblot

Soper, K. (1981) *On Human Needs*; Brighton: Harvester Press

Speck, W.A. (1975) 'Mandeville and the Eutopia Seated in the Brain', in *Mandeville Studies*, ed. I. Primer, pp. 66–79

Spengler, J. (1942) *French Predecessors of Malthus*; Durham, NC: Duke University Press

Sperber, D. (1985) *On Anthropological Knowledge*; Cambridge: Cambridge University Press

Spiegel, H.W. (1983) *The Growth of Economic Thought* (revised edition); Durham, NC.: Duke University Press

Springborg, P. (1981) *The Problem of Needs and the Critique of Civilisation*; London: G. Allen & Unwin

Strugnell, A. (1983) 'Diderot on Luxury, Commerce and the Merchant', *Voltaire Studies*, 217, 83–93

Strutt, J. (1842) *A Complete View of the Dress and Habits of the People of England*, ed. J. Planch; London: Henry Bohn

Sullivan, C.K. (1965) *The Tax on Value Added*; New York: Columbia University Press

Supple, B. (1954) 'Thomas Mun and the Commercial Crisis, 1623', *Bulletin of the Institute of Historical Research*, 27, 91–4

Syme, R. (1963) 'Ten Tribunes', *Journal of Roman Studies*, 53, 55–60

Taylor, C. (1979) 'Atomism', in *Powers, Possessions and Freedom*, ed. A. Kontos, pp. 39–61

   (1989) *Sources of the Self: The Making of the Modern Identity*; Cambridge: Cambridge University Press

Teichgraeber, R. (1986) *'Free Trade' and Moral Philosophy*; Durham, NC: Duke University Press

Thirsk, J. (1978) *Economic Policy and Projects: The Development of a Consumer Society in Early Modern England*; Oxford: Clarendon Press

Thomas, K. (1964) 'Work and Leisure in Pre-Industrial Society', *Past and Present*, 29, 50–62

Thomas, P.J. (1926) *Mercantilism and the East India Trade*; London: P.S. King

Thomson, G. (1987) *Needs*; London: Routledge & Kegan Paul

Thornton, P. (1978) *Seventeenth Century Interior Decoration in England, France and Holland*; New Haven: Yale University Press

Tomlinson, A. (1990) 'Consumer Culture and the Aura of the Commodity', in *Consumption, Identity and Style*, ed. A. Tomlinson, pp. 1–38

   (ed.) (1990) *Consumption, Identity and Style*; London: Routledge

Townsend, P. (1979) *Poverty in the United Kingdom*; Harmondsworth: Penguin Books

   (1985) 'A Sociological Approach to the Measurement of Poverty – A Reply to Professor Sen', *Oxford Economic Papers*, 37, 659–68

   (1987) 'Deprivation', *Journal of Social Policy*, 16, 125–56

Tuve, R. (1966) *Allegorical Imagery: Some Medieval Books and their Posterity*; Princeton: Princeton University Press

Vaughn, K. (1980) *John Locke: Economist and Social Scientist*; London: The Athlone Press

Veit-Wilson, J.H. (1987) 'Consensual Approaches to Poverty Lines and Social Security', *Journal of Social Policy*, 16, 183–211

Veyne, P. (1976) *Le Pain et le Cirque: Sociologie Historique d'un Pluralisme Politique*; Paris: Editions du Seuil

   (ed.) (1987) *A History of Private Life*, vol. I, tr. A. Goldhammer; Cambridge, MA: Bellknap Press

Vickers, D. (1960) *Studies in the Theory of Money*; London: Peter Owen

Viner, J. (1937) *Studies in the Theory of International Trade*; London: G. Allen & Unwin

Vlastos, G. (1940) 'Slavery in Plato's Thought', *Philosophical Review*, 50, 289–304

(1968) 'Does Slavery Exist in Plato's Republic?', *Classical Philology*, 63, 291–5

Voitle, R. (1984) *The Third Earl of Shaftesbury 1671–1713*; Baton Rouge: Louisiana State University Press

Walker, R. (1987) 'Consensual Approaches to the Definition of Poverty', *Journal of Social Policy*, 16, 213–26

Walzer, M. (1983) *Spheres of Justice*; Oxford: Blackwell

Waszek, N. (1984) 'Two Concepts of Morality: A Distinction of A. Smith's Ethics and its Stoic Origin', *Journal of the History of Ideas*, 45, 591–606

Watkins, J.W.N. (1965) *Hobbes's System of Ideas*; London: Hutchinson

Weale, A. (1983) *Political Theory and Social Policy*; London: Macmillan

Weatherill, L. (1988) *Consumer Behaviour and Material Culture in Britain 1660–1760*; London: Routledge

White, A. (1975) *Modal Thinking*; Oxford: Blackwell

Wiggins, D. (1985) 'Claims of Need', in *Morality and Objectivity*, ed. T. Honderich, pp. 149–202

Williams, G. (1962) 'Poetry in the Moral Climate of Augustan Rome', *Journal of Roman Studies*, 52, 28–46

Williams, R.H. (1982) *Dream Worlds: Mass Consumption in Late Nineteenth Century France*; Berkeley and Los Angeles: University of California Press

Wilson, C. (1959) 'The Other Face of Mercantilism', *Transactions of the Royal Historical Society* (5th series), 9, 81–101

(1965) *England's Apprenticeship 1603–1763*; London: Longmans

Winch, D. (1978) *Adam Smith's Politics*; Cambridge: Cambridge University Press

(1983) 'Adam Smith's "Enduring Particular Result"', in *Wealth and Virtue*, eds. I. Hont and M. Ignatieff, pp. 253–67

(1988) 'Adam Smith and the Liberal Tradition', *Traditions of Liberalism*, ed. K. Haakonssen, pp. 83–104

Xenos, N. (1989) *Scarcity and Modernity*; London: Routledge

Zeller, E. (1885) *Socrates and the Socratic Schools* (3rd edition), tr. O. Reichel; London: Longmans Green

Index

Titles marked with an asterisk are also available in paperback